THE PERSONALISATION OF POLITICS IN THE UK

MANCHESTER
1824

Manchester University Press

The personalisation of politics in the UK

*Mediated leadership
from Attlee to Cameron*

Ana Inés Langer

Manchester University Press

Published by Manchester University Press
Altrincham Street, Manchester M1 7JA
www.manchesteruniversitypress.co.uk

A catalogue record for this book is available from the British Library

ISBN 978 0 7190 8146 0 hardback
ISBN 978 1 5261 2284 1 paperback

First published in hardback 2011
First published in paperback 2020

Typeset by
Carnegie Book Production, Lancaster

For Orian and Sofia

Contents

List of figures and tables

Figures

Tables

Acknowledgements

I owe a massive debt of gratitude to a number of colleagues, friends and family who helped me in different ways while writing this book. First of all, I want to very specially thank Maggie Scammell, who read and commented on multiple versions of this manuscript. She was an inspiring, supportive and knowledgeable teacher and PhD supervisor, and has now become not only a great colleague but also a much-valued friend, providing useful and thought-provoking criticism and always available for encouraging advice. Thanks also to her partner, Jenks, and family for the inspiring Welsh retreats. Vanessa Cragoe's support and friendship, as well as painstaking proofreading during my PhD, were also invaluable. Other (former) members of the Media Department at the LSE have also been helpful and kind to me, especially Nick Couldry, Sonia Livingstone, Robin Mansell, Shani Orgad and the late Roger Silverstone. I am also very grateful to my current colleagues at the University of Glasgow for their feedback and support, especially Maurizio Carbone, Jane Duckett, Naomi Head, Mo Hume, Kelly Kollman, Sarah Oates, Cian O'Driscoll, Barry O'Toole, Myrto Tsakatika, Karen Wright and Alasdair Young. It is a rare privilege to work with so many nice people. Thanks also to the administrative staff, especially Lynsey McLeay, Caroline Mooney and Maggie Murray, for making my job easier, and to the team at Manchester University Press for believing in this project and for their patience and responsiveness. Finally, I am grateful to the reviewers of the manuscript and to colleagues at PSA, IPSA and IAMCR conferences for their feedback, and to students at the LSE and Glasgow for having challenged my thinking and helped me to clarify my ideas about the personalisation conundrum.

Special gratitude goes to my family, who have been a great source of love and support. To my parents who, although in very different ways, have always believed in me and encouraged me to pursue my dreams, even when it took me thousands of miles away. Thanks also for making me feel deeply loved wherever I am. To Matias for being such a good and loving 'big brother', always checking on me, especially whenever things were getting too much. To all my siblings and their partners, as well as my nieces and nephews, for their support but mostly for making me happier. We are the epitome of the 'modern' family, or dysfunctional as the *Daily Mail* would call it, and I am very proud and grateful to be part of it. To Orian's family for helping me to miss mine a good deal less. I also want to thank my lifelong friends from Buenos Aires (who are in all but genes family), those in London and the fantastic ASB & associates 'gang' here in Glasgow. *Gracias* to all for having supported me, appeased me, and amused me in my highs and lows, while minimising the effects of life as an expatriate.

Above all, I want to thank Orian Brook, who has patiently suffered the worst effects of sharing life with an academic. Without your support, encouragement and generosity this book would probably still exist (although full of wrong prepositions), but I would be half as happy and sane. With you it always feels that things can only get (even) better. I will try my hardest to re-pay you but I fear it is mission impossible. Last but not least a massive thanks to Sofia; although she still thinks that books are only for chewing, it does not matter because her smiles are of more value to me than authorship of the entire British Library.

Of course, although their support and advice have been invaluable, mistakes are mine and mine alone.

Introduction

There is no doubt that politics is a personalised game. From the US to Europe to Latin America to Russia we can hardly think of politics without thinking of presidents or prime ministers. Leaders, undoubtedly, have a good deal of symbolic and actual power in the governance of democratic countries. Not only is the business of politics personalised, but so is media coverage. Issues and policies are identified with leaders, political successes and failures attributed to them and their political and personal qualities discussed, often in detail. Campaigns are also led by leaders, who have a prominent role in both the design and the communication of (party) messages and policies, and whose personal appeals influence – directly or indirectly – a considerable number of voters. However, we need to be careful with how far we take these generalisations. It is true that leaders are powerful and predominant figures in democratic politics; it is true that this age-old feature of politics seems to have strengthened in recent times; and it is also true that personalisation is manifested across political systems and cultures. However, these are also sweeping statements, grand generalisations about the phenomenon of personalisation, which need to be unpacked, qualified and empirically investigated. Moreover, the concept of personalisation is in serious need of clarification.

These are precisely the aims of this book: to subject personalisation and these often repeated but rarely investigated assumptions to close theoretical and empirical scrutiny. The focus is on how the phenomenon has developed in the United Kingdom, with particular emphasis on Tony Blair. The UK is a case of particular relevance because it is believed that, among parliamentary democracies, it is one where personalisation has developed especially intensely. Moreover, Blair is often considered a prime example of personalisation in all its meanings. At the same time, what makes it a more interesting case is that, although in these regards the UK appears exceptional, personalisation has developed in the context of 'normal' parliamentary and partified politics; that is, in the absence of a major systemic crisis, populism or personalised parties, major constitutional or electoral reform,[1] or structural changes in media regulation. In addition, despite the burgeoning literature on the subject, systematic investigation of the British case is still limited. Previous research focused primarily on changes in the roles of leaders within the executive and parties and, when addressing political discourse, has been mostly confined to electoral periods. Furthermore, although it is only the degree of visibility of leaders that is systematically studied, research often assumes that the emphasis on their personal lives and qualities must have grown in synch. As a result, an increasing interest in the personality of leaders is merely assumed or based on anecdotal evidence that tends to emphasise rich, but exceptional, examples. There is also a remarkable lack of historical studies, which are crucial for understanding – and avoiding overestimating – change.

The book will unpack the concept of personalisation and argue that it needs to be redefined, differentiating between two distinct, albeit often overlapping, dimensions: presidentialisation and personality politics. It will focus in particular on the latter, subjecting the conventional wisdom that the personal lives and characters of leaders now dominate political discourse to systematic empirical examination. Through detailed study of press content, the book will uncover the extent, characteristics and historical development of personality politics in the UK, and how this relates to presidentialisation. Unlike most studies, it will focus on everyday coverage (i.e. outside electoral periods) and include the analysis of the presence of leaders outside political news 'proper'. It will also combine quantitative and qualitative methods and will emphasise the analysis of the evolution of the phenomenon over time, asking: what, if anything, has changed in the media portrayal of leaders? This is combined with analysis of the communication strategies of parties, which will enable us to understand how the interaction between broad socio-political changes and the shifting strategic needs of media, parties and leaders – which are often in conflict – affect the nature and degree of personalisation. The analysis pays particular attention to the role of the personal lives of leaders which, despite widespread assumptions that it is gaining exceptional importance, is a dimension of personalisation which has not yet been systematically studied. Moreover, although the book takes Blair's premierships as a catalytic moment, the approach is historical, exploring how personalisation has evolved from 1945 to the present day. This is crucial because it is only by looking at the before and after of exceptional examples that we can work out what is different (and what is not) about contemporary personalisation, and to what extent the changes associated with a particular leader are enduring or idiosyncratic.

The analysis will demonstrate that what is most distinctive about contemporary personalisation is not a general emphasis on the leaders but on their personal lives and qualities and the associated broadening of what are considered leadership qualities. This signals a move towards emphasising the private sphere and the inner self by which the 'human being' does not replace the leader but the two become harder to separate; this shift will be defined in the book as the politicisation of private persona. This is not to say either that the personal has become the most prevalent feature of public discourse, nor that it has replaced everything else in a zero-sum dynamic; it is to say that the emphasis on personal qualities and lives of leaders is the dimension of personalisation that shows the clearest change in the last two decades, especially in the case of Tony Blair. Furthermore, the personal, distinctively to our times, has become a routine element of story telling, subtly blurring the boundaries between public and private. As a result, although the personal is still dwarfed by other dimensions of the coverage, it stands out because of its ubiquity; it has entered every facet of public discourse, across genres and outlets, and it is used strategically by leaders in both on- and off-role performances.

Of course, not every leader's personal life will now be covered to the same extent as Blair's, or in the same way. How much leaders choose to reveal has to do with their biography, personality, communication styles and strategic needs, which affect also their media coverage. It is for these reasons that one should not expect the development of the politicisation of private persona to follow a linear trend. In fact, as we shall see, Blair's era was in many ways extraordinary. On the other hand, and crucially, what is 'normal' has changed, affecting all politicians regardless of style. The personal is now a routine element of media coverage and is used in the overall assessment of leadership. Moreover, the readiness, or even enthusiasm, of leaders to reveal the personal has become the new status quo and is often regarded as a necessary condition of successful performance at the ballot box. Paradoxically, however, this is not so much a consequence of the influence that the personal has in electoral choices – which is still marginal – but of a reinforcing response from journalists and politicians to what they have mutually come to define as a necessary dimension of successful contemporary leadership.

Personalisation: a conceptual muddle

Because leaders appear to dominate everything, everywhere, it is easy to get carried away about the strength and novelty of personalisation. But we need to proceed with care, avoiding grand generalisations. Firstly, for all that politics is personalised, issues and policies count a great deal: no matter how strong the personal appeal of a leader might appear to be, his or her success or failure will ultimately depend on which policies satisfy a sufficient proportion of the population and who is considered to be best placed to deliver them. Moreover, even in the most personalised of democratic systems, leaders can never govern alone. Congresses and parliaments still command a good deal of power, even if at times this might amount just to the power to constrain the leader. Furthermore, even though their role has greatly changed, political parties have not disappeared from the game. At least in countries with a history of partisan politics, leaders can rarely be elected or successfully govern without the support of the party structure and party colleagues. Media, for their part, and despite the cries of tabloidisation, generally provide good guidance not only on who espouses which policies, and who might be better qualified to deliver them, but also a fair amount of detail on what these policies are about. In short, personalisation is an important, and even a defining, feature of contemporary politics but it has not caused the importance of either policies or other political actors to disappear in its wake.

Secondly, we need to avoid overstating the novelty of the phenomenon. The discussion of personalisation undoubtedly involves change. Even if politics has to a degree always been personalised, what makes the phenomenon worth studying, and an object of strong normative concerns, is that personalisation is said to have transformed the nature of communication, electoral behaviour, the roles of parties, and even the functioning of government. But change is a question of degree and of evolution as much as transformation. If we assume radical change, we would be mistaken. If we expect personalisation to develop in a perfectly linear form, we will most likely be disappointed. To an extent, leaders have always been central to government and to communication during campaigns and everyday politics. Moreover, particular leaders and circumstantial factors make a difference, and hence change is, to an extent at least, always contingent. The question then is not: is politics personalised? What we need to investigate is to what extent politics is nowadays more personalised than in the past, and what is distinctive about contemporary forms of personalisation.

Thirdly, the personalisation of power can, and indeed does, take different forms, and these forms are strongly related to structural and cultural differences. Hugo Chavez, Silvio Berlusconi and Tony Blair are three common contemporary examples of the concentration of power in the figure of the leader, and hence of common understandings of personalisation. However, this common label obscures more than it clarifies. For all the deep socio-political changes that have affected most Western societies (i.e. partisan dealignment, the weakening of ideology, the influence of television and so on), Chavez is more like Juan Domingo Peron, and Blair more like Harold Wilson or even Winston Churchill, than they are like each other. The Venezuelan president is the prime example of a number of left-wing leaders that emerged in Latin America in the early twenty-first century. He is considered by most accounts a neo-populist or radical populist leader, who presents himself as an anti-oligarchic, anti-imperialist popular *caudillo* with a strongly ideological and antagonistic discourse (de la Torre, 2009). He has campaigned and governed outside the party system, heavily relying on mass meetings, top-down popular mobilisation and clientelistic networks. Moreover Chavez reformed – by referendum – the constitution, expanding the power of the presidency. For his part, Berlusconi, although often paired with Blair in analyses of personalisation, represents a different form of the phenomenon. An outsider to professional politics, who created his own party, he is very much an example of the political entrepreneur (Pasquino, 2007; Roncarolo, 2004): in the midst of a profound legitimacy crisis of the Italian political system, Berlusconi used his reputation, money, and access as a media and sports mogul to present himself as a right-wing neo-populist alternative to the delegitimised 'old way' of doing politics. Unlike Blair, he did not just transform the party and come to personify it: Berlusconi *is* the party. Nor did he just try to manage the media: he *owns* much of it.

Even in the case of Blair himself, personalisation takes different forms, highlighting both the multi-layered nature of the phenomenon, and the lack of conceptual clarity in how it is discussed. Blair was regularly accused of being a particularly 'presidential' prime minister, who ran a 'kitchen cabinet' government, dispensing with the cabinet tradition of *primus inter pares*. It has also often been said that Blair, and his character and personality, were outstanding foci of media coverage and central to New Labour's communication strategy, outshining the cabinet, the party, and the discussion of issues and policies. At the same time, there was also a strong *sense* of Blair the 'human being', as a father, conducting even the business of war surrounded by children's toys, as a practising Christian and husband, as an aspiring rock star and so on. All three claims highlight the central role of Blair – the leader and the person – for New Labour and in government, and hence connote personalisation, i.e. the increasing importance of leaders in the political process. However, they also reveal the analytical confusion that surrounds the term. Is it presidentialisation, i.e. a shift of power towards leaders? Is it a media focus on leaders and/or their personality traits? Is it the foregrounding of the personal as opposed to the political qualities of leaders? Is it a process of the intrusion of the private into the public sphere; or conversely an invasion of the public into the properly private affairs of public officials? In short, what is personalisation and, crucially, what is new about its contemporary manifestation?

Unpacking the concept of personalisation

The concept of the personalisation of politics is most commonly used to refer to two associated but distinctive processes: 'presidentialisation' and 'personality politics'. *Presidentialisation* refers to the process by which individual political figures become more central in the decision-making process, displacing other political actors, especially political parties and collegiate forms of government. This understanding of personalisation then focuses on the differential distribution of power, highlighting a change in relation to the autonomy and influence of different actors. Although it refers basically to the process of governing, i.e. a shift in intra-executive power to the benefit of the head of government, this process also affects the relationship of the leader with the party and the legislature (Poguntke and Webb, 2005a: 8). Moreover, it is accompanied by an intensified focus on leaders in campaigning and media coverage and in the public's assessment of political performance, including electoral choices (Mughan, 2000). More broadly, the electoral face of presidentialisation is also associated with what Foley has defined as 'leadership stretch', namely that leaders become not only more prominent but 'progressively differentiated from their organisational bases in terms of media attention, public recognition and political identity' (Foley, 2004: 293).

Personality politics, on the other hand, refers to an increasing emphasis in political discourse on the character and personal lives of politicians, which it is feared displaces the focus from records, ideological affiliation and policy. This involves the media coverage of politics as well as leader, party and government communication. Moreover, although personality politics may be most obvious during electoral campaigns, it is understood also to be manifested during day-to-day 'normal' politics. It is also assumed that an increased emphasis on personalities will have an impact on the basis of voting choices, affecting citizens' priorities when making electoral decisions. Accordingly, in comparison to presidentialisation, the discussion of personality politics tends to emphasise communication and give more significance to the role of the media, politicians and their communication advisers, and less to institutional arrangements and to the role of other political actors including parties, parliament and cabinet.

Although both aspects of the personalisation of politics are interrelated, and can be regarded as two dimensions of the same phenomenon, the analytical distinction is important. Firstly, it is a mistake to assume that the strength of one process can be automatically inferred from that of the other. Even though linked, and affecting one another, these two phenomena are not one and the same. Whereas personality politics is communication-centred and to a large extent media-driven, presidentialisation requires an actual shift – albeit without constitutional change – in the distribution of power resources. Moreover, even within discourse, these two processes are different: whereas presidentialisation requires only a greater mediated visibility of leaders, personality politics entails a specific increase in the emphasis on their personal qualities. Secondly, each concept suggests a different order of causation: whereas personality politics implies that it is the parties' and media's 'obsession' with the character of politicians that has empowered leaders and weakened other actors, presidentialisation emphasises that the prominence of leaders in political discourse is a cause, but also a result, of their increasing importance in all dimensions of the political process. Finally, addressing them separately enables a more precise empirical investigation of the phenomenon and a more refined analysis of the distinctive, even if sometimes overlapping, normative issues raised by presidentialisation and personality politics.

In this regard, there is no doubt that both phenomena provoke considerable concern. However, there are important differences. Underlying presidentialisation, the major concern is that democratic structures, such as the UK's, designed as parliamentary democracies, are being undermined. Parliament, the cabinet, and political parties are being bypassed and weakened as power is concentrated in leaders and their inner circles, who are now more dependent upon the fluctuations in public opinion. In contrast, the main issues underlying personality politics are to do with the quality of political information and democratic rationality. Electoral campaigns and politics generally are said to have become a contest between personalities and appearances rather than, as is considered normatively desirable and once assumed to be the case, a debate about competing principles and policy proposals. In short, the concern is that people are being seduced by style and therefore lack the information necessary to make rational political choices.

Presidentialisation, although a contested concept, has been better defined and more systematically studied than personality politics (Bevir and Rhodes, 2006; Foley, 1993, 2000; Heffernan, 2005b; Helms, 2005; Mughan, 2000; Poguntke and Webb, 2005b). In contrast, personality politics, although intuitively compelling, is a highly problematic concept. Firstly, it assumes (although it is rarely demonstrated) that the focus on personalities is both a novelty and detrimental, both of which are questionable claims. Has politics ever really been only about policies and issues or, rather, have leaders and their personalities always played an important role? If the latter, what is different about the contemporary form of personality politics? Moreover, is the coverage of the personality of leaders mutually exclusive from attention to 'substantive' politics? In addition, when choosing candidates or judging political alternatives, is an interest in the personal qualities and lives of politicians trivial or irrational?

Secondly, the concept is ill-defined. Personality politics is often used as a catch-all term for all the shortcomings that critics find with the state of political discourse in our age. In particular, personality politics has become synonymous with campaigns and politics as 'beauty contests' (Wattenberg, 2004), focusing on the personal appearance and telegenic appeal of leaders. It is true that good communication skills, and hence the ability to create an appealing media persona is – and in different ways has always been – an important quality of a leader. Moreover, with television now long established as the main channel of mediated representation, this skill has become both more essential and of a different nature: as politics moves from parliament to the TV studio and from the news bulletin to the talk show, leaders need to emphasise more the confessional, the mundane and the personal. But the need for communication skills and the ability to connect with the electorate, even if different in nature, are not new features in political leadership; nor are communication skills or even teleginicity simply about physical attractiveness or personal charm. Media appeal is a question of body language, rhetorical style *and* content. Moreover, to be able to connect – even on television – politicians need to appear to understand what people want, articulate problems in an accessible and engaging fashion, make them relevant to citizens' everyday life, appear capable of delivering appropriate solutions, represent people's values and priorities and so on. In other words, the leader is the message but in more complex ways than suggested by the idea of personality politics as 'beauty contest'.

In fact, personality politics refers, or should refer, to a wide range of character traits or qualities. We can differentiate analytically between two types: those directly related to the capacity for governing, such as competence, intelligence and professional experience, which we will label as leadership or political qualities;[2] and those that are generally not considered as essentially political, which we will label as personal 'private' qualities (or 'soft' qualities), such as being kind or likeable. In addition, and crucially for the aims of the book, we also need to include references in public discourse to the personal lives of leaders, such as his or her family or hobbies. These references not only provide specific information about a leader's family life or what he or she does in his or her free time but also, by showing her to be a doting parent or passionate about football or the *X Factor*, feed back into the construction of personal qualities such as being caring, accessible, or 'normal'.

We can think of this distinction as the difference between the leader as statesman and the leader as 'human being'. The emphasis on the latter is defined here as the *politicisation of private persona* (see figure I.1). This concept refers specifically to the emphasis not just on leaders or their leadership qualities but on their personal lives and on qualities that are

```
┌─────────────────────────────────────┐
│      Personalisation of Politics     │
└─────────────────────────────────────┘
```

┌──────────────────────────────┐   ┌──────────────────────────────────┐
│   **Presidentialisation**   │   │   **Personality Politics**   │
│ Shift in the distribution of power │   │   Strong(er) emphasis on leaders' │
│ towards leaders. In detriment to│◄──►│ personality traits in public discourse.│
│   political parties and   │   │ In detriment to ideological principles│
│ collegiate forms of government │   │   and policy proposals   │
└──────────────────────────────┘   └──────────────────────────────────┘

┌──────────────────────────────┐   ┌─────────────────┐ ┌─────────────────┐
│   **Leaders attain**   │   │ **Leadership**   │ │ **Politicisation of**│
│ • More power resources within the│   │ **Qualities**   │ │ **Private Persona** │
│   executive   │   │   │ │   │
│ • More autonomy from the party │   │ Strong(er) emphasis│ │ Strong(er) emphasis │
│ • Higher media visibility and distinct│ │ on leadership traits│ │ on personal life and│
│   public identity from the party │   │ and professional skills│ │ qualities   │
│ • Stronger impact on electoral behaviour│ │ (Leader as   │ │ (Leader as   │
│   │   │ statesman)   │ │ human being)   │
└──────────────────────────────┘   └─────────────────┘ └─────────────────┘

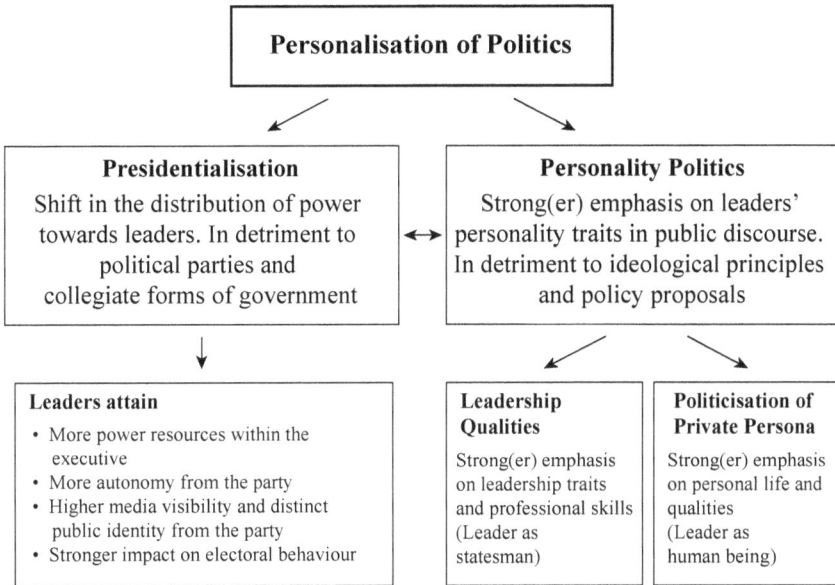

I.1 Dimensions of personalisation

not directly related to their capacity for governing, and that are generally rooted in the private sphere. Hence the politicisation of private persona emphasises the portrayals of politicians *not just* as representatives of an ideology or a party, or as statesmen, but as persons, as 'human beings'. It is the difference between learning that Barack Obama has an extraordinarily quick and in-depth grasp of complex issues and knowing that he bought a puppy for his daughters. The first is a personal characteristic but obviously desirable for a statesman; the second says nothing about his capacity to lead but is perhaps an interesting detail about who he is. Moreover, Obama and the puppy stories feed into media constructions of his personal qualities and thus affect whether or not he is portrayed as being likeable, kind or in touch.

The distinction between personal and leadership or political qualities is not clear-cut. By what criteria do we decide which qualities of a leader are politically 'relevant'? Clearly, these categories are better thought of not as discrete or in binary opposition, but as situated on a scale or continuum (Adam and Maier, 2010), where although the extremes are fairly easy to label (e.g. previous political experience at one end, and favourite rock band at the other), it is more difficult to categorise those falling closer to the medium of the continuum (e.g. being approachable or charismatic). Moreover, there are not only different degrees but also overlaps between the two spheres: integrity and empathy are generally considered leadership qualities (e.g. Miller et al., 1986; Ohr and Oscarsson, 2010) but are these based only on the behaviour in the political sphere? If a leader advocates an environmental agenda but does not recycle at home, does this impact on his or her integrity? Similarly, if a leader appears completely out of touch with popular culture, or with the lifestyle of ordinary people, could not this impact on whether he or she is regarded as empathetic? Equally, when a leader speaks about policy in the language of the private, using references to his or her life experiences, there is a clear personal element to the discourse but it does not preclude it from having 'substantial' content. Moreover, it can have an impact on whether we perceive he or she is truly committed to such a policy and capable of carrying it out. The distinction between political and personal qualities also has a circular nature: if a 'human' connection is considered a prerequisite for effective communication and electoral success, doesn't it then become – in practice if not necessarily normatively – a leadership quality? In short, there is no easy and rigid partition between the 'relevant', or what we might call leadership or political qualities, and 'irrelevant' personal qualities because these are all ultimately linked in the construction of the persona, the presentation of policy and on the assessment of leadership. Moreover, and in fact precisely as a result of how personalisation is developing, it is becoming increasingly difficult to sustain such a separation.

Why bother, then, distinguishing between the personal and the political, if this distinction creates so many problems and, in many ways, does injustice to the complexity of the phenomenon? It is a good question and one that I have asked myself. However, there are important reasons why conceptually and analytically it is useful to try to differentiate them. The reasons are threefold. Firstly, the politicisation of private persona raises distinctive normative concerns. It is clear in both punditry and academic discussion that it is the emphasis on the personal qualities and lives of leaders that provokes the most acute and distinctive anxieties about the state of contemporary political discourse. The normative concerns will be discussed in detail in Chapter 2 but for now it suffices to say that the politicisation of private persona raises in its most concentrated form anxiety at irrationality in politics, as we are invited to judge politicians through the prism of mediated intimacy and authenticity rather than through the (supposedly) rational judgements of policy, record, and ideology. Moreover, the process may affect the recruitment of political elites, as it threatens the right to privacy and becomes a deterrent to run for public office.

Secondly, there is a strong perception, both in the media and among the public, that details of the personal lives of politicians and the attention to their private qualities are now particularly pervasive in public discourse:

Politicians increasingly use personal and family details in their self presentation. Tony and Cherie Blair famously boasted of a hyperactive sex life to the *Sun* before the 2005 general election. The editorial policies – and success – of celebrity magazines like *Hello* and the show business editors of newspapers and TV shows are built on carefully calibrated relationships between the journalists and the publicists. These techniques are now spreading, inexorably, to politicians, especially to party leaders constantly in the public eye, constantly appraised on personal, familial and moral grounds by a commentariat which itself, as a body, is reluctant to draw lines between private and public actions and morality. (Hobsbawm and Lloyd, 2008: 32)

This belief is also present in academic studies both in regard to the construction of leaders' public personae and to the media coverage (for a summary see Adam and Maier, 2010). Given that we know that personalities have always played a part in democratic discourse, this perception suggests that it is the politicisation of private persona that might be most distinctive about the role of personality in contemporary political discourse. That is to say, it is not so much a focus on leaders or leadership that makes our age stand out, but the increased interest on the personal sphere and qualities of politicians. However, the emphasis on this particular aspect of leaders has been generally studied under the broad umbrella of personalisation and, hence, assumed rather than investigated. As a result, apart from rare exceptions (Adam and Maier, 2010; Rahat and Sheafer, 2007; van Zoonen, 2000; van Zoonen and Holtz-Bacha, 2000), it has seldom been researched systematically and empirically.

Last but not least, the concept of politicisation of private persona – and hence distinguishing between leadership and personal qualities – offers a clear and operationalisable definition to study personality politics. This definition will enable us to investigate systematically whether or not the common sense view of the pervasiveness of the personal is justified; to track change over time and explore not only how much but in which ways the personal is evident in the construction of leaders' public personae; and to make a more grounded assessment of whether or not the normative concerns raised by personality politics are justified. In short, the distinction between leadership qualities and personal qualities is anything but clear-cut, and yet it is important. A rigid separation is problematic in some ways, because in reality the two are often linked and their boundaries are fluid. But nonetheless their conceptual separation helps us to address the distinctive and acute normative concerns, and allows systematic investigation focused on this particular dimension of personalisation. Moreover, it is only by drawing this analytical distinction that we will be able to better understand the changing nature of the boundaries and the links between the personal and the political.

Structure of the book

Chapter 1 examines the first dimension of personalisation, the presidentialisation of power. It first defines the concept, discusses the causes of its development and scrutinises how it affects democratic politics; then it analyses how the different faces of presidentialisation (i.e. executive, party and electoral – Poguntke and Webb, 2005a) have been manifested in the United Kingdom. The review of the evidence reveals positive indicators of the party and executive faces of presidentialisation, which accelerated – but certainly did not begin – during Blair's premierships. There has been overall a strengthening of the autonomy and power resources of the prime minister within the party and the executive, but not a linear escalation because the degree of power is contingent to the leader's skills and popularity (Heffernan, 2003). With regard to the electoral face, the data provides only limited confirmation of the presence of presidentialisation. Although it is clear that leaders are a significant factor in shaping electoral choices and are massively dominant in media coverage, for the more stringent – but essential – test of presidentialisation (i.e. systematic increase over time) the evidence is not conclusive: there has been a degree of change but it is neither as marked nor as systematic as conventional wisdom suggests.

Chapter 2 presents the analytical framework for the rest of the book, highlighting what is particular and peculiar to personalisation in our age. It introduces the concept of the politicisation of private persona, discussing how and why it is related to, but different from, personality politics. It then explains the causes for its emergence, linking the modern phenomenon to socio-political, cultural and technological transformations but within a historical legacy of the continuing importance of the politician as human being. This leads to a discussion of the normative dimensions: what is the politicisation of private persona doing to democracy, and our understanding of what is right and proper in politics and citizenship? The discussion moves beyond simplistic categorisations of personal/political and rational/ emotional, addressing both the potential benefits and risks of a more personalised connection between leaders and citizens.

Chapter 3 examines the evolution of the personalisation of politics in the press in Britain. This is the first substantive longitudinal study of personalisation (1945–2009) outside electoral periods and hence a crucial empirical test of the widespread belief that there has been an increase in all dimensions of personalisation in media coverage. As in the case of election coverage (Chapter 1), in terms of the visibility of the prime ministers, although the overall trend is positive, most of the indicators fluctuate substantially between leaders rather than showing a steady increase over time. In contrast, there is a clear shift, and especially in recent decades, in relation to personality politics, and in particular in regard to the politici-sation of private persona. This is revealed by evidence of the combination of a personal turn in the assessment of character and the recent emphasis on the personal lives of the prime ministers. The degree of change, however, should not be exaggerated. The attention paid to the personal sphere of prime ministers continues to be a minor element in the overall coverage, and one that adds to, rather than replaces, the political. This applies also for Tony Blair, who is the peak of the trend.

Chapter 4 continues with the exploration of the historical development of the politicisation of private persona but now in a more qualitative fashion and with greater focus on leaders' communication strategies. It asks the following questions: beyond the scale of the coverage, how has the phenomenon evolved over time? What are the similarities and differences between past and present in how the personal was used by leaders, and reported by the media? Moreover, what do these changes tell us about the causes and evolution of the phenomenon? The chapter will show that the politicisation of private persona is neither a New Labour invention nor, although it is an influential factor, a product of television. Certainly, earlier prime ministers also made strategic use of the personal for the construction of political personae. Nonetheless, although there is a degree of continuity, the analysis of historical precedents also uncovers important changes over time in the nature of the politicisation of private persona.

Chapter 5 focuses on Tony Blair. It first analyses his communicative strategy and style, uncovering what made him distinctive in the use of the personal for the construction of his public persona. The rest of the chapter focuses on the analysis of how and why the press referred to his personal life. It will show that during Blair's era his personal life was routinely present in both political and non-political coverage, and more frequently mentioned than for any previous prime minister. Moreover, the analysis of two case studies will demonstrate how the most ordinary of personal events in his life came to be constructed as exceptional (i.e. his fiftieth birthday) and the exceptional became a routine feature of the coverage (i.e. his son Leo's birth). However, it is important to emphasise that the phenomenon of the politicisation of private persona is rather nuanced: although routinised, the references to the personal clearly did not dominate the coverage.

Chapter 6 explores how the transformations in the role of the personal experienced during Blair's era have affected the communication strategies and media coverage of his successors, Gordon Brown and David Cameron. After Blair walked out of No. 10, did the politicisation of private persona recede, back to 'normal'? More broadly, what effect has the Blair era had on journalists', politicians' and parties' understandings of the role of the personal? The analysis will demonstrate that although there are importance differences in the strategic needs, style and personality of these two leaders, both had little choice but to adapt to the new conditions, which have made the personal a 'normal' feature of political discourse.

The book's concluding chapter reviews the key theoretical arguments and discusses the past, present and future manifestation of personalisation, and especially the politicisation of private persona, in British politics. It also reassesses the normative implications of the phenomenon, arguing that although the role of the personal in political discourse is not as overwhelming as sometimes assumed, nor is it necessarily negative, its potential impacts are such that it demands a close watching brief, because it is changing our politics in ways that, even if ambiguous in part, are normatively worrying. The final section discusses the challenges to personalisation brought about by the coalition government and suggests new directions in the research agenda.

Notes

1 There have been substantial reforms at the sub-national level but not in relation to Westminster, nor in the executive-parties dimension (see Flinders, 2005).
2 They have also been defined as professional qualities (Seymour-Ure, 1995) or performance-related personality traits (Miller et al., 1986).

1

The presidentialisation of power

As established in the introduction, personalisation is an ill-defined concept, used for alluding to related but different phenomena. Thus, it is necessary to distinguish between these two interconnected but distinctive dimensions of personalisation: 'presidentialisation' and 'personality politics'. *Presidentialisation* generally refers to a shift in the distribution of power towards leaders and away from political parties and collegiate forms of government (Poguntke and Webb, 2005a). Moreover, for presidentialisation to take place, there must also be an intensification of the role of leaders in campaigning and media coverage and of their impact on voting behaviour (Mughan, 2000). *Personality politics*, on the other hand, refers to an increasing emphasis in political discourse on the character, personality and personal lives of candidates and leaders, which is said to displace the focus away from performance, ideological affiliation and policy. In addition, within personality politics it is important to distinguish between an emphasis on leadership qualities and on leaders' personal qualities and lives, the latter defined in this book as the politicisation of private persona.

This chapter will focus on the first of these concepts, i.e. the presidentialisation of power, leaving the discussion of personality politics and the politicisation of private persona for Chapter 2. The first section will define the concept and explain the causes of its development. The second section will scrutinise how presidentialisation affects democratic politics. Finally, the third section will present a critical overview of what we know about the different faces of presidentialisation (i.e. executive, party and electoral), and especially of how it has been manifested in the United Kingdom.

Defining presidentialisation

More wide ranging than personality politics, and in some ways more controversial, presidentialisation is nonetheless a more precisely defined concept. As stated in the introduction, and following the definition by Poguntke and Webb (2005a), it refers to the process by which leaders gain greater power resources and autonomy in the decision-making process, displacing other political actors, especially political parties and collegiate forms of government (cabinets and parliaments), without a formal change of regime type. Although the concept focuses on the shifts of power from the collective to the individual within the executive, the process of presidentialisation also strongly affects the relationship of the leader with the party, endowing him or her with more power within, and autonomy from, it. Moreover, the electoral process also becomes more leader-centred, with a greater focus on leaders in campaigning and in media coverage of politics, and stronger leader effects in voting behaviour (Mughan, 2000; Poguntke and Webb, 2005a). More broadly, the electoral face of presidentialisation is also associated with what Foley has defined as 'leadership stretch', which refers to the process by which leaders become not only more prominent but also increasingly detached from the party in the construction of their political identity, in media coverage and in their assessment by the public (Foley, 2004: 293). This, in turn, gives them more autonomy from other actors. The presidentialisation of power hence affects the three central arenas of democratic government: the executive face, the party face, and the electoral face (Poguntke and Webb, 2005a: 5). These three processes should not be assumed to 'run in perfect simultaneity with each other ... That said, it is expected that once one of these processes starts it will impact on the others' (Poguntke and Webb, 2005a: 16).

This is a clear definition. However, it is not how the term 'presidentialisation' is most commonly employed, especially by politicians and journalists. Instead, it is often used to condemn what is regarded as excessive and unaccountable power in the hands of the prime minister while equating it, paradoxically, to the US presidency, which – certainly compared to the UK executive – is much weaker. The analogy would arguably make more sense if the point of comparison were the delegative democracies of Latin America (O'Donnell, 1994). However, this is rarely the case, and hence precisely because of the association with the US presidency the concept is in many ways misleading. Nonetheless, because it is an established feature of contemporary political discourse, it has become the key (albeit contested) term for discussing the shifts in the distribution of power in parliamentary systems.

As understood here the concept of presidentialisation does not imply that prime ministers and (US) presidents are now indistinguishable; nor does it mean that prime ministers are omnipotent or always more powerful than they used to be. Instead, what this contested analogy conveys is that the logic of the system now 'more closely echoes presidentialist politics than was hitherto the case' (Heffernan and Webb, 2005: 56) but within the ground rules laid down by the parliamentary system, including a core degree of collegiality and different structural power dependencies (Heffernan, 2005b: 53; Heffernan and Webb, 2005: 27). In fact, in the case of the UK, the prime minister generally has more autonomy and is more powerful than the US president because of the fusion of powers between the executive and the legislature, and the dominance of the former over the latter due to the majoritarian nature of the UK's parliamentary system, its unitary state and, despite the increase in backbench rebellions (Cowley and Stuart, 2005), a much stronger party discipline (Heffernan and Webb, 2005: 43). Conversely, due to the stronger role and independence enjoyed by Congress, the functions of the Supreme Court, and the limited terms, presidents 'are far more constrained than prime ministers' (Rhodes et al., 2009: 86). On the other hand, the prime minister's autonomy is partially off-set by the fact that, unlike the president, he or she does not enjoy a fixed term in office. Moreover, prime ministers have to retain the confidence of the legislature, and hence the party. Furthermore, the executive is a collective office and cabinet members – although selected by the prime minister – are also generally elected representatives with personal followings, and have greater ministerial autonomy and resources than those endowed to ministers in presidential systems (Heffernan, 2005a).

In general terms, thus, presidentialisation refers to an increase in the autonomy and power resources of the prime minister. However, it is equally important to appreciate, as Foley (2008) rightly emphasises, that when using the presidential analogy one has to pay attention not only to the strengthening of leadership power but also to how it can help to analyse and explain its erosion and decline. Presidentialisation does not make prime ministers more powerful under all circumstances. The increasingly person-alised mandate of the leader reinforces his or her power vis-à-vis the party and cabinet when he or she is successful but also makes it weaker in times of unpopularity and defeat, as personalised leadership encourages inflated accountability of the leader (Foley, 2008: 61). In addition, it is important to stress that the power of the prime minister is still contingent, as in any system, on the political circumstances and the personal resources and skills of leaders (Heffernan, 2003). In fact, presidentialisation trends can make power more contingent as the leader is more dependent on personal popular support, and hence his or her authority is more affected by the whims of public opinion (Webb and Poguntke, 2005: 353).

In short, presidentialisation indicates a degree of convergence in how power is exercised in both systems, especially in terms of a more person-alised popular mandate, greater autonomy from the party, and stronger power resources available to the leader within the executive. But it is certainly not to say that presidents and prime ministers have become indistinguishable. Institutional and constitutional differences still (and will always) matter a great deal. Hence the role of leaders in presidential and parliamentary systems continues to be distinctive, leading not to a de facto presidential system but to 'an emergent hybrid' that fuses some dimensions of presidential politics with the forms of parliamentary democracy and cabinet government (Foley, 2000: 351). Moreover, because of systemic differences, the degree and forms of presidentialisation trends and how these affect the balance of power will significantly vary across countries.

The causes of presidentialisation

Although manifested in different degrees across countries, depending on cultural and systemic variables, there have been structural changes affecting most Western democracies that encourage a shift towards the presidentiali-sation of power. Two in particular stand out: the role of the media and the changes in the relationship between citizens and political parties.

The media, and especially electronic media, now play a massive role in democratic politics, which has led many to speak of mediated or mediatised democracies (e.g. Bennett and Entman, 2001; Meyer, 2002). However, only fifty years ago television played a tangential and deferential part in the political process. Moreover, at least in Western Europe, politicians relied heavily on direct communication and the partisan press, and the coverage across media followed a 'party logic'. In contrast, nowadays the role of partisan media has severely weakened and television (and increasingly the internet) has become the most consumed medium and the main source of political information. As a result, politicians and parties increasingly have had to adapt their strategies to the 'media logic' (Blumler and Kavanagh, 1999; Mazzoleni and Schulz, 1999). These changes are crucial on the development of presidentialisation, and personalisation more generally, because media (and especially television) tend to personalise political coverage. At the same time, parties do not just go along with the media's preferences but also try to exploit them, offering their leaders at all times and in all formats, from exclusive interviews to photo opportunities to talk show appearances.

Beyond the coverage, which is what is most generally emphasised in the literature (but see Foley, 2000; Heffernan, 2006), the central role of the media in contemporary politics also has other 'presidentialising' effects, especially in terms of leadership power resources vis-à-vis cabinets and the party. Because mediatisation is associated with a greater professionalisation and centralisation of party organisation and communication, it has empowered leaders and their core circle (Lilleker, 2005). Moreover, the media – with its inherent gravitation towards leaders – offers them key means for disinter-mediation and 'going public' (Kernell, 1997), enabling them to present themselves as 'outsiders', to build personal support from citizens, and to assemble temporary coalitions across interest groups without the need for direct intervention of other institutions, especially political parties (Foley, 2000, 2008). These trends have been deepened by the rise of 'soft' formats and the increasing prevalence of the internet, as they enable leaders to reach the public without the mediation of even professional journalists themselves. But it is not just about visibility and personal outreach. Because of the centrality of the media to contemporary politics, positive coverage buttresses the prime minister's standing in the government and the party and enables him or her to set the agenda and define the viable choices, and force ministers to stay 'on message' (Heffernan, 2006; Poguntke and Webb, 2005b; Seymour-Ure, 1994). However, equally importantly, 'the very opposite will apply in regard to negative, critical coverage' (Heffernan, 2005a: 617) as criticisms also tend to focus on leaders. So the central role of the media in contemporary democracies is a double-edged sword for leaders. As if they were on steroids, it can temporarily empower them but also, in difficult times, make them more vulnerable, diminishing their leverage and authority (see Helms, 2008).

The second factor explaining a trend towards a presidentialisation of power is the decline in party identification and membership, tied in with a weakening of clear-cut social cleavages, the decline of left–right identification and a lower ideological polarisation (see Clarke et al., 2004; Dalton and Wattenberg, 2000). This process has led to a rise of 'persuadable' or floating voters, who are more likely to be influenced by short-term factors, including the images of parties and leaders (Clarke et al., 2004). At the same time, mainstream parties have adapted to these changes, tending to converge in the centre and becoming more electorally oriented, leading to what has been defined as catch-all (Kirchheimer, 1966) or electoral-professional parties (Panebianco, 1988). This type of party tends to be less strongly ideological and more focused on valence issues. As a result, the main difference between parties becomes not so much ideology as their perceived capacity to deliver (Green, 2007: 630). In this context, leaders come to be considered an important 'selling' point both because of their role in delivering policy outcomes and their importance as cognitive shortcuts to assess the party's values and future competence in office (Clarke et al., 2004).

There have also been other factors contributing to the declining influence of collective actors. Firstly, there has been a process of fragmentation of power, with decision-making moving not only downwards (to sub-national actors) and outwards (to non-state actors) but also upwards to supranational (especially the European Union) and international organisations (e.g. G20, WTO). There has also been an increase in judicial activism in most Western democracies (Hague and Harrop, 2010). As a result, on the one hand, the overall power of national governments, including the executive, has been weakened (Rose, 2001). On the other hand, because of the rise of 'summitry' politics (Helms, 2008: 42), the power of leaders and senior government figures and their advisers is enhanced, at the expense of collective institutions, because of their role and visibility as national chief negotiators and because decisions taken elsewhere cannot be re-negotiated (Poguntke and Webb, 2005a: 14). Secondly, there has been a growth in the competence of the state, which has made it more complex and fragmented, hence demanding greater centralisation and coordination from the executive and discouraging cabinet collective responsibility (Poguntke and Webb, 2005a: 14). These two transformations essentially affect the executive face of the process of presidentialisation, although in turn reinforcing the party and electoral faces as well (Poguntke and Webb, 2005a: 16).

Presidentialisation of power: normative concerns

The process of presidentialisation of power raises strong normative concerns. Firstly, it affects the checks and balances that are aimed at dispersing power among different political actors, and especially at constraining the power of the prime minister. In particular, the issue is that presidentialisation leads to the circumvention of the key sources of restraint of individual authority: cabinet and parliament. Secondly, presidentialisation leads to the bypassing of political parties, and hence, it is feared, to a loss of democratic account-ability and the privatisation of political debate. The greater the degree of personalisation, the more the leader can claim to represent the popular mandate, gaining authority and legitimacy to decide according to his or her personal criteria and the recommendations of a small group of close allies. Moreover, because the leader is believed to be the key to electoral success, the party is compelled to refrain, at least temporarily, from challenging him or her, hence increasing the autonomy of the leader and his or her core circle and weakening the influence of dissident voices, reducing parlia-mentary scrutiny and democratic legitimacy. 'Ordinary' members and even mere sympathisers might be consulted more frequently as part of the attempt to gain personalised support and legitimacy but consultation is often merely plebiscitarian and to the detriment of those who have long-standing representation rights in party congresses or on party executives, and who are more likely to present a challenge to the leadership (see Heffernan and Webb, 2005; Mair, 2000; Scarrow et al., 2000). Moreover, participation is particularly constrained in regard to policy-making, with parties becoming like 'franchises' 'where the members are given a say over candidate and leadership selection in return for which the parliamentary leaders are left with a relatively free hand with regard to setting policy' (Scarrow et al., 2000: 145). As a result, leaders become less the spokesperson of their parties, chosen to represent pre-agreed programmes and ideas, and more their 'trustees', freer to act according to their conscience and personal judgement (Manin, 1997). On the other hand, the process of presidentialisation can actually weaken leaders and government effectiveness. Firstly, it can over-empower citizens, or at least perceived public opinion, especially among electorally crucial demographic groups:

> It may seem counter-intuitive but chief executives and party leaders in an age of presidentialization have become more vulnerable than they were in the era of partified politics ... they become more susceptible to the fickle mood swings of public opinion. (Webb and Poguntke, 2005: 353)

This development, which for many has been epitomised by Clinton's presidency and by Blair's early years, results from leaders' permanent need to preserve direct popular support, and the heavier reliance on opinion polls. Secondly, because the strengthening of a leader's autonomy from party and cabinet is conditional upon, and vulnerable to, public opinion, if individualised decision-making is taken too far it can provoke – especially when the support for the leader is weak – opposition and dissent among MPs, potentially leading to legislative gridlock and government instability (Helms, 2008: 54). Finally, presidentialisation can also diminish the efficiency of the executive and government in general, as it can lead to prime ministerial overstretch and decreasing utility of leadership intervention (Foley, 2008).

Presidentialisation also raises concerns about electoral behaviour, which share much in common with the normative anxieties associated with personality politics. The fear is that the stronger role of leaders and their greater prominence in public discourse might lead citizens to pay more attention in their voting choices to 'soft' criteria, such as a leader's telegenicity and likeability, in detriment to policy and issues positions. As a result, it is feared that the quality of leadership will erode, especially as parties, in the pursuit of electoral popularity, might choose leaders that fit these – rather than ideological or competence-centred – criteria. However, although this is one of the prime normative fears associated with personality politics, it is less emphasised in the academic debates about the presidentialisation of power. This limited interest is a result of the long-held belief in political science that leaders, and certainly 'soft' personality traits, have ultimately only a weak influence on electoral behaviour (this will be further discussed below and in Chapter 2).

Presidentialisation of power in the UK

Given the socio-political changes explored above, it is plausible to expect clear trends towards presidentialisation in the UK. Moreover, given its majoritarian and unitarian structure, which promotes strong executive power, the effects in the UK should be particularly marked. A review of the literature and available evidence confirms that this is the case, but with substantial qualifications. Firstly, concentration of power in the hands of a popular prime minister is not a recent phenomenon, nor does it make the prime minister unconditionally powerful, either within the executive or the party; the prime minister's effective use of his or her power resources, which in general terms are greater than in the past, continues to be contingent on the support of other actors and on his or her political skills. However, this support is now more heavily dependent on the prime minister's personal popularity with the electorate at large. Secondly, presidentialisation trends do not make the UK prime minister indistinguishable from presidents as the two continue to have markedly different structural power dependencies. Finally, the evidence on the electoral face of presidentialisation is anything but clear-cut, especially when one focuses the analysis – as required by the presidentialisation thesis – on the presence (or rather absence) of a persistent and systematic increase in leaders' electoral influence and prevalence in public discourse *over time*. The remainder of this chapter will discuss each of these dimensions in turn.

Party and executive face

The idea that the there is too much power concentrated in the hands of the prime minister is certainly not new in British politics. Although there were earlier concerns, it manifested more strongly during the early 1960s, when it was already referred to as 'the conventional wisdom' (Jones, 1964: 168). However, at the time the debate was not so much about presidentialisation but between two competing models associated with parliamentary government: the prime ministerial and the cabinet models. The former, associated with the work of Mackintosh (1962) and especially Crossman (1963), asserted that, although always strong, there had been such a progressive inflation of the power of prime ministers, to the detriment of the cabinet, that prime ministers could no longer be truly considered *primus inter pares* (Foley, 1993: 8; Mughan, 2000: 3). Although influential and given further credence by Harold Wilson's leadership style, this thesis was for the most part dismissed by those espousing the cabinet government model. They argued that, given the characteristics and strength of the institutional arrangements of the British system, the prime minister, unlike the president, would always be highly dependent on the support of cabinet and party. In other words, a prime minister was considered to be 'only as strong as his party, and in particular his chief colleagues, let him be' (Jones, 1964: 178). The Thatcher years re-ignited the debate. Nevertheless, many still considered her style of government as a temporary abnormality resulting from an exceptional personality and not the result of lasting changes, leaving the debate 'as a freakish idea connected to a freakish woman in freakish times' (Foley, 1993: 19). This conviction was strengthened by her fall as a result of a 'cabinet coup' and the seemingly more collegiate style of government of her successor, John Major, which restored the belief in the strength of cabinet government. However, the debate reappeared with renewed force during Blair's leadership. Moreover, it now focused less on prime ministerial vs. cabinet government and more on presidentialisation, which is a more encompassing concept. In fact, Blair came to epitomise the idea of a 'British presidency' (Allen, 2003; Foley, 2000), grounded not just in his management of the cabinet and ministers but also in the characteristics of his relationship with the civil service and the party, his (public) leadership style and the belief in his strong personal electoral appeal.

Although the way the concept is used is often problematic, the shift in the terms of the debate has been helpful. Firstly, the core executive model (Smith, 1999) has taken on more force, rejecting the notion of a zero-sum game in the distribution of power, and hence helping to overcome the sterile dichotomies implied in the cabinet vs. prime ministerial government debate. This model emphasises that both the cabinet and the prime minister can be simultaneously, but differently, powerful, and that they ultimately both depend on other state and non-state actors; hence their relative power is conditional to the alliances they build (Heffernan, 2005a). At the same time, this model should not be seen to conflate all actors as equal. Power resources are not equally distributed among actors and hence the prime minister, who is better resourced, is less dependent than other actors (although not totally independent) (Heffernan, 2003, 2005a). Secondly, instead of discussing presidentialisation *in toto* (i.e. for it to exist prime ministers must become, in all but name, the same as presidents), the focus is now more on using the presidential analogy if, and when, helpful to understand and explain the shifts in the role of leaders and leadership in British contemporary politics (Foley, 2000).

The crucial point of the presidentialisation thesis is that the system has come to operate with a more presidential dynamic or logic. In relation to the executive face, this means that the power resources available to the prime minister have been enhanced, placing him or her – when popular – in an even stronger position 'to be more than simply first among equals' (Heffernan and Webb, 2005: 28). The same arguments in regard to the structural differences between parliamentary and presidential systems still apply, and should not be forgotten. In this sense, the crucial point is that this shift takes place within the executive's predominance over the legislature that characterises the British system, hence enabling the chief executive to have potentially 'far more unchecked institutional authority than the president' (Heffernan, 2005a: 608).

Specifically, under a presidentialist dynamic, leaders should have more power within government, including greater administrative resources that enable – but do not ensure – greater prime ministerial predominance within the core executive. There is a fair degree of consensus (albeit not total – see Bevir and Rhodes, 2006) that this has been the case in the UK (e.g. Foley, 2000; Heffernan and Webb, 2005; Kavanagh and Seldom, 2008), even if many still disagree with conceptualising this shift as presidentialisation (e.g. Burch and Holliday, 2004). These changes started in the 1960s, continued during Major's and Thatcher's years and intensified during Blair's government. There is now an executive office 'in all but name' (Burch and Holliday, 2004), which combines the prime minister's and the revamped cabinet office. There was also a marked rise in the number and use of special advisers, who unlike civil servants are political appointees and hence more like presidential staffers in the US (Bevir and Rhodes, 2006: 673). Moreover, Blair paid much greater attention to, and had more control over, government communication, especially through a much stronger No. 10 Press Office and the new Strategic Communication Unit, which also coordinated the press relations of all ministers and played an important role in policy formulation (Bevir and Rhodes, 2006; Scammell, 2001). Blair also expanded the size and role of the Policy Unit (which had existed since 1974), had a special adviser with extensive powers as No. 10 Chief of Staff, created the role of Cabinet enforcer, and used 'joined up' government (including the creation of several policy-related units) to attempt to enforce his will across departments (Burch and Holliday, 2004; Rhodes, 2000). A few of these changes were reversed by Gordon Brown, in particular the authority of special advisers to instruct civil servants and the nature of the role of the Chief of Staff and of the Chief Press Secretary. But overall he retained most of No. 10's enhanced political and civil service resources, especially in relation to policy-making (Blick and Jones, 2010; Jones and Norton, 2010).

The changes in the role of the prime minister are not limited to resources. Decision-making has become dominated by ad hoc committees and 'creeping' bilateralism, and thus moved away from the full cabinet, placing the prime minister and his or her close advisers at the centre of the core executive network and the policy-making process (Heffernan, 2003: 358–60). This is of course not entirely new but bilateralism has become

'Whitehall's default setting', both reflecting and reinforcing the inflated prime ministerial authority and power (Heffernan, 2005a: 614). During the late 1940s the cabinet met on average 87 times a year, with 340 papers being formally circulated; in the 1970s, 60 times a year, with 140 papers; and by the 1990s, no more than 40 times a year, with only 20 papers (Heffernan, 2003: 359). This trend accelerated under Blair: whereas few decisions were taken – rather than merely stamped – by the full cabinet, in his first 25 months in office Blair held a total of 783 meetings with individual ministers, compared to Major's 272 (Kavanagh and Seldom, 2008: 210 and 286). This was combined with little tolerance for dissent within the cabinet (Heffernan, 2005a: 613). Of course, the British executive is still a collective body. Senior cabinet members can strongly constrain and provoke serious challenges to the prime minister, and here Gordon Brown's fierce hold over domestic policy from the Chancellor's office, practically unthinkable in a presidential system, comes immediately to mind. But authority and power resources are unequally distributed among ministers, and this distribution is to a large extent dependent on their relationship with the leader.

Moreover, the strengthened power of the prime minister spreads across the system. A stronger executive in the hands of a successful and popular prime minister expands his or her role within the party, seemingly allowing him or her 'to be as strong as he or she would wish' (Heffernan, 2005a: 615). In turn, particularly in parliamentary systems, predominance in the party facilitates greater dominance over the legislature. These trends are in part a result of the party refraining, due to electoral considerations, from challenging the authority of a popular leader. But there have also been more formal party reforms, typical of the shift from mass to electoral-professional parties, that have given leaders and their closest circles (both in power and in opposition) a much greater say over not only the choice of candidates and the marketing of the party but also policy formation (Dalton and Wattenberg, 2000; Heffernan, 2005a; Webb, 2000). These trends have been particularly marked in the case of Labour which, unlike the Conservatives, has traditionally apportioned more power outside the parliamentary leadership (Webb, 2000). However, although starting from different positions, both parties moved in similar directions during the 1980s and 1990s: in combination with a degree of confined intra-party 'democratisation', they enhanced the strategic autonomy of the leadership, especially in policy-formulation, while excluding – as much as possible – backbenchers and extra-parliamentary actors (Webb, 2000: 200).

On the one hand, the reforms gave the grassroots a stronger voice, as rank and file members now play a significant role in the leadership elections in both parties. Moreover, especially in the case of Labour, the grassroots have been consulted more often about key decisions such as the change to Clause IV, the party's constitution and key policies for the 1997 manifesto (Webb, 2000). On the other hand, this consultation is plebiscitarian rather than truly participatory, as choices are heavily pre-defined by the leadership. Nonetheless, consultation makes it harder for dissidents to dispute 'popularly' endorsed leadership decisions.

Crucially, at the same time, the influence of backbenchers, extra-parliamentary wings, and local and regional elites has been reduced, sidelining factions and potentially troublesome activists that could challenge the leader, and limiting dissent (see Heffernan and Webb, 2005; Mair, 2000; Scarrow et al., 2000). This is not to say that those who are excluded will always go quietly; in fact, backbench rebellions have grown since the 1970s (Cowley and Stuart, 2005; Norton, 2005; Webb, 2000), in part precisely as a reaction to their sidelining by the leadership. But although they can at times be problematic, especially when a leader's popularity is wavering, their impact should not be exaggerated. Most rebellions are small and by the same MPs (Cowley and Stuart, 2005); in fact, Blair did not lose a single whipped vote until 2005. Moreover, discipline and cohesive behaviour is still relatively high due to a number of factors, including the national and hierarchical organisation of parties, the electoral system and the carrots and sticks in the hands of the prime minister (Webb, 2000: 187). So, although as a reaction to presidentialisation trends MPs' independence might increase, parties have re-organised to do their best to minimise their, and other troublesome party actors', influence. Moreover, there are strong incentives for discipline when it counts because dissent threatens, unlike in presidential systems, their own survival as the party of government and MPs.

To sum up, the presidentialisation of power is meant to affect all three central arenas of democratic government: the executive face, the party face and the electoral face. The first two, as discussed, are generally accepted to have taken place in the UK, with developments accelerating (rather than starting) during Blair's premiership. Moreover, although affected by personal leadership styles, many of these changes are structural rather than idiosyncratic, and hence enduring. On the other hand, it is clear that even though the process of presidentialisation strengthens their resources and authority (within what is already a very dominant executive), leaders are not unconditionally powerful. They are still constrained by other actors – which increasingly reside outside both Westminster and Whitehall – and by the strength of their personal and political resources, which can vary greatly over time, even for the same leader. In fact, the inflated leader's personal authority can become a weakness. If his or her popularity decreases and he or she does not perform electorally, he or she will become more vulnerable within the party, affecting also his or her power within the executive and his or her control over the legislature.

The third dimension of presidentialisation, the electoral face, seems even more evident on the surface. However, as we shall see, the empirical evidence is less clear-cut. The electoral face of a presidentialised system should combine a significant *growth* in a) leadership appeals in election campaigning, b) the focus on leaders in media coverage, and c) leader effects in voting behaviour (Poguntke and Webb, 2005a: 10). Or, in Mughan's (2000: 11) terms, it should involve the presidentialisation of presentation (more leader-centred campaigns and media coverage) and the presidentialisation of impact (stronger leaders' influence on electoral behaviour). But what is actually known about the electoral face of presidentialisation? Is there compelling evidence of these processes in the British case? I shall first look at the evidence on the media coverage, secondly on party communication and finally on electoral behaviour.

The electoral face

Presidentialisation of the media coverage of campaigns

There has certainly been a lot of research about the media coverage of electoral campaigns. Even though the detailed figures vary across studies, the general conclusions point in the same direction: the overall visibility of leaders in the media coverage of recent elections strongly suggests a presidentialism of presentation (Mughan, 2000)[1] or leadership stretch (Foley, 2000: 205), with leaders taking a remarkably high proportion of the coverage given to their parties (between 35 and 65 per cent depending on the election and the indicators used). Moreover, they appear and are seen speaking or are quoted substantially more than all other party spokespersons, often including all (shadow) cabinet members added together. This applies to all three main leaders (but especially the third party's) and, with some variation, both for broadcasting (Deacon et al., 2001; Deacon et al., 2005; Foley, 1993; Goodard et al., 1998; Harrison, 1993, 1998, 2002, 2005) and for the press (Deacon et al., 2001; Deacon et al., 2005; Harrop and Scammell, 1993; Norris, 1998; Scammell and Harrop, 1998; Scammell and Semetko, 2008; Semetko et al., 1994; Seymour-Ure, 1995, 1998).

There is little doubt then that leaders have a prominent presence in the media coverage of elections. However, in order to confirm the thesis of presidentialisation, the key question is not whether election coverage focuses predominantly on leaders but rather whether there is evidence of a *systematic increase* in their relative visibility. This is a stringent test for presidentialisation as it makes sense to expect a degree of fluctuation in the role of leaders from election to election. Nonetheless, it is a crucial question because it is change – and more specifically escalation – that is at the heart of most understandings of personalisation.

Figure 1.1 Absolute number of times the prime minister and leader
of the opposition were quoted in TV news bulletins, General Elections 1964–2005
(BBC & ITV)

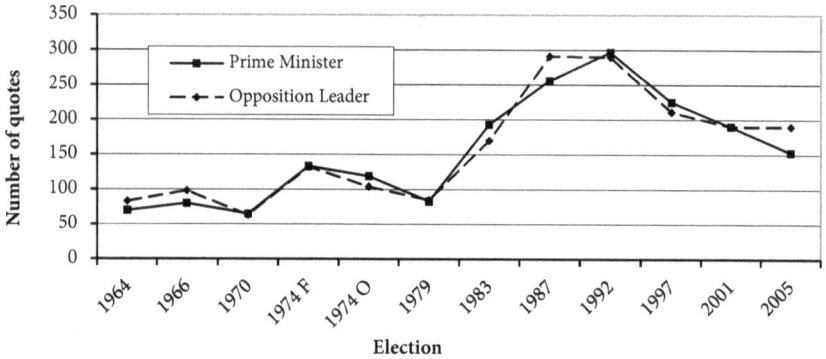

Source: Based on data from Harrison (1965, 1966, 1971, 1974, 1975, 1985, 1988, 1993, 1998, 2002 and 2005) and Pilsworth (1979) in Nuffield studies

Systematic historical analysis of media coverage of British campaigns is rare, making Harrison's studies on broadcasting coverage, which started in 1964, probably the only source of this kind. For this reason, a few researchers have relied on this data in order to uncover patterns of change in the (relative) degree of visibility of leaders (Crewe and King, 1994; Foley, 2000; Mughan, 2000; Rose, 1980). However, although relying on the same source, the conclusions are varied. Some found that, despite the presidentiali-sation thesis, 'television coverage of British campaigns *is not significantly more leader-centered* now than it was in the 1960s' (Crewe and King, 1994: 189, italics added). In contrast, others, including both Foley (2000) and Mughan (2000), concluded that there has been an increase both in the absolute and relative visibility of leaders. So, has the television coverage of British campaigns become more 'presidentialised' or not? The analysis of the evidence presented here, based on the same primary data but including every election between 1964 and 2005,[2] shows an overall positive trend for the period as a whole and *some* positive indicators for relative visibility for the most recent period in particular (1987–2005). However, the evidence does not conclusively support common assumptions that the coverage has become systematically more leader-centred.

Figure 1.1 shows that, overall, there has been an upward trend over time, especially since 1979. Moreover, although leaders' visibility has been decreasing since the peak in 1992, it has not returned to the previous low of the 1960s and 1970s. Thus these figures partially support the thesis of

Figure 1.2 Number of times the prime minister and leader of the opposition
were quoted as percentage of total number of quotes of all party spokespersons
in TV news bulletins, General Elections 1964–2005 (BBC & ITV)

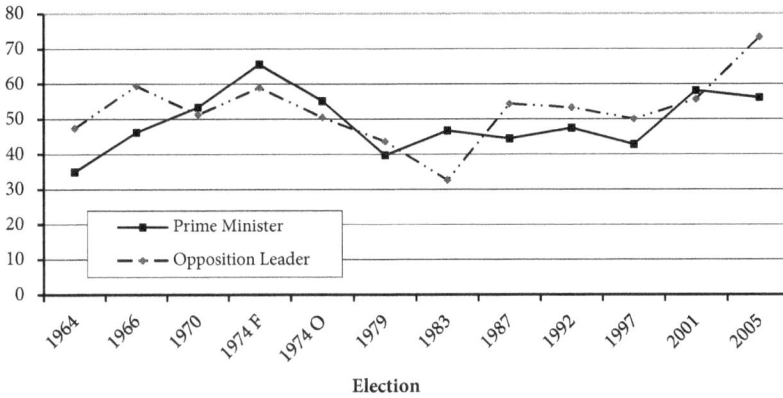

Source: Based on data from Harrison (1965, 1966, 1971, 1974, 1975, 1985, 1988,
1993, 1998, 2002 and 2005) and Pilsworth (1979) in Nuffield studies

presidentialisation of presentation, indicating a greater absolute presence of
the leaders in the news. But, because they are absolute numbers, they are
in some ways misleading. The changes might not be indicating a more or
less 'presidentialised' coverage but differences over time in editorial policy
and in the overall treatment of the election by the broadcasters.

Figure 1.2 and Figure 1.3 are better indicators because they show the
leaders' relative visibility compared to their party colleagues; Figure 1.2
as percentage of the total number of quotes of all Conservative and Labour
spokespersons, and Figure 1.3 as the ratio between the number of quotes
of the leader and of each party's five 'heavy hitters'.[3] In both cases the
analysis clearly shows that since television started covering the elections,
they have all been fairly 'presidentialised'. As can be seen in Figure 1.2, the
prime minister and the opposition leader were responsible for on average 50
per cent of their parties' quotes, the lowest combined figures being 41 per
cent in 1964 and 40 per cent in 1983 and the highest 62 per cent in 1974
(February) and 65 per cent in 2005. Although the trend is positive overall,
there is a fair degree of fluctuation. Moreover, the highest combined figures
were in the elections of 1966 and the early 1970s and not, as often imagined,
during the Thatcher or Blair years.

This finding, even though it does not confirm a systematic increase in
the predominance of the leaders over time, does make sense. It was during

Figure 1.3 Ratio of the number of quotes of the prime minister and leader of the opposition to the average for each party's top five spokespersons in TV news bulletins, General Elections 1964–2005 (BBC & ITV)

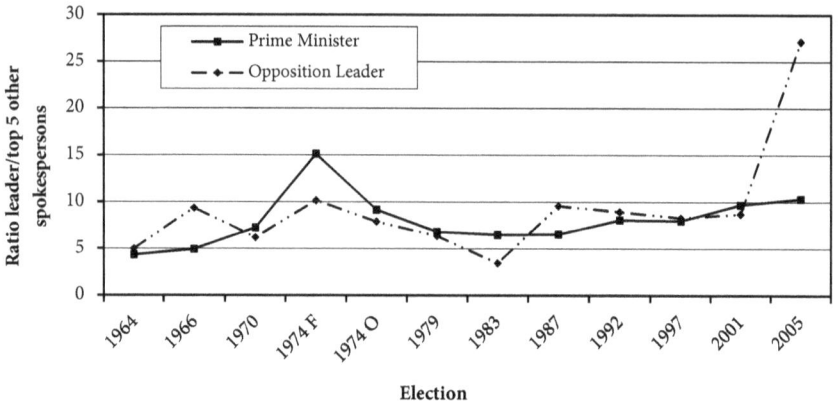

Source: Based on data from Harrison (1965, 1966, 1971, 1974, 1975, 1985, 1988, 1993, 1998, 2002 and 2005) and Pilsworth (1979) in Nuffield studies

the mid 1960s and early 1970s that television started to dictate the style of the campaign. Moreover, some these elections were particularly close, which tends to increase the focus on the leaders. Since 1987, possibly as a result of the further professionalisation of campaigns, there has been another, uneven, surge in the prominence of the leaders, especially for the Leader of the Opposition, with the last three elections higher on average than any preceding period (but see Deacon et al., 2005: 20). Moreover, the 2005 election showed the highest proportions since February 1974, but this was not as a result of an increase in the attention paid to all leaders but due to Howard's strategy, which 'came perilously close to presenting the party as a one-man band' (Harrison, 2005: 106). In combination, these figures demonstrate that the degree of personalisation has not experienced a systematic escalation; instead, it is still greatly affected by party strategy in each election, which is heavily dependent on whether or not a leader is considered the party's main electoral asset.

The absence of a systematic increase over time, and the early surge, might seem surprising. On the other hand, it can be partially explained by the fact that it is during the mid 1960s and early 1970s that television had come to dictate the style of the campaign. For this reason, one would expect the increase to be more marked in press data, especially in comparison to the pre-TV era. Although this seems to be the case for the leader vis-à-vis the party, it is less clear in relation to the (shadow) cabinet. Dalton et al. (2000)

found that, between 1959 and 1997, the ratio of the number of mentions of leaders to parties in election stories in *The Times* rose from 0.7 to 1.3. Similarly, Mughan's evidence for editorials indicates that *The Times* 'significantly increased the attention it paid to sitting prime ministers relative to their party and did likewise, albeit more mutedly, for opposition leaders relative to theirs' (Mughan, 2000: 38). On the other hand, the increase of leaders' visibility vis-à-vis their cabinets is less clear. Mughan's data, which is the only longitudinal evidence available, shows that although there was a surge in the 1980s and 1990s, the trend line is characterised by a high degree of fluctuation (Mughan, 2000: 39, figure 2.2).

In combination, this re-examination of the empirical evidence indicates that in every election a substantial part of the coverage of both television and newspapers has focused on leaders. Moreover, overall, there are some indications of an increase in the relative visibility of the leaders vis-à-vis their parties and their colleagues over time. But the increase, especially relative to other party spokespersons, is anything but as marked or systematic as conventional wisdom might suggest. Furthermore, although there is a recent upsurge in the period 1987–2005 (especially for the Leader of the Opposition), the trend lines demonstrate that this period has not been unique in regard to a consistent elevated degree of leaders' visibility. In fact, it is the 1960s and 1970s that most clearly stand out. In short, although traces of presidentialisation in the coverage over time can be found, there is no clear-cut evidence of a *systematic* increase.

These conclusions are consistent with longitudinal studies in other parliamentary systems (for overviews of the data see Adam and Maier, 2010; Karvonen, 2009; Ohr, 2010) which show on the one hand overall upward trends in the candidate-centredness of campaign coverage, but on the other that these trends are milder and more uneven than expected. In fact, rather than systematic and progressive escalation, most studies found that leaders' visibility is to a significant extent dependent on personalities and political circumstances. This in turn affects, and is affected by, party communication strategies. Moreover, despite the increase in the focus on leaders vis-à-vis parties in the UK and other parliamentary democracies, the differences with the US have become in effect not smaller but greater (Dalton et al., 2000: 51–2). This, as Ohr (2010: 24) emphasises, reminds us that one should not automatically read weak signs of gradual personalisation in parliamentary systems as total convergence between the two systems.

Presidentialisation of party communication

The last few decades have seen an abundance of research about campaign communication, especially as a result of the interest in the so-called 'Americanisation' of campaigns. In this literature, personalisation is considered to be one of the key defining characteristics of modern or post-modern campaigning (Swanson and Mancini, 1996). Nonetheless, with the limited exception of analyses of the content of TV advertisements, there is hardly any systematic evidence tracking change over time. It is possible, however, based on the review of the party material and the literature on campaigns since 1945, to conclude that there has indeed been an increase in the centrality of leaders in the UK, both in terms of their strategic role and in their visibility in campaign material. Moreover, although it has not escalated systematically, it intensified in recent years, especially with Major for the Conservatives and Blair for Labour.

Almost every post-war leader played an important part in campaigns but their role became consistently stronger in the 1960s, with the establishment of television as the key medium, leading the Nuffield studies to describe, for the first but not for the last time, the 1966 General Election as a 'strikingly presidentialised campaign' (Harrison, 1966: 131). The influence of television not only focused the attention on the leader but also affected the overall organisation of the campaign, with parties adapting to the media (and especially TV) logic. In fact, it was in 1966 that press conferences were for the first time chaired by a party leader (Ted Heath) and the leaders' speeches timed for television (Harrison, 1966: 131). Furthermore, other elements of party communication also became more leader-centric. A basic content analysis of the Conservative party's manifestos since 1945 shows that the 1966 document has, with the exception of 1992, the most frequent use of 'I'. Similarly, Harold Wilson was the first ever Labour leader to use the first person singular in a party manifesto. Moreover, it was in 1970 that the UK had its first biopic party election broadcast ('Ted Heath, a man to trust'), which offered an 'intimate' portrayal of his 'life journey' and personal qualities.

The emphasis on the leader in party communication and overall campaign strategy continued with subsequent leaders, who also became a more common object of attack by the opposition. Callaghan, although wary of television and 'American gimmicks', led a campaign run by his personal team (not the party's) that revolved heavily around him (Scammell, 1995: 78). Kinnock continued the trend and was even more central to Labour's 1987 campaign (although less so in 1992), with his face covering the manifesto and his famous biopic ('Kinnock the movie') shown twice. Thatcher, on the other hand, did not allow her biopic to be broadcast because she 'feared it was too presidential' (Scammell, 1995: 258). This might seem surprising but contrary to common assumptions, although Thatcher's campaigns were extremely professionalised they were generally less leader-centred than those of Wilson, Heath, Callaghan and Kinnock (Scammell, 1995: 53). In contrast, the supposedly more collegiate John

Figure 1.4 Percentage of time leaders vs. other party spokespersons spoke in Party Election Broadcasts, 1992–2005

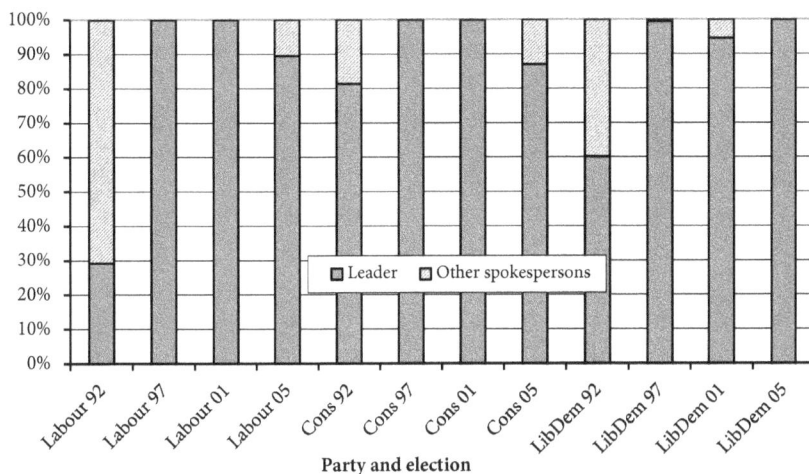

Source: Updated from Scammell and Langer (2006)

Major took personalised public leadership to new heights, setting himself, in the manner of US presidential candidates, above from the party (Scammell, 1995: 258). He ran campaigns that were 'unreservedly and unashamedly leader-centric in design and application' (Foley, 2002: 44), with his smile covering the hoardings and newspaper advertising. Moreover, the 1992 and 1997 manifestos, which he publicly defended as 'all me' (Foley, 2002: 44), had the leader's face on the cover and also had the most frequent use of 'I' of any Conservative leader.

Blair's centrality to Labour's campaign matched Major's. Moreover, the campaign's organisation and strategy were even more heavily controlled from the centre, by a cohesive and professional team closely linked to the leadership (see Gould, 1999). However, unlike in Major's case, the purpose was not to position him as separate or above the party but to generate positive associations between Blair and the 'new' party's brand. The centrality of the leader to the party's message was strikingly reflected in the manifestos of 1997 and 2001. Both had full-page pictures of Tony Blair on the cover and several others inside, and none of his colleagues. In addition, Blair used 'I' more frequently than any other leader (a striking 17 times in a short prologue in 1997), and was only the third Labour leader to use it at all. Moreover, remarkably, some of the 1997 broadcasts closed not by asking citizens to vote for Labour, but to 'Give Tony Blair your mandate'. More generally, the Party Election Broadcasts (PEBs) for both 1997 and

2001 seemed to imply that the only Labour politician was Blair: no party representative other than him appeared speaking. In fact, as shown in Figure 1.4, this is a common trend across parties: since 1997, at least 85 per cent of the words spoken by politicians in the PEBs came from the mouth of the leader.

However, it is important to put the leader-centred nature of these campaigns into perspective. Firstly, although more tightly run from the centre and controlled by leaders, campaigns in the UK are still, by and large, party affairs (Harrop, 2001). Secondly, parties and policies continue to remain central, even if these are now more often embodied by the leaders. Moreover, even though party representatives seem to be becoming endangered species, they are not always replaced by an emphasis on the leader. In the news, the major change has not been a greater focus on the leader but on the election itself, especially in the form of reports about the conduct of the campaign and opinion polls (Scammell and Semetko, 2008). In party electoral broadcasts, it is politicians as a whole that have become less prominent as they are increasingly replaced by actors, 'real people', celebrities, music and announcers (Scammell and Langer, 2007). These absences do not necessarily weaken the thesis of presidentialisation because the other party spokespersons have all but disappeared from PEBs; but as shown in Figure 1.5, it does mean that the role of leaders in PEBs is less prevalent that it might appear. In fact in some campaigns, such as the Conservatives' in 2001, leaders can be practically invisible.

Thirdly, and in line with the findings on media coverage, the personalisation trend is far from linear. Even though party campaigns have become more consistently and intensely leader-centric since the 1960s, the focus on a popular leader is not new. In 1945, the Conservative campaign revolved around Churchill's 'war-winning personality' (Butler, 1995: 5). He appeared in four out of ten Conservative broadcasts, the posters asked voters to 'Help HIM finish the job', and 95 per cent of the candidate election addresses included a eulogy of the leader (McCallum and Readman, 1947: 102). Even Attlee, who was a famously low-key leader, was at the centre of Labour's 1955 campaign, including a nationwide poster campaign telling the public 'You Can Trust Mr. Attlee' and a 'fireside chat' broadcast with his wife. At the same time, contemporary campaigns are not always leader-centred. It is true that in the era of television, professional campaigns and electoral parties the focus on the leader is the default setting. Nonetheless, the relative focus on the leader, the team and the party still varies a great deal depending on the political circumstances and the leader's style and popularity. For instance, although Labour ran very leader-centred campaigns in 1964, 1966 and 1970, in 1974 the party had come to realise that Wilson did not have the popularity he used to,

Figure 1.5 Percentage of total time where leaders spoke in Party Election Broadcasts, 1992–2005

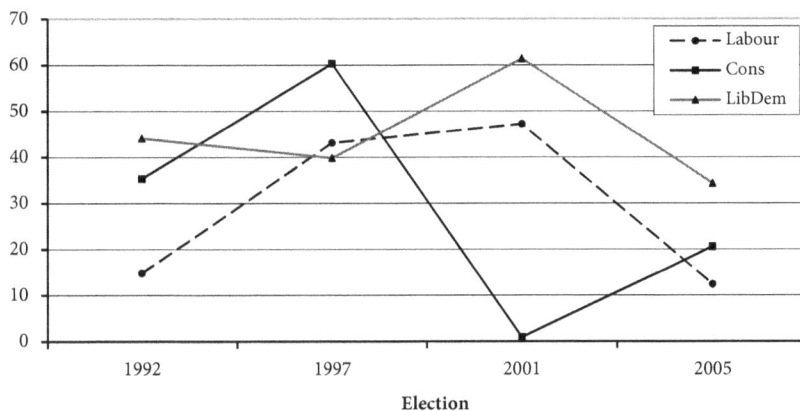

Source: Updated from Scammell and Langer (2006)

and so decided to 'focus on the team' (Cockerell, 1988: 195–6). Similarly, although at the very centre in 1987, in 1992 Kinnock was considered a liability and hence was 'packed through party publicity as the sober head of an able team' (Scammell, 1995: 256). Even Blair, widely regarded as the epitome of presidential-style campaigning, had to resort to party colleagues, and specifically to Gordon Brown, in the 2005 campaign. This alternating emphasis on the leader and the team underscores the persistent differences between presidential and parliamentary politics.

In short, the analysis suggests that leaders play an increasingly central role in controlling and presenting the party message. However, as in the case of media coverage, the centrality of leaders is neither entirely new, nor can it be said to be systematically escalating. In other words, the media and party campaign dimensions of the electoral face of presidentialisation can be only partially confirmed. On the one hand, leaders are clearly important and highly visible actors. On other hand, if we apply the stricter test, which is at the heart of most understandings of presidentialisation (i.e. systematic increase rather than high, but fluctuating, predominance), the evidence is less conclusive: within an overall upward trend, for most indicators we have also identified major fluctuations associated with structural (TV and campaign professionalisation) and transient changes (the popularity and style of leaders and the particularities of each campaign). This is in many ways unsurprising; party campaigns and media coverage are bound to adapt to the changing conditions of each election. Moreover, it is not as if nothing has changed: leader-centric campaigns are no longer anomalies associated with exceptional leaders but the default setting of contemporary elections. Nonetheless, as a whole, the evidence does call for more measured conclusions about the intensity and systematic nature of change. As much as the power of the leader within the executive and the party is now potentially greater but still contingent, so is the leader's role in campaigns. Moreover, it is worth highlighting again that, even when most leader-centred, there are still significant differences between the 'presidential' dynamics of British elections and US presidential campaigns.

Presidentialisation of electoral behaviour
The nagging suspicion that candidates can make parties win or lose elections has a long history. Most people, including politicians and journalists, have strongly believed for years that the appeal of leaders can often change the outcome of elections, even in parliamentary systems. However, academic research, especially outside the United States, has until relatively recently hardly taken this idea seriously. This omission reflected a widespread belief among political scientists that the vote was essentially determined by long-term structural variables, such as class. Moreover, it was firmly believed that leadership evaluations were themselves frequently a product of partisanship and were hence of little importance as an independent variable (Heffernan and Webb, 2005: 48–9). However, from the 1980s, in the context of weakening class cleavages and partisan dealignment, and alongside the pervasive claims of personalisation across Western democracies, it came to make increasing sense to assume that voters had become more susceptible to short-term factors of various kinds, including their perceptions of leaders. As a result research on the electoral impact of leaders substantially expanded (Bartle and Crewe, 2002; Bean, 1993; Bean and Mughan, 1989; King, 2002c; McAllister, 1996; Mughan, 2000; Stewart and Clarke, 1992).

This proliferation of research did not lead, however, to a consensual view. Or rather, although there is an agreement that the assessment of leaders plays a role in voting decisions, there are still differences between studies on the scale of their impact, its significance and, as in the case of the other dimensions of presidentialisation, to what extent this marks a systematic change from the past. Whereas some still remain sceptical, focusing on the highest possible test, i.e. the number of elections where the actual outcome has changed due to direct leader effects (see King, 2002c), there is an increasing trend to accept that party leaders matter, that overall they probably matter more than they used to, but that their impact is weaker than is popularly imagined once a wide range of factors are taken into account (McAllister, 2007). Moreover, the strength of leader effects are still (and are always likely to be) more muted than in presidential elections (Curtice and Hunjan, 2006; Mughan, 2000) and contingent because of the range of intervening factors (see Barisione, 2009a).

Aside from the discrepancies resulting from methodological variations, the most important differences are a result of how the evidence is interpreted. Overall, the research on leader effects at the individual level in the UK does agree that they are significant, but whereas for some they are modest and weaker than other factors such as social background or evaluations of issues (Bartle and Crewe, 2002: 87; Curtice and Holmberg, 2005: 245; Heffernan and Webb, 2005: 49; McAllister, 1996: 281), for others they are sizeable and often more important than most other variables, except possibly partisanship (Clarke et al., 2004: 59; Evans and Andersen, 2005: 289; Stewart and Clarke, 1992). In addition, they are stronger in the UK than in most parliamentary democracies because of the majoritarian system, which more closely mimics a presidential contest (Curtice and Holmberg, 2005: 245). On the other hand, if we focus on the outcome of elections, the conclusions are quite different. Given that the distribution of leaders' evaluations are generally not heavily favourable to one leader over another and that most elections are not that closely fought, 'whatever effects party leaders' characteristics may or may not have on individuals, those effects, at least in Britain, are only very seldom *both* on such a large scale *and* so skewed in their direction as to determine which party actually wins' (King, 2002b: 29; see also Bartle and Crewe, 2002: 93).

In the view of those with the most sceptical approach to leader effects, this evidence all but rejects the hypothesis of the electoral importance of leaders in Britain. These conclusions can, however, be contested on several grounds. Firstly, changing the outcome of elections is an extreme test. For instance, although economic perceptions are not always the difference between victory and defeat, 'few would conclude from this deterministic failure that the economy does not matter in elections' (Mughan, 2005: 3). Secondly, the fact that the evaluation of party leaders can make the crucial difference in closely fought elections can surely not be dismissed. Finally, the fact that the outcomes of a larger number of elections have not been affected certainly does not mean that (the images of) leaders do not matter. Each of the parties needs to make sure that the evaluation of their leaders is as positive as possible so that the differences in individual preferences are not translated into a negative net effect for their candidate. In short, even if leader effects have changed the outcome of 'only' a few elections, the fact that the evaluation of leaders has been found to have individual-level voter effects, and that on occasions they made the crucial difference between victory and defeat, can only mean that party leaders matter a great deal.

Equally important is that these kinds of analysis generally do not account for indirect effects. That is, they do not take into consideration either the influence of leaders within their parties, especially in terms of strategy, branding and policy; or, because of the focus on independent effects, the impact of leaders' evaluation on the party image (Clarke and Stewart, 1995; Heffernan and Webb, 2005) and on the assessment of issues, policy and government performance (Denver, 2003). This is crucial especially because the more dominant leaders become in the political process, the more likely they are to personify or act as 'surrogate' for policies and the party's capacity to deliver them (Rico, 2007; Wattenberg, 2004). In turn, this means that it is harder to ascertain the independence of these variables on the vote, and the more it makes sense to hypothesise that the causal arrow might need to be applied in the opposite direction as well (i.e. from leaders to party images). This applies not only for the policies of the party but to more intangible dimensions of a party's reputation. A powerful and decisive leader can create the impression of a strong and united party (e.g. Blair in 1997) and vice versa (e.g. Kinnock in 1992) (Heffernan and Webb, 2005: 50).

Thus, for all the disagreements, there is a good degree of consensus that leaders shape electoral choices both directly and indirectly, even if independent effects infrequently change the outcome of elections. However, as for other dimensions of personalisation, regarding whether leader effects have become *more* important over time, the evidence is less robust for most parliamentary democracies, with most studies showing mixed or negative results (for an overview see Karvonen, 2009; Schmitt and Ohr, 2000). In the case of the UK, Mughan (2000: 49) found an upward – although modest and fluctuating – trend in the magnitude of gross aggregate leaders' effects, concluding that 'party leaders matter, and they generally matter more now than in the 1960s and 1970s'. Clarke et al. (2009) also found that 'evaluations of party leaders have come to play a larger part in voters' decisions than previously' (in Denver, 2010: 605). However, other studies (that include the UK as well as other countries) are strongly sceptical, concluding 'beyond dispute' (Karvonen, 2009: 68) that 'nothing much seems to have changed' (Curtice and Holmberg, 2005: 252) and that the increase over time is 'a myth' (Holmberg and Oscarsson, 2010: 175; see also King, 2002c). In short, if anything is clear, it is that there is no consensus about the existence of a systematic increase in leader effects in electoral behaviour over time.

The lack of clear evidence is puzzling, as it goes against most people's intuition, including even political scientists (Foley, 2000: 236). Nonetheless, although the data does not offer the strongest of support for this dimension of the electoral face of presidentialisation, it does not invalidate it either. The fact is that, however ambiguous the scientific evidence is, the strong *perception* of an increase in leaders' effects means that parties will 'modify their campaign styles and structures as they come to perceive a growing *potential* for votes to be swayed by leadership evaluations' (Heffernan and Webb, 2005: 51, italics in original). Moreover, as the sceptical Anthony King himself recognises, this will also affect 'whom the parties choose as their leaders and candidates ... and how, if they win, they go on to govern' (King, 2002a: 212). These are surely not minimal effects.

Conclusion

The presidentialisation of power refers to the process by which leaders gain greater power resources and autonomy in the decision-making process, displacing other political actors, especially political parties and collegiate forms of government, without a formal change of regime type (Poguntke and Webb, 2005a). The use of the presidential analogy for parliamentary systems is controversial because it can seem to imply that the two regime types have now become indistinguishable. This is not the case. Institutional and consti-tutional structures still (and will always) matter a great deal, especially in terms of degree of collegiality and the difference in structural power dependencies (Heffernan, 2005b: 53; Heffernan and Webb, 2005: 27), which in the case of the UK makes the prime minister overall potentially more, and not as often imagined less, powerful than the US president. Instead, what presidentialisation indicates is that in some respects there are now greater similarities in how power is exercised in both systems, especially in terms of a more personalised popular mandate and legitimacy, a greater autonomy of the leader from the party, and stronger prime ministerial power resources within the executive. The prime minister can of course still be constrained by senior ministers, and often is. Moreover, the degree of autonomous power is still contingent to political circumstances and each leader's personal resources, but, as a result of presidentialisation, is potentially greater than in the past. Furthermore, the leader's autonomy within the executive and the party is now more dependent on his or her popularity with the media and the electorate at large, making him or her stronger when enjoying high public approval but also more vulnerable in hard times.

In the specific case of the UK, we have found positive indicators of the party and executive faces of presidentialisation, which accelerated – but did not start – during Blair's premierships. Firstly, the prime minister now has stronger administrative resources, a more central role at the core of the decision-making networks, and greater dominance over the cabinet. Secondly, there has been an enhancement of the strategic autonomy of the leadership within the party, especially in policy-formulation, in detriment to activists, extra-parliamentary actors and backbenchers. This development has affected both main parties but has been particularly marked in the case of Labour which, unlike the Conservatives, has traditionally apportioned more power outside the parliamentary leadership. Although these trends are not linear, because the degree of power is contingent to the leader's skills and popularity, there has been overall a clear strengthening of the autonomy and power resources of the leader within the party and the executive over time. In addition, even if at times the cabinet and the party reassert their power, the 'elastic band' – using Jones's analogy – does not simply spring back to the old norms of cabinet government. Broad socio-political transformations and formalised changes in both No. 10 and party constitutions mean that it is weak and collegiate, rather than strong and personalised, leadership that could now be regarded as 'temporary aberrations'. In other words, the pendulum of power will on occasions swing back in the direction of the party and cabinet but not as often or far as it used to.[4]

The picture is more ambiguous for the electoral face of presidentialisation. Regarding party communication, it is clear that leaders – supported by a small team of close party colleagues and professionals – are now both the face and the brain of campaigns. In general terms this predominance has increased over time as parties have become more electorally oriented and professionalised and have adapted to the 'media logic'. At the same time, although leader-centred campaigns are the norm, their prevalence can fluctuate from one election to the next. The relative focus on the leader, the team and the party can still vary a great deal depending on the political circumstances and the leader's style and popularity, with necessity calling at times for strategic – and distinctively parliamentary and partified – emphasis on the 'team'.

In terms of the influence of leaders on voting choice and their prominence in media coverage, perhaps surprisingly, the picture is less clear-cut. To be clear, there is a good deal of consensus that leaders are a significant factor in shaping electoral behaviour, even if their direct influence ultimately rarely changes the outcome of elections. Equally, it is apparent from the evidence analysed here that leaders are massively dominant in media coverage. However, for the more demanding test of presidentialisation (i.e. systematic increase over time) the answer is more complex. With regard to electoral behaviour, the conclusions are varied; some studies state that leader effects have become *more* important over time but a few others report mixed results or even conclude that nothing much has changed. There is, however, evidence of change in indirect effects, namely in the evaluation of issues and party image, and in the behaviour of parties, who have adapted who they select as leader, how they campaign and how much autonomy they give the leader to the belief in the growing potential of leaders to swing votes.

With regard to coverage, although the media do predominantly focus on leaders, there is little evidence that it is systematically more leader-centred now than in the 1960s and 1970s. In fact, at least for television, not only has there been a good degree of fluctuation from election to election, but the predominance of leaders peaked during that period and not, as would be expected if personalisation was continuously increasing, during the nineties and noughties. This is not to say that there has been no change: leader-centric campaigns are no longer exceptions associated with outstanding leaders but a standard feature of contemporary elections. But it is to say that change is neither as marked nor as systematic as often assumed.

The difficulties in identifying clear systematic change might in part be a result of the fact that – unlike the executive and the party face – there are more precise and quantifiable indicators for these dimensions of presidentialisation. As a result, instead of focusing on the overall picture, it is possible to analyse detailed trends (and fluctuations) over time and to uncover, perhaps surprisingly, the absence of systematic escalation. This might well exist but the evidence still calls for caution in how we interpret the conclusions from empirical studies and in how we characterise the phenomenon. In the same way as leaders are now potentially – but not necessarily – more powerful within the party and the executive, the leader's role in campaigns is generally greater than in the past but can, and often does, fluctuate from election to election. Moreover, even most leader-centred, and hence 'presidential', campaigns in the UK continue to be significantly different from those in the US.

In addition, the lack of conclusive evidence underscores the need for more emphasis on historical studies, greater definitional clarity, and innovative methodological approaches. In other words, the fact that signs of person-alisation in public discourse seem to be increasingly 'everywhere' but yet we cannot find the evidence that confirms a systematic increase should encourage us to determine, more precisely, under which conditions and in which regards contemporary forms of personalisation might be stronger and more distinctive, develop new ways of measuring it, and provide both more detailed and systematic comparisons with the past.

This is the challenge of the remaining chapters of the book. We will now focus on a different dimension of personalisation, personality politics, and in particular on what has been defined here as the politicisation of private persona. The re-conceptualisation and the empirical shift are essential because, it will be argued, it is the politicisation of private persona that has experienced a sharper increase in the last few decades and hence is what appears to be most distinctive about personalisation in its contemporary form in the UK. Unlike previous studies, the examination will focus on 'normal' day-to-day politics. It will also emphasise the analysis of the historical evolution of the phenomenon beyond mere visibility, asking: what, if anything, has changed in what is emphasised about leaders in public discourse, and in particular in their media portrayal? Before turning to the analysis of the empirical evidence, the next chapter defines the politicisation of private persona, clarifies how and why it is related to but different from personality politics, explains its causes and explores its normative consequences.

Notes

1 Mughan distinguishes between presidentialism and presidentialisation of presentation. Whereas the former refers to a single election, analysed in isolation, the latter implies that leaders' visibility has become stronger over a number of elections than it was in the past (2000: 9).

2 The sources of the data are the Nuffield Election studies and specifically Harrison's chapters 1964–2005 (Harrison, 1965, 1966, 1971, 1974, 1975, 1985, 1988, 1993, 1998, 2002, 2005; Pilsworth, 1979).

3 This form of calculation, replicating Foley's (2000), indicates changes in the 'leadership stretch', i.e. the difference between the visibility of the leader and the other top party figures.

4 The argument and the terminology used here draw on Foley (2000), especially pp. 332–42.

2

Personality politics
and the politicisation of private persona

As demonstrated in the previous chapter, it is clear that leaders are central to campaign communication and campaign coverage. So, even though this predominance has fluctuated rather than systematically increased, undoubtedly leaders are highly visible. But what the research on presidentialisation does not tell us is what aspects of leaders are emphasised and whether this has changed over time. Has there been an increase in the general media focus on leaders or specifically on their personal traits? Are the personal, as opposed to the political, qualities of leaders now more prevalent? How is personalisation manifested in public discourse and what is new about its contemporary form? Leaders can be highly visible but this does not mean that the emphasis on their character or personal lives will necessarily increase in synch with visibility. Nonetheless, this is a pervasive assumption; that if leaders are more dominant in political discourse so will be their personalities and personal lives. Moreover, it is this assumption that has led to the conflation of two related but distinct understandings of personalisation: presidentialisation (and especially the electoral face) and personality politics.

The concept of personality politics refers to the increasing importance of the character and personality of leaders in political discourse. Although intuitively compelling, it is a problematic concept. Personality politics is often used as a convenient shorthand for everything that critics see as wrong with contemporary political discourse and its impact on the (ir) rationality of voters. Whether the topic is the politician's competence as an organiser, orator or statesman, or whether it is a politician's family life, hobbies or religious beliefs, these are all examples of personality politics. However, these attributes are of a different nature and carry distinctive implications. Personality traits might be directly related to their role as political leaders or, on the contrary, they might have to do with the personal sphere and not be considered as essentially political. The catch-all term 'personality politics' is ill-suited to making sense of this diversity. This is why the concept of the politicisation of private persona, which is more specific, was introduced (see Figure I.1 in the Introduction). It refers to the emphasis in public discourse not just on leaders, on their overall personalities, or on their leadership traits, but on their personal lives and qualities. In other words, this concept encompasses the emphasis on politicians *not just* as representatives of an ideology or a party, or as statesmen, but also as persons, as human beings.

Of course, a rigid separation between the personal and the political is anything but clear-cut because in reality these two are often linked and their boundaries are fluid. Yet their conceptual separation is important because it allows systematic empirical investigation of this particular dimension of personalisation, which is said to be pervasive in contemporary political discourse. Moreover, it helps us to address the distinctive and more troubling normative concerns that it provokes. Whereas an emphasis on leadership qualities is now generally more accepted as having a virtually inescapable role in modern, de-aligned mediated politics, the emphasis on the personal seems more problematic. Firstly, there is a strong preoccupation with regard to the impact on the rationality of electoral behaviour and the quality of leadership. What happens if the characteristics of the system consistently promote those who are better able to present themselves as nice people or caring parents ahead of those who have the abilities, regardless of how they behave in the private sphere, that have been traditionally associated with political leadership? Secondly, the phenomenon might contribute to an erosion of the public sphere by offering pseudo-insights into leaders' personal lives and inner selves that distract the public from matters of principle. This is regarded as deceptive, not only because it offers an image of the candidate that is based on trivial aspects, but also because this image does not reflect the 'real' person; it is manufactured and staged for the consumption of spectator-like citizens. In short, personality politics, and especially the focus on the personal qualities and lives of leaders, is said to encourage the 'packaging' of leaders, impoverish the quality of political information, divert the attention of the electorate from policy, record and competence, and erode the bases for rational electoral behaviour.

But are these concerns justified? The discussions about personality politics assume that the focus on personalities is both new and damaging. Both are, however, questionable claims. Has politics ever really been only, or even mostly, about policies? Or have leaders and their personalities always played a prominent part? If so, what is distinctive about personality politics in our age and why has it changed? Moreover, is an interest in their personal lives necessarily a distraction from 'substantive' politics and an irrationality-inducing basis for political choices?

This chapter will argue that the importance of leaders as persons is inherent to democratic politics and, as a consequence, so has been the interest in the personal and the leaders' management of the self. At the same time it will show that, even if not a new phenomenon, broad socio-political, cultural and technological changes have made it more essential. Secondly, the chapter will demonstrate that the public personae of leaders is neither a fake marketing invention nor the 'real' thing; instead, it is a product of who they are, how they present themselves in the public eye and how the media re-construes it. Thirdly, the chapter will argue that although the politicisation of private persona has much in common with 'celebrity politics', the former is a better way of conceptualising the phenomenon because, while accounting for the overlap with popular culture and celebrity discourse, it also underlines what is distinctive about the political sphere. Finally, this chapter will address the implications of the politicisation of private persona for democratic politics. It will argue that many of the normative concerns associated with this phenomenon are overstated and based in narrow ideals of what democratic politics should be. These notions might not only be inadequate for appraising the potential benefits of change but are also, in many cases, based on nostalgia for a past that actually never existed. Thus, instead of merely going along with the narrative of decline and accepting without question that emphasis on the personal is 'bad' for politics, it is necessary to reappraise the normative concerns commonly associated with the phenomenon. In doing so, the aim is to show that, when these rigid assumptions are challenged, plausible reasons for revisiting, although not necessarily 'defeating', the quasi-dominant pessimism are revealed.

What is new? Why now?
Socio-political, cultural and media transformations

The centrality of the figure of the leader in the political system is long-lived and so has been, as a consequence, the importance of their public personae. Indeed, scholars of political and cultural history provide multiple examples – often in the words of the much-quoted Machiavelli – of the importance that both autocratic and elected leaders have given to the construction of public personae, and hence to style and appearance. From busts, coins and painted portraits to photography, film and television, rulers have for centuries been concerned with how they are perceived by citizens, and have tried to use and manipulate the available means of mediation to (re)present themselves in the best possible light (see Barker, 2001; Braudy, 1986; Bruce, 1992; see also discussion in Corner, 2000 and Street, 2004).

The methods and styles of performing and managing the self have radically changed, along with cultural and technological transformations.

But the personae of leaders have long mattered because politics has always been constructed around, and legitimised by, individual figures (Barker, 2001). Moreover, although relevant for leaders in non-democratic regimes, the emphasis on leaders is inherent in representative democracy. Firstly because legitimate and willing consent is more essential for democratic governments, and secondly because it is embedded in the very mechanism of election of representatives. As Manin (1997: 142) argues, elections have always been in some ways irreducibly 'a choice of persons'. Even while voters may also compare parties and policy programmes, because representatives are not selected by lottery, 'the personalities of the contenders inevitably play a part'. Thus candidates are compelled to show that they are endowed with positively valued characteristics, what Manin calls the *principle of distinction*, which sets them apart from the rest of the population.

Historically, the principle of distinction has not been restricted to strict criteria such as competence or record. The persona of leaders has mattered beyond what it tells us about their capacity to design or deliver policies because democratic representatives have always been more than sources of political agency. As Corner explains, there is a 'symbolic excess at work in the figure of the politician', which serves to condense 'the political' for those they represent, playing the physical and symbolic foci of political values and ideas in a way that 'exceeds rationalistic commitments to particular programmes and even perceived levels of competence in the performance of public office' (2000: 398). If leaders are to represent us, citizens need to think *and* feel that they are not only authoritative and capable persons but also attractive objects of identification and personal trust. As a result, leaders have always had to pursue 'representative adequacy' (Corner, 2000: 388): a delicate balance between the ordinary and extraordinary, between distance and proximity, between resemblance and difference, and to project themselves, somehow, as both human and heroic. But although the need to pursue 'representative adequacy' is not new, leaders now have to do it under different conditions: under the dazzling lights of electronic media, a fiercely competitive media market, weakening ideological principles, declining partisan alignments, waning deference for authority, and an unprecedentedly intense celebrity culture. Each of these changes entails complex consequences for the modern process of personalisation.

The first important change concerns the relationship between citizens and political parties. Modernity, individualisation and secularisation have led to well-documented structural changes, including a more autonomous media, a marked decline of traditional social cleavages and binding ideologies, the weakening of mass parties, and partisan de-alignment and a consequent rise in the number of floating voters (Swanson and Mancini, 1996). These changes have encouraged parties to crowd the ideological centre ground, leaving fewer sharp ideological or social distinctions between them. As a result, leaders are increasingly used as unique selling points, effectively party 'brand differentiators'. Moreover, lower ideological polarisation and declining partisanship have also affected the characteristics of the trust-building process between representatives and represented, increasing the potential significance not only of leaders but also of their projection as 'human beings':

> We know that we are presented with choices between candidates as objects of trust as well as between parties with different policies ... However, this factor of trust is now becoming increasingly personalized, as alternative bases of trust in party traditions (whether based in economic interest, ideology or vague sentiment) become ever weaker ... So political leaders have, to an increasing extent, the task of presenting themselves as persons to be trusted for their intrinsic qualities. (Richards, 2004: 348)

We need to remember that in party-based democracy, parties have heavily mediated the development of trust. Their role as mediators has been twofold. Firstly, trust originated in the symbolic representation of the community or the imagined community represented by the party: '*belonging* is invoked as a non-experiential assessment rule for trustworthiness. Invoking the shared belonging to some community ... and its presumably distinctive history, identity, or spirit, may also trigger the chain effect of trusting, recollection, obligation, and reproduction of the trust relation' (Offe, 1999: 63). Secondly, political parties operated as the chief agencies for judging the trustworthiness of politicians: 'they could supply citizens with the knowledge they needed to determine whether candidates were trustworthy even when the citizens could not directly know the candidates well enough to make such assessments on their own' (Hardin, 1999: 36). With the weakening of the role of parties, the projection of leaders as 'personalities' is necessarily foregrounded, and a range of elements – including those from the private sphere – become increasingly useful as potential shortcuts to define the leader in an accessible way and to assess his or her trustworthiness and values.

Related to these transformations, there have also been changes in the cultural boundaries of the political, which have led to more individualised and personalised forms of democratic representation and participation (Coleman, 2006: 475). Personal identity is, to a significant extent, replacing collective identity as the basis for contemporary political engagement (Bennett, 1998: 755). Moreover, nowadays the political, particularly in wealthy countries, has broadened to include a range of post-material issues, such as environmental quality, lifestyle choices, and women's and consumer rights (Bennett, 1998; Dalton et al., 2000; Giddens, 1991; Inglehart, 1990,

1997) in which our personal behaviour is regarded as an authentication of one's political stance (Elshtain, 1997: 171). In other words, what we – as well as leaders – eat and wear, and where we go on holiday, can be, and often is, part of the political. Furthermore, the shift to the personal goes beyond behaviour. Contemporary societies place a premium on the expression and management of emotion, with personal experiences and the affective dimensions of life, previously reserved mostly for the private intimate domain, becoming an essential component of public culture (Richards, 2007: 32–4; see also Sennett, 1977 for a broader and more critical appraisal of these developments). As a result, there is an expectation on leaders to show awareness of the emotional dimensions of everyday life (Richards, 2004: 349) and an unprecedented public interest in their inner strengths, struggles and frailties (Coleman, 2006: 469).

The second major transformation encouraging the emphasis on the personal is the change in the role of the media in the political process. The media, and especially electronic media, now play a crucial part in democratic politics, and it is well known that media, and television in particular, tend to personalise political coverage. Moreover, the characteristics of Western media systems have been transformed in the last few decades. The combination of neo-liberalism, the revolution in communications technology and changes in media consumption patterns (fragmentation of audiences, decline in newspaper readership, 'smart' TV boxes, etc.) have greatly increased competitive pressures, affecting not only commercial media but also public service broadcasters, including even the BBC. These changes have led to an expansion in the number and range of media outlets, as well as changes in their style and content, offering more space for both in-depth political coverage and light entertainment content. Moreover, coupled with celebrity culture, a decreasing interest in institutional politics and an expansion in the meaning of the political, these developments have made the boundaries between information and entertainment, political and non-political programmes, and 'serious' news and popular culture evermore permeable. The point here is not to lament 'tabloidisation', but to highlight that there is greater scope and appetite in contemporary media for the discussion of the personal lives and qualities of politicians.

Significantly, the impact of the media on the characteristics of the political process goes beyond content. The nature of the dominant means of communication greatly conditions the terms of political representation and the favoured style of leadership performance. As Hall Jamieson points out, when the main means of communication between leaders and citizens were print and live oratory, grand 'manly' rhetoric was required. Speeches needed to be passionate, authoritative and combative, using the rhetoric of 'fire and sword' (Hall Jamieson, 1988: 80). Leaders also routinely suppressed their private identity in public speeches (Hall Jamieson, 1988: 62) and had little problem in keeping the 'back stage' out of sight (Meyrowitz, 1985). Moreover, there was a good deal of symbolic distance between the leader – literally on the stage – and the audience. Although this style has not disappeared, the arrival of broadcasting media has favoured a different kind of rhetoric and performance, the one associated with the 'fireside chat' first perfected by Franklin Roosevelt: emotionally open, conciliatory, scattered with autobiographical references and personal anecdotes, and relying more on the language of everyday life (see Hart, 1987; Hall Jamieson, 1988). Moreover, for those politicians who master them, electronic media give them the opportunity of developing millions of 'personal' connections, enabling them to:

> present themselves not just as leaders but as human beings, as ordinary individuals who could address their subjects as fellow citizens, selectively disclosing aspects of their lives and their character in a conversational or even confessional mode [...] Political leaders acquired the capacity to present themselves as 'one of us'. (Thompson, 2000: 40)

In fact, it is not only that television *enables* it; if they are to appear comfortable and at ease, it actually *requires* politicians to reveal some of their 'authentic' selves, 'unself-consciously disclosing' the personal and drawing 'public discourse out of the private self' (Hall Jamieson, 1988: 80–4). Furthermore, the internet has strengthened these trends, enhancing both the possibilities and pitfalls of self-disclosure and mediated intimacy and the risks of unbounded public visibility.

In short, the role of electronic media in politics has radically altered the preferred modes of mediated representation and hence the nature of the construction of the public personae of leaders. It has enabled, and in fact encouraged, mediated intimacy and the emphasis on the personal sphere of politicians. It has also changed the social conditions of privacy, blurring the boundaries between off-stage and on-stage behaviour and significantly increasing the degree of public visibility of the personal sphere, and hence the potential for millions of 'intimate' connections but also the ever-present risk of scandal (see Castells, 2009; Meyrowitz, 1985; Thompson, 2000).

Electronic media has also affected the criteria of evaluation of key leadership qualities, which is especially noticeable in the definition of charisma. Charisma is certainly not a new category in the evaluation of leaders but it has experienced a redefinition. In its classic meaning, following Weber, charisma applies 'to a certain quality of an individual personality by virtue of which he is considered extraordinary and treated as endowed with supernatural, superhuman, or at least specifically exceptional powers or qualities' (Weber, 1968: 241). Common understandings of charisma have been generally laxer than this, but it is clear that the attribution of charismatic appeal is now broader and 'lighter' than in the past, as charisma has been informalised or, in Sennett's terminology, secularised with 'the little man ... now hero to other little men' (Sennett, 1977: 293). Charisma is now less heroic and more human, less mythical and more transparent, less distant and more intimate, and with the emphasis placed less on extraordinariness and difference and more on 'normality' and authenticity, and hence on virtues which draw from the private realm and on psychological categories (Sennett, 1977).

There is much in common here with the construction of the celebrity persona, and more generally with celebrity culture. In fact, the celebrity and the political world appear now to be so closely linked that many have defined personalisation of politics as celebrity politics, and the personalised leader as a celebrity politician (e.g. Meyer, 2002; West and Orman, 2002). There is no doubt that there are links between these two contemporary phenomena, but the relationship is remarkably complex and this complexity can be obscured by the casual use of these labels. In an over-simplistic version, the association between celebrity and politics suggests that leaders and celebrities are constructed with, and assessed by, the same attributes: their media appeal, how famous they are, who they hang out with, what they wear, and so on. In other words, celebrity politics is often used as another pejorative term to refer to what critics fear most about 'personality politics': that the trivial details of performance, presentation and appearance replace policy, principles and 'proper' leadership qualities. This is not entirely incorrect but it is a limited understanding of personality politics, and of the complexity of celebrity and the literature that examines it.

There are, however, other more sophisticated ways of thinking about these links. Firstly, as Street (2004) has shown, there is a fluid degree of circulation between the two spheres, which is symptomatic of the broader link between politics and popular aesthetics that characterises contemporary culture: celebrities are doing politics and, in some cases, becoming politicians; and 'traditional' politicians now more often use icons, conventions, techniques and practitioners of popular culture as campaign and branding resources. Additionally, there are *some* parallels between the societal role of leaders and celebrities in late capitalism. With the decline of binding ideologies, grand narratives and great heroes, celebrities offer a new focus of secular identification and affective engagement (see Marshall, 1997). And politicians, unable to rely on traditional partisan attachments and incapable of playing the role of 'single God-like leaders' (Corner and Pels, 2003a: 10), come *partly* to occupy a similar space to celebrities; one among many similar 'little gods' who quickly rise and fall in public estimation (Corner and Pels, 2003a: 10). Furthermore, there are the similarities between celebrity and political personae. As in politics, celebrities have had to adapt to changes in communication and the conditions of privacy, trying to manage and strategically exploit the exposure of their previously out of sight lives. In fact, it is characteristic of contemporary celebrity discourse to draw upon the resources of private life to create a public persona that appears authentic and 'normal', inviting the media to sort out the star from the 'real' person, and hence constructing their private sphere as the ultimate site of truth for understanding their conduct in the public sphere (Gamson 1994; Marshall 1997; Ponce de Leon 2002). Finally, there is the impact of celebrity culture upon society at large. The so-called democratisation of celebrity (especially as manifested in the success of reality TV and the DIY celebrity of the internet) have made the need for ordinariness, off/on stage consistency and unrehearsed authenticity in the personae of public figures even more marked. More generally, celebrity culture, where the primary emphasis is increasingly on a person's 'private life' or lifestyle, rather than their professional role (Holmes and Redmond, 2006: 11), has led us to routinely expect, and the media to search for, intimate details of the personal sphere and inner selves of public figures; sometimes scandalous, sometimes mildly embarrassing but, more often than not, only to 'reveal' the mundane experiences of everyday life.

However, it must be emphasised that, despite the similarities, the world of politics and celebrity are not one and the same. The areas of overlap are limited to *some* of the dimensions of political discourse and political persona. It has been suggested that celebrity 'may increasingly be a "generic" mode of representation, a set of discursive structures through which the famous [regardless of the origin of their fame] are constructed, shuttled and consumed' (Holmes and Redmond, 2006: 12). This discursive structure might be increasingly applied to politics but it co-exists, sometimes prominently, sometimes marginally, with modes of representation that are based on the sphere of government and political action, and hence are linked but fundamentally distinct (see Corner, 2000).

This is not surprising given that, unlike celebrities, leaders represent us not only symbolically but also as agents of political choice and action. Politicians declare war and peace, write our laws, and make decisions on taxation, health and education. In other words, unlike most celebrities, they can greatly affect the material conditions of people's lives, and hence politicians' jobs and reputations are still heavily based on the work they do in the political sphere.[1] These fundamental differences are also reflected in the construction of their public personae and in media coverage, as well as in how citizens assess them at the ballot box, where they look for a combination of attributes, including 'soft' personal qualities but also competence, strength and experience as well as policy and values. In other words, even if the discursive structure of celebrity discourse appears to have become more prevalent, it is by no means the only dimension of political discourse; nor are the personal elements in a politician's persona dissociated from his or her policies, values and political qualities.

The politicisation of private persona: it takes two to tango

All these changes are hugely important. However, it would be a mistake to regard personalisation as a one-way street: politicians are not merely docile and passive recipients of external factors. On the one hand, not all politicians engage with the politics of the personal. Some merely try to cope with these changes, revealing as little of the personal as possible, while attempting to minimise the negative effects of going against the flow of the changing conditions of representation. In other cultural conditions the changes will be less marked, or tempered by other variables such as proportional representation, strong legal provisions for the protection of privacy, or weaker popular media, making it both less necessary and less advantageous to take this route (see Kuhn, 2007; Stanyer and Wring, 2004b). There also short-term tactical factors that might discourage 'going personal'. For instance, if the previous leader has been heavily criticised for his or her emphasis on the personal, the incoming leader – especially if it suits his or her personality – might try to develop his or her public persona in opposition, or even as an 'antidote' (Foley, 2002: 194), to that of his or her predecessor. There will be also times of crisis, which will call for more traditional leadership styles.

Notwithstanding these qualifications, there are strong incentives and opportunities in contemporary politics to make strategic use of the personal. Moreover, even for those who are less inclined to do so, it is becoming increasingly costly to conceal the private self, dragging many reluctant politicians, 'sometimes kicking and screaming, into the sphere of mediated intimacy' (Coleman, 2006: 468). As a matter of fact, the perceived potential benefits of selectively exploiting personal disclosure – and, just as importantly, the risks of not doing so – have become such conventional wisdom that this strategy has grown to be seen, in many countries, as an indispensable tool and prerequisite for electoral success (Stanyer and Wring, 2004a: 5; van Zoonen, 1998a: 116).

Leaders can use, and politicise, the personal and emphasise the 'human' aspects of their personae on many different stages: campaign material (e.g. manifestos, posters, TV ads), speeches, media interviews, blogs, video diaries, photo-opportunities, press releases, and so on. Some of these are under their control but, more frequently, the content will depend on the genre, what they are asked, and on how their responses are mediated and later reproduced by other media. Moreover, the content transcends the verbal as the personal is also 'read' from other aspects of the presentation of the self, such as their accents and rhetorical style (Do they sound like 'normal' people?), the context (Is the interview at home? Do they drink from a cup or a mug?), non-verbal expressions (Are they comfortable playing with the dog? Do they appear emotionally open when talking about their children?), and their personal appearance (Are they sporty, healthy, stuffy or stiff?).

In terms of verbalised discourse, and drawing on van Zoonen and Holtz-Bacha (2000), there are three related ways in which politicians can use the personal.[2] Most plainly, they can speak as 'human beings' (i.e. from a personal position) about their private lives and experiences: who does the washing up, who they cheer for in *American Idol*, or how much they love their children. However, the personal and political, both in terms of positioning and content, are more commonly combined. Firstly, politicians can speak (or be spoken about) from their position as leaders but in the discussion of personal issues: how their political careers affect their health or their family lives, or expose their inner feelings about difficult political decisions. Secondly, they can speak from their personal positions – as parents, spouses, or children – about politics. There are numerous examples of this: show how they feel *as parents*, about a soldier's death, as Tony Blair and George W. Bush did repeatedly during the invasions of Iraq; explain their stand on policy through their parental role, as did Ségolène Royal with her 'motherly' opposition to pornography (Kuhn, 2007); discuss how their biographical experiences have affected their political views, as with Neil Kinnock's support for public education, or Obama's commitment to universal health, motivated by what their relatives lacked; or show us how they enact, or even embody, their political positions and values in their personal lives as with David Cameron's support for environmental policies symbolised in his cycling, or Palin's opposition to abortion embodied by her Downs Syndrome child. Rhetorical style is also important. The use of the personal in a politician's discourse works better if the language of the private sphere, or at least a fluid combination between public and private language, is used. Otherwise, this 'personal objectified discourse' produces an awkward form of personalisation (van Zoonen and Holtz-Bacha, 2000: 49) which, as will be discussed in Chapter 6, tends to occur when reserved politicians such as Gordon Brown are invited to talk as 'human beings' about the personal, but continuously try to bring back the conversation to the language of the public and to the policy sphere.

There are other combinations and certainly numerous other examples. But schematically we can identify three interlinked functions that politicising the personal can perform for politicians: manage media coverage; develop identification and emotional connections and enhance the perception of positive personal *and* political qualities; and authenticate and personify policies and political values (see also Holtz-Bacha, 2004). Firstly, emphasising the personal can enable leaders to gain 'softer' (less adversarial) media coverage. Moreover, via alternative outlets and through the appeal of 'non-political' rhetoric, it can help leaders to reach those who are less interested in formal politics. Secondly, details of a leader's personal life can 'humanise' a leader's persona, highlighting their 'normality' and enabling them to display a degree of vulnerability and emotional reflexivity. Moreover, it can also impact on the public's perception of their political qualities. For instance, a virtuous private and, especially, family life can help to infuse a leader's persona with leadership attributes such as integrity, kindness, and reliability, while at the same time reinforcing authoritativeness (Marshall, 1997: 218; van Zoonen, 1998a: 116). Finally, the personal sphere can help them to authenticate, through the force of personal experiences and example, their political positions. Their policy stances become *more real, more genuine* if related to relevant personal experience. Moreover, as leaders are increasingly expected not only to represent the party's views but also to embody the party brand, their personal lives can personify the party's values, priorities and policies and be the common thread that links what can often appear as an ideologically incoherent set of policies. Furthermore, even seemingly tiny and trivial details such as their style of dress or musical taste can perform an invaluable role in strengthening brand coherence and differentiation (Scammell, 2007).

However, for all the potential advantages, there are, of course, also risks for politicians. The media are not an empty stage, where politicians can freely perform their preferred publicity strategy. The media's interest in the personal results from multiple factors: commercial imperatives, conventions of newsworthiness, organisational routines, and journalistic understandings of normative duties. Some of these, not least the 'watchdog' duty, often conflict with the aims of politicians' publicity strategies, especially in the context of an ever more marked adversarial culture between politicians and journalists (Blumler and Gurevitch, 1995; Cappella and Hall Jamieson, 1997; Patterson, 1993). Moreover, the media increasingly 'defame and decry' the very same people they celebrate, often focusing on 'bringing the heavenly star or glitzy celebrity back down to earth with an almighty "bang".' (Redmond, 2006: 32). Therefore, the making of a leader's persona needs to be understood as a complex and dynamic process, in which the media play an active and powerful role that can both strengthen and erode carefully built reputations, and where both journalists and politicians try to exert control and pursue their interests and agendas. Accordingly, while media interest encourages the strategic publicity of the personal, it also demands careful planning of how this is performed, leading to a strategy centred 'not just on image projection and self-promotion, but also on image control and self-protection' (Kuhn, 2004: 33).

Thus, when leaders appear in 'human being mode' it is not simply a reflection of their 'true' selves. On the one hand, this persona, that is the public version(s) of their private selves, tends to be constructed based upon their personalities, life history and experience so as to avoid moving too far from their sense of self (van Zoonen, 2005: 74). At the same time, their biographical narrative and personal attributes are honed on the advice of political communication experts to make them not only more appealing but also to try to ensure that, when combined with political statements, issue stances and policy proposals, they form a coherent package (Kuhn, 2007: 193–4). On the other hand, what the media choose to publicise, and how they frame and interpret it, shapes a leader's public persona, helping to determine which character traits will prevail in the public mind (Cornog, 2004; Hall Jamieson and Waldman, 2003) and ultimately impacting on voters' choices (Hacker, 2004; Miller et al., 1986; Ohr and Oscarsson, 2010).

In short, the 'public' private personae of politicians are the result of a battle between who they are, the version(s) of their 'true' selves they present for public consumption across different stages and genres, and the version constructed by the media. And it is this 'virtual person' (Gaffney, 2001: 130), which is neither fake nor the 'real thing', that provides the grounds for leaders to try to make themselves attractive, to legitimise their policies, and for citizens to make their judgements about politicians as 'human beings'.

Challenging normative assumptions

There is a sense in which the politicisation of private persona seems inevitable. In part, it might seem so because of historical precedents, i.e. the long-standing importance of leaders and their personae in democratic politics. But mostly, the feeling of inevitability seems a result of broad technological, socio-political and cultural changes, which have produced strong rational incentives for both politicians and journalists to increasingly publicise the personal. However, as Street (2004: 441) remarks in relation to celebrity politics, to explain and rationalise the attention to leaders as persons on the grounds of historical precedents or as an inevitable product of social and political change does not make it, per se, a positive development. One still needs to question whether, in principle, the politicisation of private persona is more likely to enhance or to erode the quality of representative democracy.

This is a difficult question, which raises significant disagreement. On the one hand, the process of politicisation of private persona is regarded as challenging important normative principles that underpin and legitimise representative democracy. On the other hand, there are a number of scholars who have started to draw attention to the potential benefits of the phenomenon (e.g. Coleman, 2006; Corner, 2000; Richards, 2004; Street, 2004; van Zoonen, 2005). Although those who support this view are still relatively marginal in mainstream political communication, this position has gained importance during the last few years. Their views do not necessarily conform to a single coherent argument, nor have some of the theoretical claims been subjected to enough empirical scrutiny. Nonetheless, the attraction of this approach is that it makes apparent the extent to which many of the normative concerns associated with the politicisation of private persona, and personalisation more generally, are grounded in rigid notions of what democratic politics should be. Instead of merely going along with the narrative of decline and accepting without question that the emphasis on the personal is 'bad' for politics, it is necessary to reprise the normative concerns commonly associated with the phenomenon. Specifically, the politicisation of private persona raises several troubling questions. Firstly, how does it affect the quality of political information and, more broadly, the public sphere? Secondly, how does it influence electoral behaviour and, in particularly, the highly- (it will be argued over-) prized value of rationality? Thirdly, how does it impact on the relationship between citizens and leaders, representation and civic engagement? Finally, how does it affect the recruitment and quality of political elites?

The first concern has to do with the quality of political information and debate. It is based on the idea of 'style over substance', and specifically with the fear that trivial – and often heavily 'packaged' or 'staged' – information about the personal lives and qualities of leaders is replacing the discussion of issues, policy and 'hard' leadership qualities (see e.g. Franklin, 2004; Meyer, 2002). It is obviously troubling to imagine political discourse swamped with details of what leaders wear, eat or watch on TV, replacing everything of substance. And indeed, some of the detail that we are fed about the personal sphere of politicians is plainly trivial. Moreover, many of these personal 'revelations' are strategically managed and the 'human' side of leaders groomed. However, to leave it there is to assume the worst-case scenario. This is mistaken because we should not presume that the personal and the political interact in a zero-sum game. Public discourse is a realm of interaction, where these two spheres are linked: sometimes overlapping, sometimes displacing, and sometimes bringing a personal angle to the discussion of 'properly' political issues. More broadly, a hasty rejection of style and performance, and a rigid definition of what is 'proper' or 'worthy' information and what is not, are misguided. It fails to engage with some of the key – and legitimate – components employed by contemporary citizens to make sense of politics. In fact, in principle, the presence of the personal in public discourse should not be regarded as interference or threat, but as a call to recognise, and even to welcome, the fact that rigid dichotomical distinctions between the personal and political, emotions and rationality, style and substance, are (if they ever were) no longer valid.

In fact, research in electoral behaviour and political psychology demonstrate that there is no reason to assume that citizens cannot use the personal to help them to make sound, albeit not purely rationality-based, political choices. As discussed in Chapter 1, most research on electoral behaviour now shows that in most countries leaders matter, and arguably matter more than they used to (Clarke et al., 2004; McAllister, 2007; Mughan, 2000). At the same time, however, this influence is weaker than often assumed, once a wider range of factors are taken into account (McAllister, 2007). Moreover, the assessment of leaders is not necessarily based on their personalities; in fact, research in the US has shown that leaders have, over time, become increasingly liked/disliked more for their association with issues than due to citizens' evaluation of their personal and political qualities (Wattenberg, 2004). Furthermore, research on political psychology has demonstrated that to make *reasoned* choices people do not need substantial amounts of detailed information and facts (Lupia and McCubbins, 1998; Popkin, 1991). Indeed, they have found that given the complexity of contemporary politics, the character of the candidate might be as or more important for the electorate than detailed information on specific issues, because they are cognitive shortcuts that help them to predict what the candidate will do once in office (Just et al., 1996: 216). Moreover, tellingly, they found that 'sophisticated' citizens, i.e., those who are more politically active, knowledgeable and educated, often make greater use of these kinds of shortcuts.

There have also been some studies focused on establishing which particular traits of the personalities of leaders have a greater impact on the vote, and whether these are idiosyncratic or enduring. This research clearly suggests that voters are more strongly influenced by what Miller et al. (1986) define as *performance-related* criteria such as competence (the most influential character trait in most studies), caring/empathy, integrity/honesty, effectiveness, responsiveness and reliability (Bean, 1993; Bean and Mughan, 1989; Jones and Hudson, 1996; Just et al., 1996; Miller et al., 1986; Ohr and Oscarsson, 2010). Conversely, *personal 'soft' qualities* such as likeability and charm, and *personal characteristics* such as background, family life and appearance, appear to have a weaker direct influence on voting behaviour. In addition, the criteria used by voters are, by and large, limited and stable over time, following a fairly rigid cognitive schemata (Miller et al., 1986), even while showing some variation in salience in response to the uniqueness of particular candidates, and the focus of the campaign and media coverage (Kaase, 1994; Miller et al., 1986: 529; Ohr and Oscarsson, 2010: 208–9). This degree of consistency challenges the common assumption – and strong object of concern – that leaders, by emphasising and 'packaging' certain aspects of their public personae, could easily induce voters to make a decision based on superficial or 'irrational' bases. Significantly, these conclusions apply across different types of leaders and parliamentary and presidential democracies, including the US, the UK, Australia, New Zealand, Spain and Sweden (see Ohr and Oscarsson, 2010 for a useful overview).

These findings are in many ways reassuring and show that citizens are much less easily distracted than is often feared. At the same time, they do not feel entirely right: do (perceptions of) the personal qualities and lives of leaders really make so little difference? Aren't we missing something? In part, it is possible that the impact of personal qualities is underestimated as a result of the methodology (which is usually concerned with direct independent effects after controlling for other variables) and the social desirability bias of survey responses[3] (Wattenberg, 2004: 149). There are also other limitations to this approach: the interpretation of these results reproduces in some ways rigid distinctions between personal and political, and rational and emotional. How citizens evaluate leaders and politics is a complex and messy process. For instance, 'caring' was found to be the strongest constitutive element of responsiveness (Mughan, 2000: 64; Stewart and Clarke, 1992: 455). Moreover, Miller et al. (1986: 531) found that people 'draw inferences about competence, integrity, reliability and charisma of a candidate form the candidate's personal characteristics'. This is not to say that citizens evaluate politicians as they do friends or lovers but rather that they link personal attributes to their assessment of a politician's professional qualifications (Just et al., 1996: 216–18). Furthermore, the personal qualities of the leaders are also interlinked with the assessment of policies and the images of the parties as they 'serve to embody in a walking, talking and changing presence the whole set of values, priorities and policies that the party stands for' (Dunleavy et al., 2006: 8).

In short, concerns about the impact of the emphasis on the personal on the rationality of electoral behaviour should not be entirely dismissed, even if they are overstated. Leaders matter but are by no means the only consideration in voting. Moreover, citizens use a range of issues and character dimensions to assess their leaders, and the 'soft' personal qualities and personal lives are not the predominant ones. Citizens use them in combination with other character and issue information to assess a politician's leadership qualities as well as to infer his or her policies and political values. This probably does not live up to the 'gold standard' of pure rationality but neither should personal considerations be dismissed as 'lazy, unsophisticated, and apolitical' (Just et al., 1996: 216). Within the constraints of the information environment, personal details are actively reinterpreted by citizens, who use them to make political inferences about the candidates, and vice versa. Even 'gut feelings' of passionate personal like or dislike for a politician, although influenced by the personal, are generally a reflection of whether or not they share citizens' values, priorities and concerns. Moreover, these kinds of emotions, because they mobilise the expressive or affective dimension of political choice, can facilitate rationality and deliberation (Brennan and Hamlin, 2000; Marcus, 2002; Marcus et al., 2000).

If the jury is still out (not guilty albeit not quite innocent) in relation to the rationality of electoral behaviour, there are more positive prospects in regard to the impact on mobilisation and civic engagement. As a few scholars have recently argued, certain types of emphasis on the personal may actually help to reinvigorate representative democracy (Coleman, 2003, 2006; Corner and Pels, 2003b; Richards, 2004; van Zoonen, 2005). Before we can accept this more optimistic assessment, however, we need to revise the definitions of the 'authentically' political and, closely linked, the characterisation of 'proper' political discourse.

Typically, 'proper' political discourse and participation involves the clear demarcation between the personal and the political and, simultaneously, between the rational and the emotional, and information and entertainment. This is particularly clear in the debate about the Habermasian public sphere which, although heavily criticised (see, for instance, Calhoun, 1997; Livingstone and Lunt, 1993; Young, 1996), has been the predominant position in much of the normative thinking in media and communications research in the last few decades. From this point of view, emotions, and those aspects of people's lives that particularise their interests, are seen as inappropriate when discussing the political. If one is to participate 'properly', it is necessary to rise above, or set aside, one's personal (or subjective) interests and expressive nature (Warner, 2002: 40). Moreover, entertainment, popular culture and even pleasure are better omitted as they can distract us and prevent rational thinking. This need for stressing rationality and impersonality is strongly associated with the principles on which the legitimisation of democracy as a system is based, and reflects the Enlightenment legacy of the links between rationality and democratic ideals (Mouffe, 1996: 245).

It is, however, a flawed ideal, even if in some ways normatively inspiring. By sidelining the significance of the personal and the emotional, this 'one-sided cerebral' (Pels, 2003) approach to politics fails to recognise some of the key components citizens can employ to relate to the political and has 'the effect of narrowing the repertoire of political citizenship' (Coleman, 2006: 458). In part this involves the recognition that most people are not 'perfect' citizens; but the point is stronger than that. As is now widely accepted in political psychology, emotion and reason do not preclude one another: they are intertwined (Marcus, 2002; Neuman et al.,

2007). Moreover, '[t]o invite emotional engagement is to facilitate rational discourse, not to banish it' (Richards, 2004: 340). This does not mean that following our emotions will always lead to the best possible judgement; but rather that emotions are a necessary and mobilising component of political action, and that they do *not* need to preclude rational choices.

Thus, instead of condemning it because it does not meet the dubious gold standard of 'proper' political discourse, it is important to recognise that the projection of leaders as 'human beings', as attractive persons with feelings, style and personal lives, who can incorporate the language of emotions and everyday life in the discussion of issues and polices, can motivate citizens to participate; possibly more than if these elements are absent. It can also make citizens feel more (or better) represented (Coleman, 2006; Corner, 2000; Mazzoleni, 2000; Pels, 2003; Richards, 2004; Street, 2003; van Zoonen, 2005). This is not to give up on rationality or the discussion of policies and issues, but neither is it to consider the use of the emotional and the personal as second best, as sweeteners for those citizens who are otherwise seemingly incapable of swallowing 'real' politics. It is to emphasise, as the authors above have argued, that there can be a positive synergy, which takes place without necessarily undermining their capacity for judgement or rational considerations, or transforming citizens into brainless followers. Conversely, failing to do so can erode the affective motivation indispensable for political involvement and participation, especially now that leaders carry a greater burden for encouraging mobilisation, as this was traditionally one of the crucial functions of mass political parties.

However, there is a catch. The pursuit of this positive synergy can become self-defeating. The persona of a leader is conditioned by their personality, biography and political resources; heavily shaped by the conditions of mediation; and, of course, ultimately dependent on how citizens perceive it. Appearing to be trying hard to be seen as 'human' will not make many citizens feel more connected or better represented by leaders; rather the opposite. Moreover, there are different incentives and expectations at play for politicians, journalists and citizens, which often act against the development of a positive personal and emotionalised connection. Even if we assumed that politicians might try to do their best to engage and mobilise, what is required for the personal to re-engage and reinvigorate trust is complex, and in many ways at odds with the characteristics of contemporary political communication.

The first thing to watch for is accusations of hypocrisy, and in its heightened version, the likelihood of scandal (Castells, 2009; Thompson, 2000). Of course, politicians have always had to show a degree of consistency between political values, public statements and personal choices. But the more the personal is strategically emphasised, the greater the risk of accusations of insincerity and hypocrisy, especially given the increasing mediated publicness of private behaviour (Thompson, 2000: 37). This kind of hypocrisy is why John Major's Conservatives, with their emphasis on 'Back to Basics' (moral values), were so chastened by the revelation of sexual 'misbehaviour', and also helps in part to explain why Nixon, who had placed great emphasis on 'moral probity', had little chance of surviving Watergate (Just and Crigler, 2000). But it is not enough to avoid this kind of inconsistency: William Hague was heavily ridiculed by the media for claiming to drink fourteen pints of beer in a night and Gordon Brown for appearing to suggest that he liked the rock band Arctic Monkeys. A politician can appear to be perfectly honourable and still appear insincere or packaged. Conversely, he or she might have a few personal flaws and still be accepted, and liked, by citizens.

The body of literature that emphasises the potential of the emotional and the personal for the reinvigoration of representative democracy recognises this, emphasising that as much as the (inevitable) use of personal, emotional or aesthetic elements is not per se detrimental, its democratic value ultimately depends on the nature and quality of the performance or the appeal (Coleman, 2006; Richards, 2004; Scammell and Langer, 2006; Street, 2004; van Zoonen, 2004). What this means in practice is hard to define but, at its core, it seems to me that the normative hopes are pinned on politicians prioritising connection and mobilisation over instrumental and short-term electoral aims. But without wishing to dismiss the normative value of these proposals, which I have myself advocated elsewhere (see Scammell and Langer, 2006), it is necessary to recognise that the structural conditions that shape political communication practices make this hard to achieve. Among other things, the personae of leaders, and how they are constructed, need to combine ordinariness and extraordinariness, to be grounded in everyday life, be attractive, genuine/real, individual, emotionally sophisticated and intelligent, and so on. For instance, leaders should be prepared to acknowledge error and vulnerability, and be honest about (inevitable) failure, as opposed to hiding these in the impossible pursuit of the perfect heroic image (Richards, 2004: 349). Given the mixed expectations of extraordinariness and ordinariness embedded in our relationships with leaders, this is not easy at the best of times, but is especially hard in the presence of a relentlessly adversarial media, who often interpret a change of mind as an embarrassing U-turn. Personal frailties are more often condoned, and might be even sympathised with, but the boundaries between private and public behaviour are increasingly porous, with flaws in either sphere often impacting on the other (Sennett, 1977).

Some of these difficulties are offset by the premium placed on authenticity. In fact, a cross-reading of the 'literature of hope' suggests that, if citizens are to reinvigorate their relationship with politicians, this might be the most crucial component of the persona. Authenticity is a hard concept to pin down (see Cornejo, 2008 for an excellent discussion). It is both cognitive and affective (Coleman, 2006; Cornejo, 2008; Couldry, 2004). Moreover, it is performed, not possessed (Ruddock, 2006: 294) and this performance has to do with the content of what is said, the attributes of the speaker (with 'being' rather than saying) and with the development of a connection between speaker and audience, which links voters' concerns and public discourse, making the latter meaningful to the former (Cornejo, 2008: 31). In addition, the performance has to appear unrehearsed and unscripted, and display a high degree of consistency between conscious and unconscious action. In other words, for leaders to be authentic, they must appear to reveal their 'real' selves in public as they would do in private. In turn, this 'real self' must be consistently true to (our image of) who they are, and connect with what we care about.

Research pertaining to celebrities, and especially reality TV contestants (e.g. Hill, 2002; Holmes and Redmond, 2006), indicates that authenticity is indeed increasingly valued. Moreover, according to the rare studies that have explored this empirically for politics (Coleman, 2003, 2006), this might also apply to leaders. People do not expect public figures to be perfect or even 'normal', but 'real'. In other words, many people seem to value authenticity over mimetic resemblance and flawless character: to be authentic politicians do not need to be perfect or a replica of us – although emotional resonance and a degree of trustful recognition and identification are necessary (Coleman, 2003: 754–7; Pels, 2003: 59) – but to be open, sincere and unspun and reveal the 'real' self in public in a creative fashion. This emphasis on authenticity explains partly why Bill Clinton's reputation was not as damaged as might have been expected by the Lewinsky affair (although more so by the lying)[4] or why Silvio Berlusconi's grand collection of gaffes or Boris Johnson's 'naughty public schoolboy' (Ruddock, 2007) blunders have not made them unelectable. The revelations, although showing character flaws, for many did not conflict with the overall perceptions of their personae or core political values. In fact, they showed a degree of unconventionality, openness and particular kind of sincerity (even about lying) that matched with our images of their 'real' selves.

However, the pursuit of authenticity may too easily become, in practice, a contradiction in terms. Even if there are elements of (self) expressive motives in what leaders communicate, there is inescapably a dominant instrumental agenda in both their performances and in how they are mediated. This creates a paradox. To be 'genuine', 'naturally human' and 'showing the real person',[5] politicians have to appear unrehearsed and unscripted, display a high degree of consistency between public and private performances and effortlessly adapt their personae to the demands of different stages and genres. But for how many politicians and for how long, especially in office, is it possible to be consistently true to (our images of) their 'real' selves? As Goffman (1959) has demonstrated, human interaction always involves an element of performance that enables us to adjust to the requirements of different settings. However, politicians do not have the same degree of freedom as us 'civilians'. Both their public and private behaviour are increasingly scrutinised. Moreover, they have to navigate between on- and off-role modes, between the formality of the news programme and the informality of the talk show, and between the 'full sincerity' of the personal and the necessary compromise and quota of deceit that is essential to democratic politics (Corner, 2000); all while under unprecedented mediated visibility and guarded by an unrelentingly adversarial media, furiously searching for inconsistency and traces of 'packaging'. These conditions call not for authenticity, but for carefully staged and multiple – and hence prone to inconsistency – public presentations of their selves. Some politicians seem intrinsically incapable of 'unrehearsed authenticity' (Coleman, 2006: 466), others manage it some of the time. Overall, however, although the relevance attributed to authenticity both partly explains apathy and disengagement and 'contains the seed for a renovation', it is clear that 'far from offering simple answers to the current problems [...] the constructed nature of authenticity could make the new relationship as artificial as the situation that it was devised to improve' (Cornejo, 2008: 34–5).

There are also other troubling issues raised by the need for authenticity and more generally by the emphasis on the personal. How does the politicisation of private persona impact on the quality and recruitment of political elites? The first clear hurdle is that the emphasis on, and critical scrutiny of, the personal can discourage perfectly qualified people from standing for public office (Elcock, 2001: 14–5; Lichtenberg, 1989; Seaton, 2003; Thompson, 2000). Secondly, the emphasis on personal authenticity gives preference to a particular type of character: those who are capable of revealing, 'sincerely' and attractively, their private selves. Of course, favouring some qualities in leaders over others is not unique to contemporary politics, nor is the need for politicians to perform; rather, as Runciman puts it, 'the masks they wear must suit they age in which they find themselves' (2008: 210). But in this age of unprecedented media visibility and scrutiny and permanent campaigning, the mask – or rather the ability to appear not to be wearing one – has become a much more central component of the armoury of leadership, affecting not only the construction of the persona but, crucially, also whom parties select as leaders (and, as importantly, whom they do not). This is a result not so much of the criteria that citizens use to assess their leaders but of the effects that the belief in the importance of leaders as 'human beings' has on whom parties select and the criteria the media use to judge them.

Conclusion

The aim of this chapter has been to provide the theoretical underpinning for the investigation of personality politics, to offer elucidation on what it is, its causes and why it matters. In particular, it focused on one of its dimensions, which is the main subject of the book: the politicisation of private persona. The task was threefold. Firstly, expanding on the Introduction, the chapter has defined and explained the concept and why it is preferable to alternative conceptualisations. Specifically, the politicisation of private persona was differentiated, firstly, from the broader and ill-defined 'personality politics', to underscore what appears to be unique about contemporary forms of personalisation: not just the focus on leaders, or on their leadership qualities, but on their personal lives and qualities, on leaders as 'human beings'; secondly, the politicisation of private persona was distinguished from 'celebrity politics' to underline that although there are important overlaps between politics, popular culture and celebrity discourse, these are only partial and the emphasis on celebrity can obscure what is distinctive about the political sphere.

Secondly, the chapter has explained the socio-political, cultural and media changes that have encouraged the emphasis on the personal lives and inner selves of politicians. It would be a mistake, however, to assume that these transformations led to a new and sudden attention to leaders as persons, because this interest is long-lived and inherent to representative democracy. Moreover, not all politicians engage to the same extent with the politics of the personal. It still depends on culturally specific conditions, the leader's personality, short-term tactical factors, and political circumstances. But, even if neither entirely new nor automatically applying to all, the fact is that there are now stronger rational incentives for both politicians and journalists to increasingly publicise the personal, and to do so with different intensity, methods and style than in the past. These incentives are, however, based on the different interests and agendas of the media and politicians, which while encouraging the strategic publicity of the personal also demand a careful planning of how this is performed. Moreover, the pressures of these transformations mean that it is increasingly inadvisable to flatly refuse to reveal the private self, notwithstanding how reluctant or uncomfortable a politician might be with being drawn into the sphere of mediated intimacy.

Finally, the chapter has discussed the normative implications of the politicisation of private persona for democratic politics. The default assumption is that the phenomenon has a negative impact, encouraging the manufacturing of leaders' personae, distracting citizens from policy, record and competence, tainting the integrity of the public sphere, and undermining the electorate's ability to make rational decisions. However, too often normative concerns associated with this phenomenon are overstated and based on restricted ideas about what democratic politics should be. There is no reason to assume that the personal and the political are mutually exclusive. Research has found that in shaping voters' choices, leaders – and certainly their soft qualities – are not as important as often imagined and that, when citizens take into consideration the personal, they do not do so in isolation: they use it to make inferences about the leadership qualities and political values of the candidates. Moreover, even what might appear to be apolitical feelings of like and dislike for leaders are in fact linked to political considerations about their values. Furthermore, because these feelings bring into play the expressive dimension of political choice, they can mobilise citizens to participate and even, potentially, encourage rationality and deliberation.

More broadly, the chapter has argued that the presence of the personal in public discourse is neither necessarily misplaced nor normatively detrimental. However, to refuse to dismiss the personal as improper or unworthy should not lead to overstating its potential benefits. It would be naive to think that if only politicians could be more expressive, authentic and 'human', trust and engagement would be immediately restored. The problems of representative democracy are too deep and complex to be 'resolved' by this. Moreover, unless the characteristics of political communication radically change, given the way it is mediated and strategically practised, the politicisation of private persona is likely – at best – to only occasionally and fleetingly help to restore the relationship between citizens and representatives. Furthermore, and worryingly, the emphasis on the inner lives of politicians makes success harder for those who, even if competent in other regards, are unwilling or incapable of 'authentically' revealing their private selves. Of course, politicians have always needed to perform, portraying a version of themselves in tune with the preferred modes of leadership persona; but this need is now ever more critical. In short, the politicisation of private persona is not new but it is expected to have intensified and changed, along with cultural, socio-political and technological transformations. Moreover, normatively speaking, it is neither intrinsically wrong nor a democratic panacea.

These arguments are important but the discussion in this chapter, as is also the case in a lot of the literature on the subject, has been restricted to theoretical arguments. However, without actually exploring whether or not the phenomenon is really taking place and how; or more precisely, given historical precedents, whether it is more intense and/or different from before, the arguments will remain conjectural. This is problematic. The discussion of normative concerns must at some point consider whether the personal is as ubiquitous as it is feared, whether it *replaces* or *adds to* the debate about issues, policies and leadership qualities, and *how* it is (or is not) *linked to the political*. These are ultimately empirical questions, to which we now turn. Not all answers to these complex normative questions can be provided by empirical analysis, including that carried out in this book, which is focused on the analysis of media coverage and party communications. Moreover, it is limited by a research design that relies heavily on quantitative content analysis, which is crucial to examine trends over time and avoid 'cherry picking' the most telling examples but also necessarily reduces complex concepts and processes to what it is possible to measure. But, notwithstanding these limitations, the analysis provided in the next four chapters will offer a much better grounding to understand the nature of the politicisation of private persona, whether and in which regards it entails change, how much it has to do with structural factors and how much is idiosyncratic, and ultimately help us to reassess its normative implications; because the assumption that the personal is pervasive in political discourse, *detached* from the political and *replacing* everything of substance in a devastating storm of triviality, is only that: an assumption. But it is one that has provided the basis – like a frightening spectre – for much of the discussion about personality politics, the concerns that it provokes, and the counter-arguments of those who come to 'defend' it.

Notes

1 Some 'famed non-politicos' (or CP 2 in Street's terms), such as Bono, Angelina Jolie or Jamie Oliver, also participate in the political sphere. But for all their potential ability to articulate popular sentiment and even mobilise political action, unless they run for public office, their influence in the material conditions of people's lives is generally limited. Moreover, although involvement in political causes is becoming increasingly common, this kind of celebrity is still the exception rather than the norm.
2 This is an adapted version of a very useful, and more complex, typology developed by van Zoonen and Holtz-Bacha (2000).
3 People's responses might inflate the 'serious' traits and underestimate those that are considered, by political scientists but also by most people, as 'unsophisticated'.
4 This was of course not the only reason. The positive performance of the economy is generally considered the most crucial element in the 'survival' of Bill Clinton's presidency (see Just and Crigler, 2000; Zaller, 1998).
5 These are some of the qualities that the panel members in Coleman's study (2006: 469) said would motivate them to support a candidate.

3

Personalisation(s) of politics in the press: British prime ministers 1945–2009[1]

This chapter is the first step towards the goal of providing a historical and empirically grounded understanding of the characteristics of the politicisation of private persona in the UK, whether and in which ways it is changing, and how it is linked to other dimensions of personalisation. This phase of the research is based on a longitudinal content analysis of routine press coverage in Britain over a 64-year period. In addition to offering much-needed empirical scrutiny of what is generally referred to as 'personality politics', the chapter will provide evidence about the media dimension of presidentialisation during 'normal' day-to-day coverage, which is currently lacking.

In order to fulfil these aims, and to better identify change, the exploration will differentiate between three related but distinctive analytical dimensions of personalisation. These, as defined in previous chapters, are: i) presidentialisation of power/presentation, i.e. greater prime ministerial predominance and hence increased visibility in media coverage; ii) leadership focus, i.e. increased emphasis on leaders' personality traits and skills directly related to their competence for governing; and iii) politicisation of private persona, i.e. increased emphasis on leaders *not* just as a representative of an ideology or a party, or as statesmen, but as 'human beings'.

These distinctions are crucial because it has often been assumed that the existence or strength of one process can be automatically inferred from those of the other. In fact, there are several related assumptions which pervade the literature. Firstly, it is expected that leaders will have a very strong presence in public discourse, both in their own right and as compared to the party itself, other party spokespersons and cabinet members. This assumption, as we have seen in Chapter 1, has been tested quite thoroughly but, bar a few limited exceptions (Foley, 2000; Langer, 2007; Rose, 1980), only in relation to campaign periods. Moreover, there is no conclusive evidence of a systematic increase. Secondly, it is assumed that there is now a strong emphasis in the media on a leader's personality traits both in terms of leadership (e.g. competence) and personal qualities (e.g. likeability) as well as on the details of their personal lives. This assumption is at the core of the claims of the rise of 'personality politics', but has hardly been systematically studied for the UK. Thirdly, and crucially, underlying each of these assumptions there is a clear notion of change, and specifically of escalation over time. However, apart from Langer (2007), previous longitudinal research has only measured the overall and relative visibility of leaders, and thus has not empirically explored the changes in the attention paid to different kinds of personality traits or the prevalence (or lack) of references to their personal lives. In other words, there has been little systematic research focused specifically on the historical evolution of 'personality politics' and the politicisation of private persona. Finally, there is a strong supposition that the different dimensions of personalisation are inherently synchronised (or contagious) and that they develop with a zero-sum dynamic in relation to other political coverage. In other words, the implication is that if there is a systematic and substantial increase in the extent to which leaders appear in the media, this must be accompanied by an even stronger focus on their leadership qualities and on their personal lives and 'private' qualities. Again, with exception of Langer (2007), to my knowledge no study has explored this assumption in the UK.

In short, longitudinal studies in the UK are rare and those available have focused on electoral periods and almost solely on leaders' visibility. As a result, although there have been interesting analyses of the causes and the potential consequences of personality politics and the politicisation of private persona for democratic politics, these have been mostly confined to theoretical arguments that essentially reflect normative positions but that rarely provide systematic empirical information to underpin them. There has been, however, some research of this kind during electoral periods for other countries including Croatia (Grbeša, 2008), Israel (Rahat and Sheafer, 2007), the United States (Sigelman and Bullock, 1991; Wattenberg, 1991) and especially Germany (Holtz-Bacha, 2004; Kleinnijenhuis et al., 2001; Reinemann and Wilke, 2007; Schulz and Zeh, 2004). Holtz-Bacha's (2004: 48) analysis of the campaign coverage in national dailies and political magazines between 1949 and 2002 in Germany found that since the 1990s press attention to candidates' personal lives has become more noticeable. But most other systematic studies have found that although the presence of the candidates in the news increased, the assumption that candidates are increasingly portrayed more according to their non-political characteristics than their political competence and performance could not be confirmed (see references above), even in the US (Sigelman, 2001).

This chapter will offer, similarly to these studies, an analysis of the historical evolution of personalisation, including 'personality politics' and the politicisation of private persona. However, the approach adopted here is innovative in significant ways. Firstly, to explore personalisation as an everyday phenomenon, it focuses on non-election periods. Secondly, in order to capture the changing nature of coverage, it analyses all kinds of articles that refer to the leaders, rather than only those that could narrowly be defined as political news. Thirdly, in order to test the 'contagion' effect, it pays particular attention to the synchronicity (or lack thereof) in the variation between the different dimensions of media personalisation. Finally, although looking for overall patterns of change, it pays particular attention to the identification of more subtle manifestations of personalisation and nuanced variations over time.

This approach rose from frustration with the mismatch between the lack of categorical findings in quantitative studies and the strong perceptions of pervasiveness of the personal in journalistic as well academic discourse (e.g. Corner, 2000; Corner and Pels, 2003b; Finlayson, 2002; Kuhn, 2007; Seaton, 2003; Stanyer, 2007; Stanyer and Wring, 2004b; Street, 2001; van Zoonen, 1998b). It is clear that in part the sense of ubiquity is a result of a tendency to highlight the most clear examples of 'personality politics', even if they are atypical, as well as to infer the degree of coverage devoted to the personal from the overall visibility of leaders. However, even if there are remarkable examples of exposure of the personal 'everywhere', it is important not to get carried away and assume, based on these high profile examples, the novelty, pervasiveness or normative significance of this phenomenon. On the other hand, this sense of pervasiveness cannot be ignored. The lack of evidence to back it up partly indicates an absence of radical change. But, it seems to me, it is also a result of reading the evidence through the prisms of flawed expectations. There can be significant change even if the phenomenon is not entirely new, does not have a linear trajectory, or has not become all-encompassing and systematically replaced all other elements of political discourse. Moreover, proportions are important but so are absolute numbers and high-impact instances of personalisation. In addition, because systematic studies generally focus only on a restricted definition of political news, they are likely to underestimate the presence of the personal.

In order to address these issues, it is necessary to use a combination of approaches. Content analysis is undoubtedly the most suitable method for the identification of patterns of stability and change over time, and it will thus be used for the analysis of the longitudinal evidence. But it also has well-known limitations especially because of its focus on manifest content and the necessary rigidity of the analytical categories, which can lead to overlooking nuanced indicators of change. Moreover, content analysis allocates the same value to every piece, regardless of the impact a particular article might have (or not) on other journalists, politicians or, indeed, the readers. This limitation, I believe, partly explains the incongruence between the strong feeling of pervasiveness of the personal and the lack of conclusive evidence emerging from quantitative studies. The use of more qualitative forms of textual analysis in the subsequent chapters will enable us to tackle some of these issues although, given that this study does not include audience research, we will be unable to analyse the effects of the coverage on the readers.

Methodology

The data is based on a historical quantitative content analysis of articles from two newspapers: the *Guardian* and *The Times*. Although the choice of outlets limits the generalisability of the results, the study still offers much-needed empirical evidence about the evolution of the different dimensions of media personalisation over time. In this regard, this selection offers some strong methodological advantages. Both papers are available for the entire period through a combination of digital archives, which enables the efficient gathering of data for the entire period under study.[2] Moreover, it also permits the use of electronic search functions, which are essential for answering these research questions in such a large data corpus.[3]

These two titles, however, are obviously not representative of the British media, or even of the press as a whole. Television is generally considered a crucial cause of personalisation and is also the most consumed source of information. Moreover, within the press, although the *Guardian* is centre-left and *The Times* centre-right, they are both broadsheets in a market where tabloids have a much greater circulation. These are undoubtedly important limitations. Nonetheless, and crucially, if as believed personalisation has become such a defining feature of contemporary politics, it must be manifested across media. In fact, as tabloids have historically been more personalised and emphasised the 'human interest' angle, *change* should be more marked in broadsheets. Moreover, including both titles increases the validity of the results. Most previous research of this kind (Foley, 2000; Mughan, 2000), including my own (Langer, 2007; Langer, 2010), analysed only articles from *The Times*. Because it is considered the newspaper of record, evidence from *The Times* 'cannot be regarded as an isolated anomaly but rather as symptomatic of broader changes in the nature of political coverage, the prime ministerial office and politics more generally' (Langer, 2007: 374). At the same time, however, *The Times* has changed more during the period under study than most other newspapers, especially because of change in ownership, and the decline of its traditional emphasis on 'hard' political news. In contrast the *Guardian*, although not immune to political and content changes over such a long period, because it is owned by a not-for-profit trust is expected to have a stronger stylistic continuity and have better resisted commercialisation pressures. Therefore, the combined evidence from both newspapers should give strong indications of whether or not there have been structural changes in the nature of political coverage.

The research starts in 1945, with the first post-war prime minister, Clement Attlee, and finishes with Gordon Brown. However, premiers who were in office for less than three years were excluded (i.e. Anthony Eden, (Sir) Alec Douglas-Home and James Callaghan).[4] This was based on the rationale that only by covering each of the first three years in office was it possible to ensure that the articles were representative of 'normal' periods (i.e. not unbalanced towards either the start or the end of the premiership), while at the same time including the 'novelty period' (i.e. the first year).

The data sample of 5,139 articles (2,698 for the *Guardian* and 2,441 for *The Times*), includes every article across all sections that mentions the then prime minister (by name or post) during two equivalent weeks in each November of their first three years in office (i.e. six weeks per prime minister) . This choice of dates enables us to avoid electoral campaigns, parliamentary recesses, wars and summer holidays, and hence to generate a sample that was both representative of the 'normal' coverage of the prime ministers and as comparable as possible. In order to test the reliability of the coding frame, a trained second coder coded a 10 per cent random sub-sample of the articles (i.e. 510 pieces). The overall inter-coder reliability, calculated using Holsti's formula, is 0.95 with individual variable scores ranging from 0.82 to 1.

Discussion of the results is structured as follows: the first section looks at trends in regard to the overall presence of the prime ministers. The second section reports the analysis of the references to leadership and personal qualities. This is followed by the findings in regard to the references to leaders' personal lives, which will provide a much-needed empirically grounded answer to the question of whether or not it is possible to talk about a progressive trend towards the politicisation of private persona.

Prime ministers' visibility

A combination of variables was used to explore the overall visibility of the prime ministers over time, while controlling for page inflation and the shortening in the length of the articles: absolute number of articles referring to each of the premiers and their parties; the proportion of articles referring to the leaders and parties as a proportion of all articles published by the newspapers; the total number of references to the prime ministers as a proportion of the total number of words; the ratio between the number of articles mentioning the leaders and the numbers mentioning parties in both headlines and the entire article; and the ratio between the number of articles defining the government according to party or the prime minister (e.g. Attlee's government vs. the Labour government).

There are some noteworthy differences in the results for each of these variables, which will be discussed below. However, overall, the results are consistent and in many ways surprising. Firstly, by and large, the trends for both newspapers have strikingly similar trajectories. This indicates that the changes over time are a result of structural factors and not of isolated changes in the style of each of the papers. Secondly, as would be anticipated from the presidentialisation thesis, the absolute visibility of the prime ministers has increased, and there is overall a positive trend for their proportional presence over time and relative to their parties. However, most of the indicators do not show a consistent, systematic increase in the presence of the prime ministers; rather, there are substantial peaks and troughs for individual leaders. This is not to say that the leaders are not prominent in the coverage: they are very prevalent over the entire period and especially after the 1960s, and their visibility is often as high as, and at times even higher than, their parties as a whole. But there is no conclusive evidence to confirm the widespread assumption that their relative visibility has substantially and consistently increased over time. Instead, the presence of the prime ministers in the coverage shows a good deal of fluctuation, and appears to be dependent on the leader's style, his or her political strength and popularity, and the different nature of the most pressing issues affecting each of the premierships. Finally, the evidence unequivocally indicates that parties are still central actors in British politics.

The departing point for the analysis is that, as part of presidentialisation trends, the prime minister increasingly becomes the main public face of the party and the cabinet and, thus, his or her presence in public discourse expands. The first step in establishing visibility patterns was to count the number of articles that refers to each of the prime ministers (key words *last name*, e.g. Attlee, Major AND/OR *prime minister* AND/OR *premier*[5]) during the six weeks under study.[6] In the period 1945–2009 there is a clear increase in the average number of articles per week: from 21 to 68 for *The Times* and from 24 to 76 for the *Guardian*, in both cases peaking with Blair. Moreover, as Figure 3.1 shows, over the entire period there is a fairly neat positive trend in the presence of the prime ministers in both titles. However, this change in the visibility of the prime ministers is likely to be a consequence more of page inflation than of presidentialisation. Nonetheless, the increase in visibility of the leaders in absolute terms cannot be dismissed because it indicates a much stronger presence of the prime ministers in public discourse overall.

The variations in the size of the newspapers over this period have been substantial. During the first premierships, because of post-war rationing of paper, the number of pages per day was limited (Wieten, 1988), which affected, although only mildly, the number of news items printed in

Figure 3.1 Average number of articles mentioning the prime ministers per week in the *Guardian* and *The Times*, 1945–2009

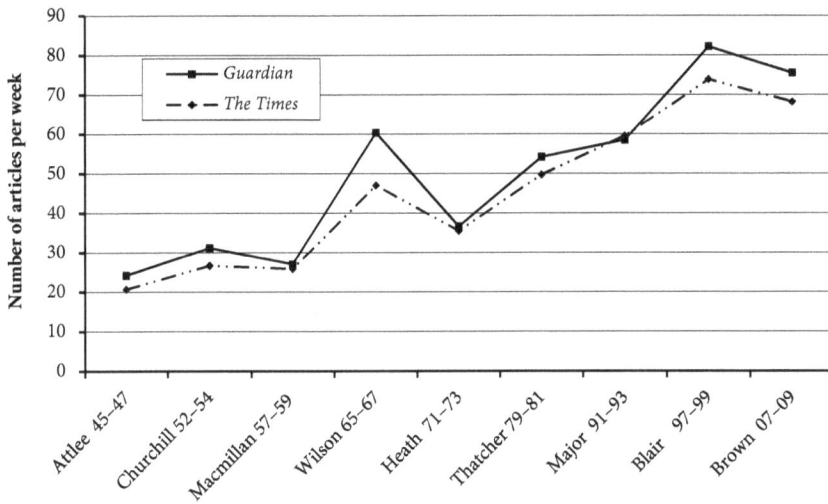

Source: Content analysis by the author

the newspapers (Curran and Seaton, 1981). More significantly, across the period newspapers have massively increased their pagination, although not necessarily their political news content. The most considerable growth took place during the last two decades, when the average number of news pages (i.e. ads excluded) grew in *The Times* from 19.8 (1985) to 34.9 (1995) to 56.4 (2006) and in the *Guardian* from 17.8 (1985) to 32 (1995) to 57.7 (2006) (Lewis et al., 2008). To account for this, in Figure 3.2, the number of articles referring to each of the prime ministers is standardised by the total number of articles published in the newspaper. This way, it is possible to track changes in visibility while controlling for pagination inflation. The figure should then be read as the number of articles referring to each prime minister per 100 published articles for the six weeks under study.

Several findings emerge from this figure. Firstly, although the proportion of articles referring to the prime ministers in the *Guardian*'s coverage is overall greater than in *The Times*, the trend lines of the two papers are again strikingly similar. Secondly, there is an overall pattern of a higher prominence of leaders since the 1960s, which coincides with the coming of age of television in politics and the start of the 'presidentialisation' concerns. However, the trend line does not show a systematic increase over time, and few would have perhaps predicted that Wilson would be as prominent as, or more so, than all other leaders in the past forty-five years (this is particularly noticeable in the *Guardian*).

The personalisation of politics in the UK

Figure 3.2 Percentage of articles that refer to the prime ministers
in the *Guardian* and *The Times*, 1945–2009

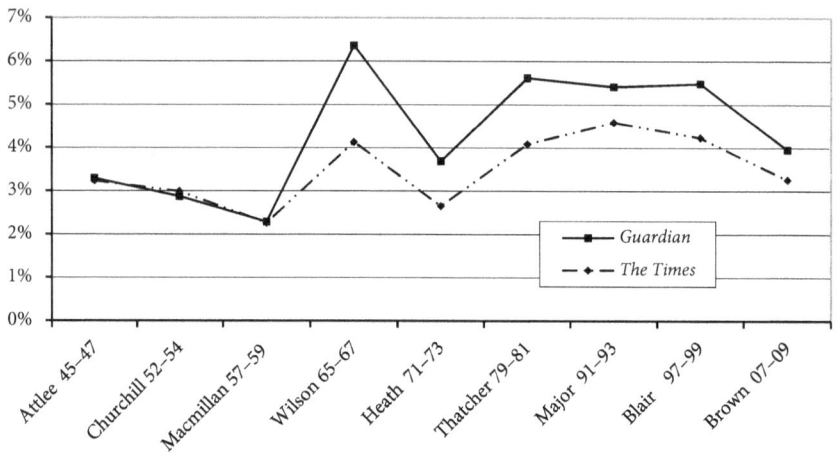

Source: Content analysis by the author

For a fuller picture, however, this evidence needs to be combined with a measurement of the salience of the prime ministers within the articles. Figure 3.3 presents the ratio between the number of mentions of each of the prime ministers during the six weeks over the total number of words in the same articles (measured in 10,000). This form of calculation is unaffected by the variations in the proportion of the coverage devoted to politics, and also controls for the differences in the lengths of the articles over the period under study.

Although the trajectory is different, in general terms the evidence here suggests a similar conclusion to the previous figure. There is indeed overall a positive trend over time, especially for *The Times*, but there is no conclusive evidence of a systematic escalation. The emphasis on the leaders consistently increases in the 1950s and the 1960s (peaking with Wilson), there is then a downward trend for Heath and Thatcher, and in *The Times* it markedly rises again during the last three premierships. The recent figures for the *Guardian* are more puzzling. However, they reveal, particularly for Blair, a different and crucial side of presidentialisation. On average, the presence of the prime minister within the articles is lower precisely, even if counter-intuitively, because he appears 'everywhere'. Specifically, because as a result of presidentialisation trends the prime minister is now personally associated with most of the government's initiatives, he is mentioned, albeit briefly, in a wider range of policy areas. In addition, unlike the earlier prime ministers, recent leaders (and especially Blair) are more frequently

Figure 3.3 Number of references to prime ministers per 10,000 words in the *Guardian* and *The Times*, 1945–2009

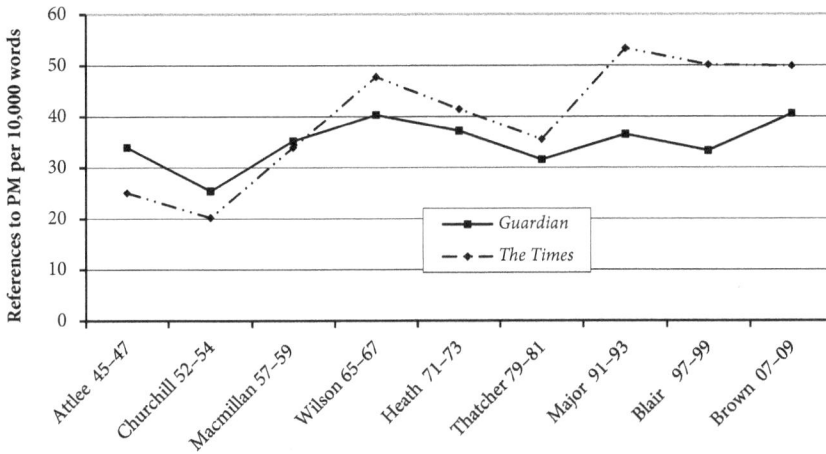

Source: Content analysis by the author

mentioned, albeit in passing, in articles outside political news such as society and entertainment (Langer, 2007). As a result, the presence of the leader within the articles is less prominent on average but, overall, it is more pervasive when considering the paper as a whole.

If we analyse the three figures in more detail, and contextualise them within the historical circumstances, it becomes clear that, within an overall personalisation trend, there are several factors that affect the degree of visibility of the prime minister. The case of Wilson is particularly illustrative in this regard. Firstly, although the role of television in British politics was consolidated in the late 1950s and early 1960s, Wilson is generally considered the first prime minister who really understood how to use the medium to his advantage, affecting the nature of coverage across media. Secondly, he had a highly personalised leadership style, especially during his first premiership. Thirdly, and crucially, each of the three years covered for Wilson was affected by major political developments that were not only newsworthy, hence expanding the amount of political coverage, but also of the kind that are more likely to result in the personal involvement of the leader: the Rhodesia/Zimbabwe crisis, the UK's entry to the European Economic Community (EEC) and the devaluation of the pound. In other words, the combination of structural changes, Wilson's personal style, and the presence of a (mismanaged) crisis and major international issues made his mediated presence particularly prominent.

However, often only some of these variables are present at any one time.

For instance, Attlee had a higher presence than Churchill and, in some regards, than Macmillan. Although he was a pre-television and a remarkably low-key personality, Attlee's visibility was relatively high because of the post-war context of critical negotiations with international leaders, which were both personalised and newsworthy. In contrast, although Heath was prime minister during the coming of age of television, and like Wilson had also to deal with the EEC, he deemed the emphasis on the public projection of leadership as 'confined largely to the vulgarities of the electoral process' (Foley, 1993: 107). As a result, his visibility was lower than Wilson's.

In short, the evidence suggests that, in step with the presidentialisation thesis, the overall presence of the prime ministers in the newspapers has grown over time and, as a result, so has their presence in the mediated public domain. However, against expectations, the increase is neither substantial nor systematic. The most notable increase occurred in the 1960s. Moreover, there has been a good degree of fluctuation. This indicates that although structural changes, including the internationalisation of politics and the impact of television on the characteristics of political communication, are important drivers of personalisation, the degree of visibility – as with presidentialisation – is ultimately also associated with short-term political circumstances and the leadership style of the prime minister.

Leaders compared to parties

Figure 3.4 shows the ratio between the number of articles mentioning the prime minister and the number referring to his/her party over the three years covered for each prime minister.[7] When articles refer to both, they were counted for both variables. In the manner that it was calculated (party÷leader), ratios >1 indicate that the leader appeared in more articles than the party, whereas ratios <1 show the reverse. The analysis does not offer categorical support to the thesis of presidentialisation in media coverage either, although for *The Times* the average is higher in recent decades. In addition to the omnipresent fluctuations, which underscore again the impact of individual leadership styles and the political context, it also demonstrates that even within the presidentialisation trend, parties have an enduring importance in British politics and its media coverage.

Firstly, even considering the latest peak, given that the ratios vary only between 0.57 and 1.27, it is clear that in many regards leaders and parties have always been, and still are, inseparable in British politics. This is not to say that leaders are not important; in fact, considering that any mention of the party in any kind of article was included, the high ratios across the period show the remarkable and consistently high visibility of the prime minister vis-à-vis the party, especially when Attlee is excluded. But, even if

Figure 3.4 Ratio of articles mentioning prime ministers to articles mentioning their party in the *Guardian* and *The Times*, 1945–2009

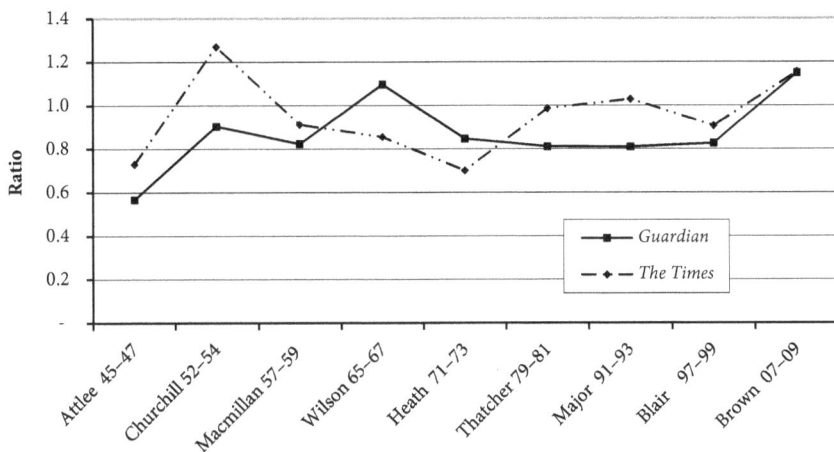

Source: Content analysis by the author

as a result of the presidentialisation of power prime ministers have become more prominent, they are still heavily identified with their parties. When strong, they act as proxy of, and carry, the party brand as demonstrated in particular by Blair's relatively low score: New Labour and Blair became practically synonymous. When weak, the coverage focuses on how the party, the cabinet and the backbenchers are turning against the leader. Secondly, as before, there is a good deal of fluctuation. Given their leadership styles, unsurprisingly, Attlee and Heath had the weakest visibility vis-à-vis their parties. In contrast Churchill, although weak as prime minister in his second term in office (in part because of health reasons), had came to be considered in many regards as above party politics. In the case of Brown the rise, which is more surprising, has probably to do with the state of almost permanent (and personalised) crisis of his short-lived premiership.

The analysis so far offers only inconclusive evidence of presidentiali-sation in media coverage; however, there is one indicator that confirms that there has been a sizeable and systematic increase in the importance of leaders relative to their parties. In fact, together with the evidence for absolute number of articles mentioning the prime ministers, this is the only indicator that closely matches the expectations associated with person-alisation. Figure 3.5 shows the ratio between the number of articles that describe the government according to its party (e.g. the Tory administration or Conservative government) or its leader (Major's government or Blair's administration).[8] In the manner that it was calculated (party÷leader), a

Figure 3.5 Ratio of number of articles describing the government according to its party vs. its leader in the *Guardian* and *The Times*, 1945–2009

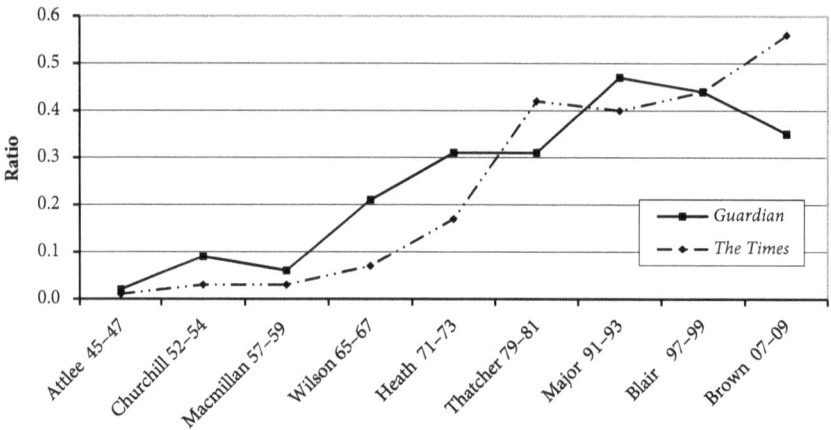

Source: Content analysis by the author

higher ratio indicates a greater proportion of references to the government as 'belonging' to the prime minister rather than the party.

The trend is strikingly clear and reveals a remarkable shift in how journalists interpret the role and power of the prime minister, who has come to personify government. Whereas for the first few premierships the government was hardly ever referred to as 'belonging' to the prime minister, the ratios start to gradually increase from the 1960s, reaching the highest point during the most recent governments. Given the previous evidence about the fluctuation of leaders' visibility and the consistently strong presence of parties in the coverage, this might seem in some ways puzzling. But, in fact, it uncovers a crucial finding. It reveals that even though the prime minister's visibility fluctuates depending on political circumstances and personalities, the allocation of responsibility for both successes and failures has become increasingly personalised. Moreover, although prime ministers continue to be strongly associated with their parties, they have increasingly come to be considered the leading partners in the relationship. In other words, the parties still clearly matter but, in the eyes of the media, the symbolic importance of the prime minister as the leader of both the party and the government has escalated.

Overall, the combined evidence reveals a complex picture. On the one hand, it does indicate an overall upward trend in the salience of the prime ministers in the coverage. This is particularly clear in regard to their absolute visibility which, even if a result partly of the substantial size inflation of the papers, still constitutes an escalation in the sheer presence of the prime ministers in public discourse. Moreover, although political coverage has proportionally decreased, the leaders are now also appearing across other sections of the newspapers, which adds to the sense of their pervasiveness. In addition, there has been a remarkable escalation in the power attributed to the prime ministers: recent premiers not only lead but also personify and 'own' government. On the other hand, very few of the indicators show a substantial and systematic increase of the kind often assumed. Firstly, leaders have dominated coverage throughout and, if one had to identify a single turning point, it would be the 1960s rather than the most recent premierships. Secondly, although noteworthy in absolute terms, the growth in leaders' visibility over time has not been on a massive scale. Thirdly, the trends are clearly not linear, indicating that the impact of structural changes in the nature of the coverage is not impervious to the particularities of each prime minister and political circumstances. Finally, although the presence of the leaders relative to their parties has also increased, it is clear that parties continue to play a crucial material and symbolic role in British politics. This is generally in line with the findings for electoral periods, presented in Chapter 1.

In terms of the comparison between newspapers, both generally follow strikingly similar trajectories. This indicates a remarkable consistency across the titles in the degree of newsworthiness and importance attributed to politics and leaders, which has varied depending on the changes in the size of the newspapers, the style of coverage and political circumstances. There are some differences, however, in regard to relative salience within the articles and leaders' visibility vis-à-vis the parties. Although the trajectories are also similar, with marked upsurges in the 1960s, the trends are more markedly positive in recent years for *The Times* than for the *Guardian.* In other words, whereas the latter increased its focus on the prime ministers in the 1960s, the evidence for *The Times* better matches conventional wisdom, showing a more sustained presidentialisation of presentation in the last decades.

Personality politics: leadership and personal qualities

The increase in the overall visibility of leaders is generally believed to go in synch with a greater emphasis on 'personality politics'. However, although this might seem common sense, it need not be the case. In many of the stories the references to leaders are in the context of the discussion of issues, policies and strategy, and make no reference to their personalities. In fact, as we have seen, research during elections in several countries has indicated that more candidate-centred campaigning is not necessarily associated with a greater emphasis on the leaders' personal qualities, even in the US. In other words, campaigns with coverage centred on the leader do not need to become 'beauty contests' (Wattenberg, 2004). On the other hand, given the deep political, cultural and media transformations experienced in the final decades of the twentieth century, it is reasonable to expect a degree of change in the attention paid to the personal qualities and lives of leaders.

In order to find out how these two dimensions of personalisation (presidentialisation of media coverage and personality politics) are associated, we will now explore the patterns of stability and change in the emphasis on leaders' personalities, both in terms of their political (leadership) and personal qualities, as well as their personal lives. By tracking these patterns over time it will be possible to investigate not only the evolution of personality politics but also whether, as is assumed, there is a 'contagion' effect, i.e. an increase in a leader's visibility leading to a greater emphasis on personality politics. Moreover, distinguishing between different types of qualities will enable us to establish what kinds of traits have become more prominent over time.

This exploration presents us with some methodological challenges. Firstly, the reliability of content analysis is dependent on measuring only manifest content. So implicit references to the personality traits of leaders that could be found in the overall tone of the article, but that are not overt or specific, will not be accounted for. Moreover, the qualities have to refer specifically to the leader, not just to the government he or she leads or its policies. It could be argued that a more inclusive definition could have been used. However, this stricter definition was chosen because it ensures that every article across the entire period can be coded reliably and systematically.

Secondly, the research questions require us to distinguish between different personality traits: leadership/political (or hard, performance-related) qualities and personal/private (or soft) qualities, and between a leader's personal and professional life. This is anything but straightforward because, in practice, the personal and the political are continuous rather than dichotomous categories (Adam and Maier, 2010) and they are not neatly separated in the media's or public's assessment of leaders (Just et al., 1996). Moreover, what might have been a personal quality during the earlier premierships could have come to be considered a leadership quality in recent years. In fact, the mutable nature of these boundaries are at the heart of personality politics; namely, how the political and personal, role and person, public and private are intertwined in the construction of a leader's public persona, and how this has changed. In order to enable the reliable tracking of patterns over time it was necessary to develop an operationalised definition that distinguishes the two types of qualities as clearly as possible. At the same time, however, the qualities were defined as a continuum ranging from clear-cut leadership or political traits (e.g. intelligence) to personal or 'soft' traits (e.g.

being nice or interesting) with mixed political/personal qualities in between (e.g. social skills). In combination, these definitions enable us to measure the relative presence of different kinds of personality traits in the coverage while, at the same time, capturing qualitative changes in the most prevalent dimensions of personality politics over time. The high intercoder reliability scores indicate that, in spite of the potential difficulties, the definition and operationalisation of the coding categories worked satisfactorily.[9]

First, we measured the proportion of articles that include references to a prime minister's qualities, both political and personal. In order to strengthen both validity and reliability, the list of qualities was constructed drawing on coding categories used by previous studies (Bean, 1993; Bean and Mughan, 1989; Hart et al., 1996; Just et al., 1996; Miller et al., 1986; Ohr and Oscarsson, 2010; Wattenberg, 1991) but adapted to the specific aims of this research. However, as mentioned above, rather than defining political (or leadership) and personal qualities as dichotomous oppositions, the different dimensions of character were re-grouped into three categories to represent more of a continuum (see Figure 3.6).

A category was created for pure leadership qualities (i.e. personality traits that have a direct link to the leader's fitness and capability to govern) including references to competence, intelligence, strength and integrity. These characteristics are relatively easy to distinguish from personal qualities and straightforward to code. However, most studies also include charisma and communication skills as leadership qualities. These proved more complex and shifting concepts, and it is in particular for these types of qualities that the interest in the personality of leaders has taken a more personal turn. Whereas previously these traits would have been discussed mostly in relation to a leader's stature as statesman, or skills in discussing policies and communicating with colleagues, more recently the same types of qualities are discussed in terms of interpersonal skills, their 'normality' and their ability to connect with ordinary people. To enable us to account for this change, any mention of charisma as having (or not) the 'aura', 'heroic character' or the 'stature' of statesmanship and public communication skills were coded as leadership qualities, whereas interpersonal and para-social communication skills and personal appeal (or informal charisma) were coded as personal or private qualities. In addition, psychological traits, which appeared only recently in the coverage, were also coded as personal or private qualities.

Figure 3.7 presents the proportion of all articles mentioning the prime ministers (N=5,139) that refer to any of these qualities (both positive and negative). The results were combined for both newspapers for presentation purposes. However, although the *Guardian* appeared to have paid slightly greater attention to the personality of leaders across the entire period, the

Figure 3.6 Dimensions of leadership and personal qualities

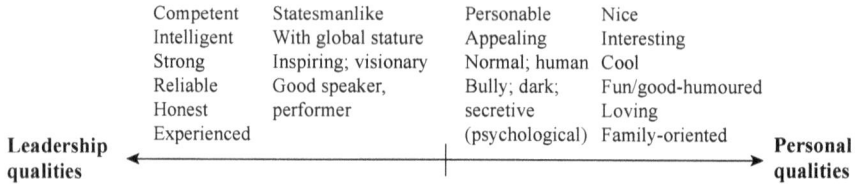

Competent	Statesmanlike	Personable	Nice
Intelligent	With global stature	Appealing	Interesting
Strong	Inspiring; visionary	Normal; human	Cool
Reliable	Good speaker,	Bully; dark;	Fun/good-humoured
Honest	performer	secretive	Loving
Experienced		(psychological)	Family-oriented

Leadership ←————————————————|————————————————→ **Personal**
qualities   **qualities**

patterns for both titles were similar. The solid grey represents leadership or 'hard' qualities and the patterned grey represents personal or 'soft' qualities. If the story included both, the article was coded in the latter category.

As the figure shows, the explicit references to leadership qualities (solid grey) were relatively infrequent across the entire period. Although this is in part a result of methodological choices (i.e. to include all articles mentioning the prime ministers regardless of the main subject and to code only for manifest references), it is nonetheless clear that during day-to-day politics the emphasis on leadership qualities is not pervasive. They were mentioned in only between 2 and 6 per cent of the total number of articles referring to the prime ministers. Secondly, there is not, as expected, a systematic increase over time.

The picture changes, however, when leadership qualities (solid grey) are joined with personal qualities (patterned grey). Whereas leadership qualities have been present throughout the period, and have not systematically increased, the references to personal qualities (e.g. nice, dour, charming, human, socially inept, loony, etc.) are all but absent for any prime minister before John Major. Because of this difference, when we combine both types of qualities, we can detect a positive trend from the 1990s, pushing all three most recent leaders, for the first time, over the 5 per cent line, with Brown the clear peak of the trend. This evidence gives some support to the personality politics thesis; although still far from pervasive, the recent emergence of personal qualities in the coverage indicates a noteworthy quantitative change. More significantly, the evidence reveals important qualitative changes in what is regarded as relevant traits. We have moved from a restricted definition of leadership qualities and skills, clearly associated with the fitness to govern, to one that also encompasses more personal aspects of leaders' personalities and which paints a picture of the overall character of the leader, including emotional, temperamental and psychological traits. This signals a shift towards the private sphere, the inner self and the leader as 'human being'.

However, these personal qualities do not come to systematically replace leadership qualities such as competence, charisma or communication skills, nor are they assessed in isolation from the prime ministers' performances

Figure 3.7 Percentage of articles mentioning the prime ministers that refer to their leadership and personal qualities in the *Guardian* and *The Times*, 1945–2009

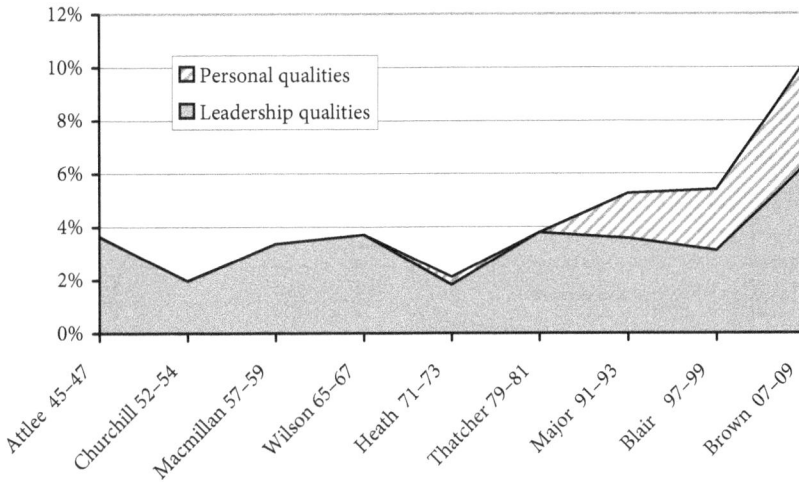

Source: Content analysis by the author

as leaders. In fact, the opposite is true; the two have become much harder to distinguish as personal qualities are presented precisely as a requirement of contemporary leadership. So, for instance, communication skills are now assessed not only by a leader's rhetorical ability in parliament but also by his or her para-social interpersonal skills, especially the capacity to communicate and 'personally' connect with the public at large in mediated performances. Likewise, charisma, always a difficult quality to define, is now less focused on the enigmatic attraction of heroic or statesmanship qualities (à la Churchill and closer to Webber's conceptualisation of the term) and more on the capacity to generate a degree of personal identification based on a leader's 'human' qualities, such as the ability to charm, entertain or to appear 'normal'. In other words, as we move from specific skills and qualities to character and personality, the human being does not replace the leader, but the two become harder to distinguish.

The coverage of the personal lives of leaders

The analysis of the references to the prime ministers' qualities has shown a recent move towards to the more personal aspects of their personalities. But to what extent has the shift towards the leader qua human being also been reflected in a greater interest in their personal lives? In other words, has the personal, as implied by the idea of the politicisation of private

The personalisation of politics in the UK

Figure 3.8 Percentage of articles mentioning the prime ministers that refer to their personal lives in the *Guardian* and *The Times*, 1945–2009

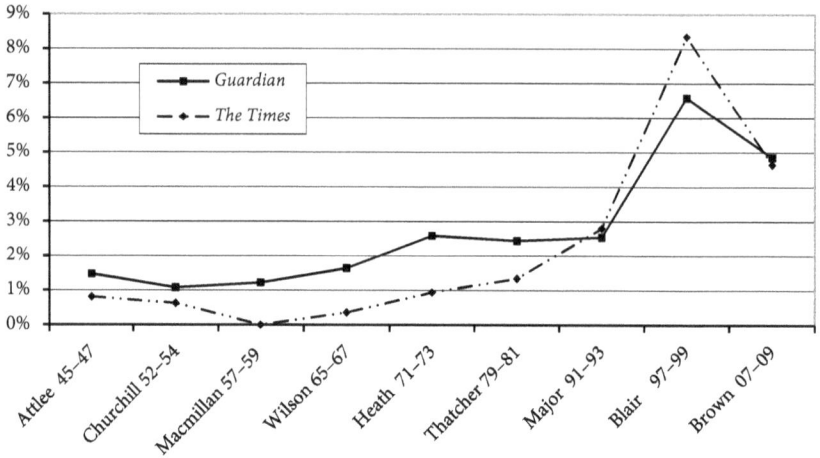

Source: Content analysis by the author

persona, become politicised? In order to answer these questions, this section presents the analysis of patterns of stability and change in the references to the personal lives of the prime ministers. As in Langer (2007), the coding frame combined five variables in an index: family life, personal appearance, lifestyle (i.e. hobbies, personal likes/dislikes and recreational activities), upbringing and religion. References to the relatives of the prime ministers which referred *solely* to the presence of family members in protocol activities and/or partners' professional lives were coded separately. Figure 3.8 shows the proportion of articles including references to any of these variables as a proportion of the total of articles referring to each of the prime ministers. If the same article referred to more than one of these themes it was counted once only.

Figure 3.8 shows that overall the figures for both newspapers again have similar trajectories. However, whereas the *Guardian* has paid consistently more attention to the personal lives of the prime ministers since Heath, the increase is more gradual in *The Times*. Beyond this difference, it is evident that there is a clear increase in both papers: the personal lives of leaders are more prominent in the coverage now than in the past, with Tony Blair the clear apex of this trend. However, even for the very reserved Brown, the figures do not return to pre-Blair levels. This upward trend is particularly remarkable given that, from a contemporary perspective, the early prime ministers' family lives had some clearly newsworthy dimensions: Attlee's wife famously voted Conservative and Macmillan's had an illegitimate child by a member of his government (Seaton, 2003: 177). Moreover, as we shall see in the next chapter, Wilson is considered the first prime minister to have systematically used his personal life for strategic publicity, to portray himself as a down-to-earth, family man. In other words, it is not that the lives of the leaders have become more interesting but rather that the media are now more interested in them.

In addition to the overall upward trend, there are important implications from this Figure for the assumption of a 'contagion' effect. Firstly, given Attlee's and especially Wilson's low scores, the evidence shows that in the past a higher degree of visibility did not translate to a greater interest in leaders' personal lives. In other words, the association between presidentialisation and the politicisation of private persona is a relatively new phenomenon. This is also consistent with the recent personal turn in the assessment of character. Secondly, although the trend is clearly upward and smoother than previous figures, as for other dimensions of personalisation, it is also contingent: the personal style of leaders does make a difference. Blair is the only prime minister for whom the proportion of articles mentioning his personal life was greater than those referring to his leadership qualities. Moreover, his family had a particularly high profile: whereas his relatives were mentioned in 8 per cent of the articles, Major's and Brown's were only present in 2 and 3 per cent respectively. In fact, Attlee's and Churchill's wives were mentioned more frequently than theirs, although these references were practically always in the context of official duties and made no comments on their personal lives (Langer, 2007). It is worth noting that Blair's youngest son (Leo) had not been born, nor Cherie's pregnancy announced, during the timeframe under study. Moreover, if references to religion are excluded from the index, Blair's figure is only marginally affected. Hence, the growth for Blair cannot be attributed simply to these arguably exceptional personal circumstances. As will be explored in more detailed in Chapter 5, Blair was a special case but not because of the characteristics of his personal life. Instead, the peak was a result of a combination of structural socio-political and media changes, and Blair's skilful and eager (selective) use of his personal life for strategic publicity. It is also important to note that the limited details about the personal life of the very private Brown did not stop the interest: not only was his personal life mentioned more frequently than for any prime minister other than Blair, but his reserve also raised, as reflected in Figure 3.7, frequent questions about his personal qualities (or rather lack thereof). This will be explored in detail in Chapter 6.

There are two additional elements that make these findings more significant in terms of a trend towards the politicisation of private persona.

Firstly, the average lengths of the articles have approximately halved in the period 1945–2009. Yet, even with fewer words to spare, journalists managed to mention these issues more often. At the same time, in recent premierships the presence of the leaders in the newspapers has escaped the narrow confines of politics. Whereas in the past prime ministers appeared almost solely in articles directly linked to public affairs, it has recently become more common for leaders to be mentioned in stories about politics more broadly defined (e.g. sports funding or society) as well as in those that bear little relation to the duties of the office such as fashion, travel or entertainment (Langer, 2007: 376). So, although because of length the available space within the articles has shrunk, new sections and themes in the newspaper have opened up to the presence of the prime ministers, giving more, and more fitting, opportunities for the exposure of leaders' personal lives.

Secondly, although it is important to work with relative figures to control for changes in the degree of visibility and page inflation, the sheer differences in absolute numbers cannot be dismissed. Whereas proportionally Blair's personal life is mentioned at least three times more than any of his predecessors (excluding Major), in absolute terms the difference expands to at least eight times. This is crucial because the absolute number of articles indicates the overall mediated exposure of the prime minister's personal life and the amount of information available in the public sphere for the use not only of citizens but also of journalists, who often recycle stories published elsewhere in an ever more competitive and expanding media market. In fact, many of the stories with references to the personal lives of the prime ministers were prompted by pieces in other, generally 'lighter', media outlets. In a sense, what we find in these newspapers is only the tip of a deeper trend. Although in relative terms the leaders continue to appear much more frequently in outlets focused on news and public affairs than in other genres, their presence in the latter has increased (Stanyer, 2007; Street, 2001). Moreover, when interviewed in genres such as talk shows or in women's magazines, leaders almost inevitably talk (albeit not exclusively) about their personal lives, which is then often picked up by other media. When we take into consideration the combination of these factors (the proportional increase, the rise in the absolute number of references to the personal and the presence of the leaders in other genres) we can start to understand the mismatch between the small quantitative change uncovered by systematic studies of political coverage and the widespread perception, backed by more qualitative studies, that the personal lives of leaders have become a pervasive feature of public discourse. There is truth to both because they are not mutually exclusive.

The degree of change in regard to the overall coverage, however, should not be overstated. Although changes in the media and in the communication strategies of leaders have affected the newspaper coverage of the prime ministers, the details of their personal lives are far from being the most dominant dimension and have not systematically displaced substantive political stories. This is the case even for Blair, who is the peak of the trend. Firstly, most of the personal references played only a minor role in the articles, with only 22 per cent of this sub-sample focusing on his personal life. Secondly, a large percentage of these references were found in articles that focused on 'non-political' issues such as society and celebrities (44 per cent). This suggests that the 'human being' has not replaced the leader; instead the coverage of the prime ministers has stretched and diversified, now more often reaching beyond narrow definitions of leadership or the political. The latter supports, to an extent, the idea of politicians as celebrities.

> We can map the precise moment a public figure becomes a celebrity. It occurs at the point at which media interest in their activities is transferred from reporting on their public role ... to investigating the detail of their private lives. (Turner, 2004: 8 quoted in Holmes and Redmond, 2006: 11)

As with those from the world of sports, fashion and entertainment, the prime minister's music preferences, dressing style and parenting approach is now the object of media interest and scrutiny. Moreover, as in the coverage of celebrities, there has been a clear re-definition of the boundaries between public and private (Holmes and Redmond, 2006: 11). But we should not overstate the parallels. Unlike most celebrities, prime ministers are not famous mostly for being famous and do perform a very public and important professional role, which is reflected in the still overwhelmingly politics-centred nature of the coverage.

Conclusion

This chapter examined the historical evolution of three dimensions of personalisation in day-to-day press coverage over a period of 64 years: the overall visibility of the prime ministers (and in comparison to parties); the emphasis on their leadership and personal qualities; and the references to their personal lives. While the evidence does not offer entirely conclusive results, it does uncover the complexity of the phenomenon and underscores the need to distinguish more precisely between different dimensions of personalisation and to pay attention to nuanced indicators of change. As the presidentialisation thesis would predict, the absolute visibility of the prime ministers increased between 1945 and 2009, as did their proportional presence over time and relative to their parties. However, as in the case of election coverage (Chapter 1), most of the analyses do not reveal a consistent increase, but considerable variation for individual leaders. This indicates that although structural changes are important drivers of personalisation, each leader's visibility is influenced by their style, political strength and popularity, and the nature of the significant events that dominate their premierships. Moreover, the period with most rapid increase was the 1960s rather than the most recent premierships, with Wilson (and not as expected Thatcher or Blair) receiving the highest figures for several of the indicators of presidentialisation.

At the same time, there are other findings that do show more gradual and recent change and that hence tally with the assumptions associated with presidentialisation in media coverage. Firstly, there has been a clear escalation in the prime ministers' absolute visibility. This increase has less to do with the effects of presidentialisation and more with the growth in the newspapers' paginations and with the more frequent presence of the leaders outside the political pages (e.g. society, fashion, sports); nonetheless, it is still significant because it has expanded the visibility of the prime ministers in public discourse. Secondly, as identified by the marked gradual increase in the references to the government as 'belonging' to the prime minister (instead of to the party), leaders have been increasingly *attributed* more power, which matches the perceptions of an increasingly personalised government. This is a remarkable finding because it shows that although – as manifested in the overall analysis of the coverage – parties and other actors are still central to day-to-day government, the media have increasingly come to consider the prime ministers as leading partners in the relationship and more personally accountable for both successes and failures.

The most remarkable shift over time and especially in recent decades is, however, in relation to personality politics, and in particular in regard to the politicisation of private persona. In terms of 'pure' leadership qualities, there is no evidence of systematic quantitative change. However, there are significant qualitative differences in relation to the last three prime ministers. Whereas leadership qualities have been present throughout the period, the references to personal qualities are practically absent for any prime minister before John Major. This indicates important changes in the definition of relevant character traits: it has broadened from an almost exclusive focus on skills and qualities directly linked to fitness to govern to providing a more rounded picture of the overall personalities of the prime ministers, as leaders *and* human beings. The emphasis on *and* is important because, rather than replacing them, personal qualities have become enmeshed with leadership qualities and successful politicians are expected to combine positive traits of both kinds.

The shift towards the leader *qua* human being is also manifested in the proportion of articles that included references to the personal lives of the prime ministers. While rare early on – even for highly visible prime ministers – the proportion of articles referring to their family lives, upbringing, lifestyle and so on has increased over time, especially from the 1990s. This indicates that it is only for recent leaders that a higher visibility is associated with a greater emphasis on the personal. Moreover, the combination of the personal turn in the assessment of character and the recent emphasis on personal lives reveal that, of all three dimensions of personalisation, it is the politicisation of private persona that has experienced the clearest changes. The escalation is not, however, perfectly linear. Although the trend is more clearly upward and smoother than for the other indicators, as for other dimensions of personalisation, the emphasis on the personal is also contingent: the fact that Blair is still the apex of the trend confirms that the style of leaders does make a difference. And yet, even for the reticent Brown the figures do not return to pre-Blair levels: not only was his personal life mentioned more frequently than for any prime minister other than Blair, but his reserve and hence lack of a public personal life also raised frequent questions about his personal qualities and his fitness for contemporary leadership.

The extent of change, however, should not be overstated. Coverage of the personal sphere of leaders is in addition to, rather than replacing, the political, and is still a minor element. Even for Tony Blair, the proportion of articles mentioning his personal life is relatively small, most of these references were only brief, and almost half were made within 'non-political' stories. Nonetheless, even though the personal has neither become the most dominant feature of the coverage nor replaced everything else in a zero-sum dynamic, it is clear that the politicisation of private persona is the most distinctively contemporary form of personalisation. Thus, it needs to be explored further, especially as manifested during Blair's premiership, the highest point, and its 'aftermath'. However, it is first necessary to look at the historical precedents to better understand what has changed (and what has not) and why; these are the aims of the next chapter.

Notes

1 This chapter draws partially on data and analysis of *The Times* first published in Langer (2007).
2 The archives are: Thompson-Gale Times Digital Archive (1945–1985), Times Archive CD Rom (1990–2000), The Guardian Digital Archive (1945–1999) and NewsBank and Lexis-Nexis for the later period (1999–2009) for both titles.
3 There are, as Deacon (2007) points out, some important validity and reliability issues associated with the use of digital archives. However, painstaking care

was taken to minimise these problems. The search key words were piloted and the choices were sensitive to historical changes. So, for instance, both the last name of the leaders but also prime minister and premier were used as key words. Secondly, there was no exclusive dependence on the results of key word searches. Every result list was manually checked to exclude duplicated articles and spurious 'hits'. Moreover, the results of searches within the articles were also individually examined. Thirdly, the inter- and intra-archive reliability was strengthened by the use of the archives produced by the newspapers themselves, which have greater internal consistency. Moreover, given the unavoidable need to change the archive source for the most recent period, the searches were carried out in both NewsBank and Lexis-Nexis. In the few cases where there were noteworthy inconsistencies between the archives, a more thorough and detailed examination of the results was carried out.

4 Gordon Brown was prime minister for just under three years but was nonetheless included because of his contemporary relevance.

5 In the case of Churchill, for the last two years, *Sir Winston* was also included as key word.

6 Articles that mentioned the office rather than the person occupying it (e.g. when an article discusses the constitutional role of the premier with no reference to the way in which the current incumbent fulfils that role) were excluded.

7 Although not entirely reliable because of changes in their style and length, the presence/absence of references to the prime minister and the parties in the headlines were also measured. No clear trend (either upward or downward) was identified.

8 In order to increase the size of the sub-samples (many of the articles do not refer to the government in either of these forms), the period for each prime minister per year was expanded from two weeks to two months. The total number of articles (N) for this calculation is 702.

9 The author coded all articles and a trained second coder independently coded a randomly selected sub-set of articles for each leader (20 per cent). The intercoder reliability calculated using Holsti's formula is 0.96.

4

The historical evolution
of the politicisation of private persona:
Baldwin to Major

The previous chapter revealed that there has been a clear escalation in the emphasis on the personal in the last few decades although, even at its peak, it was not pervasive. At the same time, the longitudinal analysis also suggested that the presence of the personal in public discourse is not an entirely new phenomenon. References to the personal lives of leaders that preceded Blair, and even Major, were not altogether absent. This indicates that although it has taken on a different scale and form in recent times, the politicisation of private persona has been present for decades. In fact, this chapter will show that as well as significant change, there has been continuity in the role of the personal in public discourse. Moreover, although it has become more intense over time, the evolution has not been linear because it depends on the particularities of leaders and the political circumstances.

The fact is that to make strategic publicity of the personal for the construction of a public persona is an enduring – arguably age-old – feature of democratic politics. But, at the same time, there is also something clearly different about its contemporary form. Thus, the questions that emerge, and which this chapter will focus on, are: beyond the scale of the coverage (i.e. the quantitative increase), how has the politicisation of private persona evolved over time? What are the similarities and differences between past and present in how the personal was used by leaders, and reported by the media? Moreover, what do these changes tell us about the causes and the evolution of the phenomenon? Unlike the previous chapter, which uncovered broad quantitative trends, this chapter will present a qualitative historical analysis. Moreover, the discussion, while addressing changes in the nature of the coverage, will focus on how parties and their leaders have used the personal for the construction of political personae, from Stanley Baldwin to John Major. The aim is to reflect on crucial historical precedents, and to start uncovering breaks and continuities with the past in the nature of the politicisation of private persona. This exploration continues in Chapters 5 and 6, which focus on Blair, and Brown and Cameron respectively.

The inter-wars version of 'one of us': Stanley Baldwin

Although a pre-war leader, the exploration starts with Stanley Baldwin, who served three separate terms as Conservative prime minister between 1923 and 1937. His significance in this context resides in the fact that he constitutes an important early historical precedent of the politicisation of private persona. Sometimes referred in his time as 'honest Stan' or 'farmer Stan' (Miles and Smith, 1987), Baldwin has been compared to Blair in being equally determined 'to present himself as a friendly, trustworthy, "ordinary person", unskilled in the arts of professional politics and uncorrupted by them' (Marquand, 2000: 76). Moreover, as Blair, he also tried to invoke a special relationship of personal trust between himself and the electorate, claiming 'special insights into the thoughts of the common people' (Williamson, 1982: 389). Baldwin's personality partly explains this approach, although not his background which, as those of most leaders, was far from that of the average citizen. But, more importantly, and in a pattern that will be repeated later on, his time as leader combined three key developments that encouraged this strategy: a radical transformation of the political environment that called for the re-positioning of the party; transformative changes in political persuasion, including the emergence, and Baldwin's mastering, of new forms of mediation; and a strong belief in the party on Baldwin's personal popular appeal.

Firstly, and crucially, this period saw a massive expansion of the franchise, increasing the electorate from less than eight million to around twenty million. It was also the time of a rapid growth in Labour's appeal which, in combination with the Liberals' split, brought a serious challenge to the Conservatives' electoral position. Baldwin, looking for a wider support base to include the newly enfranchised, greatly changed the party and its doctrine, and put himself at the centre of this transformation, articulating and embodying this 'New Conservatism' (Taylor, 2005: 450). In this context, Baldwin portrayed himself as 'plain, honest, and commonsensical', above and beyond parties and class (Williamson, 1999: 155), using at times an informal and self-deprecating rhetorical style and select details of his biography and personal life to sustain this persona. In particular, he heavily emphasised the soundness of the English tradition, which he linked especially to a nostalgic love of the countryside where he was born (Worcester), as well as with cricket and football (Miles and Smith, 1987: 53). Moreover, in spite of his background and position, he often portrayed himself as a non-political, anti-intellectual, countryman:

> Mr Baldwin, M.P., opened the new library of Gray's Inn yesterday [...] There is no greater bore in the world, said Mr. Baldwin, than those who asked you, 'What is the best book you have read lately? What book has helped you most?'

[...] '[In the library of the House of Commons] there are rooms full of books none of which should I ever look at were I alone on a desert island for the rest of my life [...] A library cannot be too catholic. A library should be a place into which you can find your own pasturage. It should be to me as the briar patch was to Brer Rabbit'. (Mr. Baldwin on the Ideal Library, the *Guardian*, 19 July 1929: 8)

Baldwin's strategy was enabled by the Conservatives' belief in his popular appeal. The party considered him, particularly during the early years, 'our chief asset' and the campaign for the 1929 General Election was 'almost in fact a one man show' (a former chief whip quoted in Williamson, 1982: 407). Secondly, and crucial, was the fact that Baldwin was exceptionally skilful in the use of the new communication technologies: sound film and radio. He was the first, and for a long time the only, leader to go to a BBC studio to record especially tailored talks for radio, for which he prepared in great detail. Moreover, although not quite Franklin Roosevelt, Baldwin was able to converse in a relaxed and convivial fashion, and was widely praised for his 'naturalness' (Rosenbaum, 1997). Likewise, he was a skilled performer in the newsreel, which he used successfully to build his leader persona (Scammell, 1995: 35). He even used it to publicise more informal (but of course staged) appearances such as receiving, with his family, the 'Old Berkley' pack of hunting dogs at Chequers.

Yet the similarities with the present have to be qualified. Whereas in contemporary forms of personalisation there is much emphasis on the construction of leaders' 'normality' and 'ordinariness', in Baldwin's persona the differences and distance between the leader and the people, in both style and position, remained at the forefront. So, although he spoke of himself as a 'plain man of the common people' (Williamson, 1999: 194), in the 'golden age of paternalism' his favoured roles were those of the moralist and the teacher (Williamson, 1999: 195). Moreover, from a contemporary perspective, the attention paid by the media to the personal sphere of the leader would be hardly noticeable and its tone strikingly deferential. He was a 'star' of the newsreel but, in comparative terms, the medium's presence in people's everyday lives was fairly limited. There was no television, radio was only in its infancy, and newspapers heavily focused on reporting parliamentary debates, confining politicians to the political pages.

Moreover, the infrequent references to the personal were generally triggered by, and appeared almost exclusively in, Baldwin's own words, with little media discussion of his personal qualities. Similarly, Baldwin's family life was rarely in the public domain. Mrs Baldwin, who was quite outspoken, appeared in the press when making public appeals for her charitable causes or partisan pleas to the female vote. But articles mentioning Mrs Baldwin rarely discussed any aspect of their family life. Moreover, the reporting was dry and matter of fact, occasionally breaking the mould to describe – but never judge – her outfits or to ask her about 'women's issues'. Likewise, the prime minister's holidays were briefly reported by the press every year but, unlike nowadays, there was no analysis of the reasons (personal or strategic) for his choice, or details of the activities he carried out. Even when Baldwin's mother died in 1925, although it was reported, there was no reference to the prime minister's feelings or how it might affect him.

Notwithstanding these differences, Baldwin is an important reminder that the portrayal of ordinariness and outsider status by a leader is neither a product of television, nor certainly a Blair invention. Moreover, the analysis of his case sheds light on the patterns that tend to encourage strategies of this kind: transformations in the political environment and changes in the conditions of political mediation that call for new forms of representation and political style; the party's tactical needs; and a popular leader with good media skills. At the same time, Baldwin's case starts to uncover the differences, both in scale and style, between earlier and more contemporary forms of politicisation of private persona. Not only was the leader's persona, and how the personal was used in its construction, very different; the media coverage was in comparison minimal and only reported, with detachment and uncritically, on the limited aspects of his personal life that the leader *chose* to reveal.

The post-war era: 1945–1960

Although Baldwin set a significant historical precedent in the use of the personal for the construction of his leader persona, he was for decades more the exception than the rule. The two first post-war prime ministers, Clement Attlee (Labour, 1945–1951) and Winston Churchill (Conservative, 1940–1945, 1951–1955) were, because of the crucial historical moment as well as their personalities and political skills, both powerful leaders. At the same time, they were very different: Churchill, a larger-than-life character, epitome of the heroic and charismatic leader; and Attlee who, in the words of Peter Hennessey, was 'breathtakingly unbreathtaking'.[1] Neither of them, however, placed much emphasis on the personal sphere, nor did the media on the reporting of their premierships.

Attlee was notably shy and reserved. Moreover, although central to Labour's electioneering, he was also famously 'hopeless at all aspects of the media' (Seymour-Ure, 1996: 209). His campaigns, travelling around the country in the family saloon car erratically driven by his wife, came to epitomise the 'pre-modern' electioneering (Bartle and Griffiths, 2001). In fact, Attlee's campaign 'adventures' in the family car were probably the best-known feature of his personal life, regularly mentioned, especially during election periods, in the press. This aside, his personal sphere was kept consistently private, with the exception of the by then standard brief references to the leader's holidays and relatively frequent, but dry and unrevealing, references to Mrs Attlee and her participation in official and charity events.

There was, however, a telling exception to this firm distinction between private and public. During the 1955 campaign, with the Conservatives in power and with TV rapidly becoming widespread,[2] Mr Attlee appeared with his wife chatting to a 'friend'[3] in a Party Election Broadcast (PEB). With Mr Attlee talking exclusively about political issues, and with Mrs Attlee mostly as 'an attentive listener', this 'intimate' broadcast was hardly revealing in personal content.[4] Nonetheless, the PEB triggered commentary in most papers, hence bringing some attention to issues such as Mrs Attlee's personal style and the decoration of their home. The scale of the reaction was relatively small, and the broadcast peripheral to Labour's campaign and to the construction of Attlee's persona. Yet the PEB and the media's reaction to it presage important aspects of the development of this dimension of personalisation. Firstly, it emphasises the reciprocal influence and highly reactive nature of party and leader competition (Foley, 2002). This PEB would probably not have been shown by the Labour Party had Attlee not been considered personally liked and a strong electoral asset, nor if Anthony Eden – younger and a more skilled TV performer – had not replaced Churchill as Conservative leader and prime minister. Secondly, it underscores the importance of electronic media in encouraging, or even 'forcing', leaders to pursue mediated intimacy. Finally, it draws attention to how staged personal appearances by leaders can stimulate coverage in several outlets, because of self-referentiality across media (Thompson, 2000).

For his part, Churchill was clearly much more comfortable with the politics of personality than Attlee, as were the Conservatives as compared to Labour, as they believed that 'more in politics must be left to the discretion of leaders' (McCallum and Readman, 1947: 102). Moreover, there is no doubt that the campaigns, especially in 1945, were heavily focused on him. But the overwhelming emphasis both in the party's communication and in the press coverage was on the leader, and not on the 'human being' underneath. Moreover, Churchill made little attempt to appear 'ordinary' or 'in touch', focusing precisely on what made him remarkably different from the common people: his war leader and world statesman reputation.

By the end of 1955 both Churchill and Attlee had resigned and had been replaced by younger leaders (Anthony Eden and Hugh Gaitskell respectively). Political communication was also changing rapidly, moving from an era dominated by print and live oratory to one where television predominated. The influence of television was also being felt in the press coverage of politics, which started to become more nationalised and with stronger focus on the top figures of the party hierarchy (Butler and Rose, 1960). The use of communication and marketing professionals, although not really new nor yet at its apex, was also becoming increasingly central to the parties' strategies, especially in the case of the Conservatives under Harold Macmillan (prime minister 1957–1963), who is considered by many as the first modern political marketer (Scammell, 1995: 47). Moreover, leaders slowly started to make better and more strategic use of television, adapting their rhetorical style in the process.[5] Macmillan in particular broke new ground, including the first ever interview by a prime minister in a studio, the landmark live (but heavily rehearsed) televised 'chat' with president Eisenhower at No. 10 in 1959, the face-to-face 'casual' interviews at Heathrow before and after foreign trips, and the first ever Party Election Broadcast showing the 'behind the scenes' of television production (Bruce, 1992; Cockerell, 1989). His mastery and strategic use of the medium led his biographer to describe Macmillan as 'the first incumbent of Number 10 to emerge as a TV personality' (Horne quoted in Cockerell, 1988: 94).

Part of his success was due to the fact that Macmillan realised, as Baldwin had done a few decades before for radio, that broadcasting 'is not a speech but a conversation' (Macmillan quoted in Francis, 2002: 367) in which the audience should be treated 'like an intimate dinner companion' (Cockerell, 1988: 63). Macmillan also understood that he and the party had little choice but to deal efficiently with television and other dimensions of modern political communication. He was the first British leader to be subjected to the 'Hollywood makeover', including new well-cut suits, haircut and spectacles (Bruce, 1992: 30). More importantly, during this period, the party started to conduct systematic public opinion surveys, to begin campaigning well in advance of polling day (over two years before the 1959 election) and to pay serious attention to the production of PEBs (Scammell, 1995; Wring, 1996). Moreover, crucially for the development of personalisation, and especially for the use of the personal for strategic publicity, a few forward-thinking experts in the Conservative party started to realise the importance of getting ministers to participate in entertainment programmes so that citizens could identify government with 'problems people feel and understand' while at the same time avoiding the 'fuss about balance' (Deedes quoted in Cockerell, 1988: 82).

But this was still very much a period of transition. On the one hand, the prime minister's image, personality and mannerisms were more publicly exposed than ever before (Cockerell, 1988). Moreover, as epitomised by the Profumo affair but also, for instance, by how much more quickly Eden's and Macmillan's health problems were reported compared to

Churchill's, it was clear that the social conditions of privacy were radically changing, to a large extent because of television (Thompson, 2000). On the other hand, leaders were still distant figures, whose representation and self-representation were characterised by a great deal of formality, detachment and emotional restraint. Their discourses, albeit differentiated by their personal style, made little reference to inner feelings or their experiences in the private sphere, which was consistent with dominant normative modes of masculinity, and hence of leadership (Francis, 2002). They still limited their appearances in the media almost exclusively to news and public affairs outlets and to 'on-role' modes. Moreover, despite more interest in the private, and a more probing approach in the context of scandal especially post-Profumo, the routine coverage was still focused practically exclusively on the public sphere of leaders. Furthermore, when touching on the personal, the press continued to use a detached and deferential tone, occasionally offering them the opportunity to 'reveal', but on their own terms.

The Wilson–Heath era

Although there were important historical precedents prior to this era, it is the 1960s and 1970s that constitute the crucial turning point. Labour's Harold Wilson, twice prime minister (1964–1970 and 1974–1976), and Conservative Edward 'Ted' Heath (1970–1974), were party leaders over four general elections, in which both were heavily emphasised, although also taking a more 'team-focused' strategy when their popularity was in decline (Harrison, 1965, 1966, 1971). Moreover, as we have seen in Chapter 1, the longitudinal evidence showed that, in terms of coverage, they were the most 'presidential' pair of leaders ever, representing in combination the highest average visibility in campaign television news for the last forty-five years. Not coincidentally, these changes took place at the same time as groundbreaking professionalisation of campaigning and election-eering – especially for Labour which, after three successive defeats, was now catching up (Wring, 2005) – and major transformations in the forms of political mediation, particularly because of the now consolidated role of television in politics (Bartle and Griffiths, 2001). In fact, so important had the 'new' medium come to be considered that the preceding prime minister, Sir Alec Douglas-Home (Conservative 1963–1964), a poor media performer with a stilted, aloof persona, is regarded by many as 'the first party leader whom television helped to destroy' (Seymour-Ure, 1996: 206).

The changes were neither restricted to campaign periods nor, regarding personalisation, to a higher degree of visibility or mere general emphasis on the leader. On the contrary, it is clear that the 1960s, especially as represented by the figure of Harold Wilson, constituted a crucial watershed for the development of the politicisation of private persona in the UK. Wilson made use of the personal with an intensity, enthusiasm and strategic intent not seen before in British politics. In fact, he was the first to employ, in a systematic fashion, many of the strategies for humanising leaders and portraying themselves as 'one of us' that would later become embedded in political communication practices. Moreover, Wilson did this from the very start of his leadership, and as a deliberate and positive strategy, rather than adopting it later to counteract an 'image' problem. Even before being elected leader, he had for a long time been 'at pains to appear a plain man of simple tastes, who in every respect except his ability and vocation, resembled the average voter' (Pimlott, 1992: 266). Furthermore, in an inter-party/leader competitive dynamic that we will see repeated later on, his use of the personal put great pressure on Edward Heath to 'go personal' himself. In fact, the emphasis on the personal sphere came to be seem as so prevalent that Enoch Powell referred to the contest between these two leaders as one where people were asked to choose between 'a man with a pipe and a man with a boat' (quoted in Rosenbaum, 1997: 192).

Many of the strategies used by Wilson seem now not only familiar but unsophisticated, and indeed in time they came to symbolise affectation and deceit, the very opposite of what they were intended to portray (Pimlott, 1992: 267). But their initial value should not be underestimated. Wilson used several dimensions of his personal sphere for portraying himself as an 'ordinary bloke'; from moulding his personal appearance (a mass-market Gannex raincoat and the 'classless' pipe, although in private he preferred cigars) to publicising some of his eating habits (a much emphasised fondness for HP sauce and home-made food), interests outside politics (*Coronation Street*, thrillers and his hometown football club Huddersfield FC) and family beach holidays always in the same bungalow in the Scilly Isles. His Labrador, Paddy, also got affectionate references and cameo roles, following in the steps of Fala and Checkers (Roosevelt's and Nixon's dogs). Moreover, the northern folksiness was built around his well-preserved 'working class' Yorkshire accent, and his touches of colloquial language. He also aligned himself with popular culture, giving an MBE to the Beatles, posing with James Bond, and singing a duet with a star from *Coronation Street*. All of this was combined with a strategic emphasis on his family, and in particularly on his wife, which he knew gave him a competitive edge: 'It's a positive advantage to us that I and Mary appear together and Heath has nothing' (Marcia Williams 1975, quoted in Rosenbaum, 1997: 192). Even on the day of his resignation, Wilson arranged a photo-call as 'farewell', where he appeared with Mary and Paddy and dropped in for a pint in his local (Cockerell, 1988: 226).

In fact, Wilson was so convinced of the importance of his family to his public persona that he came to believe that the BBC had a secret ban on Mary, to help Heath (Cockerell, 1988: 151). Although Mary was not too keen on the public exposure, not only did she participate prominently in campaign tours, which as we have seen was fairly standard, but she also took part in several interviews in a range of media, including some talking about their domestic and romantic life.

Wilson also pioneered another crucial element in the use of the personal for strategic publicity: the participation of politicians in programmes outside traditional news and public affairs genres, where the leader is shown in 'natural' settings and 'off-role'. He showed his 'life journey' in a visit to his hometown with Granada TV, including his childhood homes, schools, football club and friends (Howard and West, 1965: 40). He also provided a few 'intimate' shots for a *Panorama* profile, such as one repairing his son's bike in their living room, hence showing himself to be both practical and family oriented (Cockerell, 1988: 87). Wilson also gave, for the first time, full camera access both to Downing Street and Chequers. In combination, these kinds of programmes enabled Wilson to get friendly media exposure, engage with a different audience, and to attempt to project, simultaneously, prime ministerial authority and unassuming 'normality'. Moreover, in a strategy that was to be much repeated later on, he used the bargaining power of these exclusive 'intimate' interviews for punishing particular journalists or outlets, and in his case particularly the BBC, with whom he had an acrimonious relationship during most of his premiership.

These developments were to an extent idiosyncratic. Wilson was the first prime minister to truly appreciate the power of television and was a very skilled performer and shrewd self-publicist (Cockerell, 1988; Seymour-Ure, 1996; Wring, 2005). He also had a strong tactical motivation, as his personal sphere provided useful strategic differentiation with the two Conservative leaders he had to compete against: Douglas-Home, who was much older and aristocratic, and Ted Heath, who was reserved and a bachelor. Moreover, international trends and early signs of 'Americanisation' also had an effect: Wilson was a great admirer of John F. Kennedy and tried to emulate several aspects of his moderniser, youthful and family-man persona.

But, as much as he was an astute political communicator, to explain the changes merely as a result of Wilson's skill or personality is to misunderstand the nature of the phenomenon. Wilson's public persona and communication style were intimately tied up with the wider transformations in society, culture, media and politics of the 1960s. In the age of the death of deference, with the explosion in satire and the rise of the 'angry young men', Wilson 'harnessed the tide to his advantage', positioning himself not just as an ordinary man whom voters could relate to, but as one who positively rejected the 'drawing rooms of Belgravia' – a man 'with a chip on his shoulder', who preferred tinned to smoked salmon and beer to champagne (Pimlott, 1992: 267). In this sense, his version of the 'ordinary' man was an explicit rejection of the Establishment and a clear strategic contrast to the personae of Conservative leaders. Moreover, the emphasis was not so much on aspiration, which as we shall see will be a key dimension of the personae of 'post-ideological' leaders such as Blair, but on pride in his 'working class' roots. Crucially, Wilson's style also fitted the coming of age of television in Britain. The rise of mediated visibility and intimacy were changing the relationship between public figures and the people, as even the Queen agreed to herself and her family being filmed as 'human beings' in the 'fly-on-the-wall' style documentary where she appeared making a salad and buying ice cream for her son. In this context, Wilson revelled in disclosing his 'authentic' and 'ordinary' self in a way that neither Douglas-Home nor Heath did.

But Heath could not avoid being affected by these developments. The same societal changes, as well as added pressure to 'go personal' because of the reactive nature of leader competition, came to affect him. In fact, as much as Wilson's strategic use of the personal, what marks the period is how it also helped to define the construction of Heath's leader persona. Heath was not only a bachelor but was also a reserved character and rather uncomfortable with television, especially in the more informal and 'off-role' settings. In a different era, as we have seen, this would not have been much of an issue. But in a period of great leader-centredness, under the pressure of the new style of mediation, and as compared with Wilson, his reserve and lack of a *public* personal life (including a wife) made him appear – or so his advisers believed – aloof and out of touch with 'ordinary' people. The press also emphasised this narrative, assuming that this could be the crucial difference between winning and losing the election:

> Like many of the electorate, the woman saw the election as a contest between Wilson and Heath. The pundits may well be right that his problem is his aloofness, his lack of charisma, and his disinclination to go for the jugular vein, but in Dudley none of this worries the working class. What worries them is the lack of a wife. It is the first criticism made by both men and women. (Dean, the *Guardian*, 17 June 1970: 8)

As a result, 'the Heath problem', as it became known in the Conservative office, heavily weighed on the discussion of Heath's public persona, and attempts to 'solve' it and make him appear more 'human' had a considerable influence on the party's communication strategy (Cockerell, 1988). Unlike Wilson, Heath certainly did not engage with this enthusiastically and, as with most of the communication advice he received, he came to mostly ignore it once he got to No. 10. But despite his distaste for these 'gimmicks', he invited TV cameras to film him on holidays and tried to be seen with, and to talk about, children as much as possible (Scammell, 1995). He also emphasised his love for classical music and made much of his achievements in competitive sailing. Moreover, in the quest to make Heath a 'more attractive and accessible figure' (Cockerell, 1988: 147), and taking advantage of technical advances and a very professionalised advertising team, he was the first party leader to appear in a fly-on-the-wall Party Political Broadcast (1968), 'enjoying' himself in ordinary settings and with ordinary people (pub, shops, football, etc.). Heath also starred in what can be considered the first UK biopic spot, a PEB for the 1970 election that highlighted Heath's political and personal achievements (much centred around his triumph at the Sydney to Hobart yacht race), and showed the public more of 'the private man – the real man':

> Cold, aloof, distant. These were the kind of words the press were always ready to trot out about Ted Heath. But as the election got into its stride they began to use them less. Heath was a man come to life and clearly enjoying himself. Even enjoying the ever-present camera, the back-slapping, the hand-shaking. The public had never seen the private man in quite this way before and they liked what they saw. Someone said, 'He's a man you can trust' [...] Heath has rarely managed to convey the convictions he so easily expresses in private. He doesn't believe that a leader need necessarily be an entertainer as well. But, as the months have gone by audiences have seen more of the private man – the real man. (Conservative PEB for the 1970 General Election, voice-over by Christopher Chataway quoted in Kimber, 2010)

This greater role of the personal in the marketing of leaders began slowly to be reflected in the nature and tone of the media coverage, although not yet in a palpable increase in quantitative terms, as we saw in the previous chapter. The straight reporting of 'plain' personal facts started to give way to some colourful 'revealing' intimacy, and detachment to a degree of sentimentality and analysis of inner feelings. Although the press had been reporting the prime minister's holidays for some time, it started to provide more 'intimate' details of Wilson's family's holiday routine as well as of the 'behind the scenes'. Similarly, after the 1970 elections, the press offered some colourful analysis of the emotional impact on the leaders of triumph and defeat, spotting teary eyes on both the winner and the loser.

Moreover, the strategic use of the personal by leaders also provoked other reactions in the media, which will come to be characteristic of the politicisation of private persona. Firstly, 'intimate' media appearances of the leaders triggered recycled coverage in other outlets, including in satirical form, which amplified the overall presence of reporting of a personal nature in public discourse. In comparison to the contemporary media environment, the sites for this kind of coverage were much more limited as the line between information and entertainment was less porous and the number of outlets, overall, much smaller. Moreover, personal disclosure was by and large concentrated in electoral periods. Hence, the personal never reached today's sense of pervasiveness. Nonetheless, leaders' 'intimate' moments still generated a good degree of self-referentiality and amplification.

Secondly, the more leaders used the personal for strategic publicity, the more incentive the media found to search for traces of 'packaging' and their true 'real' selves, increasing strategic coverage, and hence prevalence, as well as a need for staging. Not coincidentally, Wilson was the first prime minister whom the media heavily criticised on the grounds of personal insincerity and lack of authenticity (Seaton, 2003: 177), starting to ask 'What sort of man is he, really?' (*The Times*, 13 February 1964: 6) even before he had become prime minister. Relatively speaking, journalistic culture (especially in broadcasting) was still broadly deferential and the interest in celebrities, and its culture of revelation, nowhere near today's. Nonetheless, the seeds of strategic coverage, adversarialism and the battle of the (in)authentic were already present.

Finally, Wilson's public persona – combined with the Kennedy effect – started to affect the criteria of leadership assessment. It helped to raise the belief, among journalists and party advisers, that this kind of 'human' portrayal might make a crucial difference at election time. This is of course, at most, only partially true and it was even less the case four decades ago. In fact, in 1970, in the most 'presidential' campaign for Wilson, where he heavily emphasised Mary and his ease with ordinary people, and where the Conservatives struggled to 'humanise' Heath, Labour lost an election that they were expected to win. Of course, there were very good reasons for this defeat: the economic situation had seriously deteriorated, including devaluation; Labour and Wilson had become increasingly unpopular; and the Conservatives ran a very professional and long campaign. But this unexpected result underscores, on the one hand, how parties and the media started to believe that humanising, especially when the opposition has an 'appealing' leader, is a requisite for electoral success, and on the other, how personal qualities in themselves do not really win or lose elections.

The Conservative years: the Iron Lady and Mr Grey

The role of the personal in public discourse continued to develop after the Wilson–Heath era. Leaders kept on using selected elements of their personal lives in the construction of their public personae. The media, for their part, also started to pay more attention to the private sphere, especially in the growing number of entertainment outlets and programmes; although, as shown in the previous chapter, not yet as much in routine press coverage. However, even though in many ways the role of the personal became more central and sophisticated, it would be a mistake to regard this evolution as linear. For instance, unlike Wilson and later Neil Kinnock (1983–1992), the two next Labour leaders (James Callaghan, 1976–1980, and Michael Foot, 1980–1983) rarely relied on 'going personal', which was consistent with their reluctance to thoroughly engage with most dimensions of modern political communication. More interestingly, Margaret Thatcher (Conservative 1979–1990) and John Major (Conservative 1990–1997), both of whom made careful and considerable use of the personal for strategic publicity, did so to different degrees, and with varying styles and strategies. This should not be very surprising.

On the one hand, because of the socio-political, media and cultural transformations that took place during these decades, the incentives, as well as the pressures, to show the 'human' side of leaders became more marked over time. Moreover, there is an imitative effect to innovations in political communication practices, which affects both what parties believe it is necessary to do to get elected and what the media think is interesting and acceptable to report. Thus, the personal had become a more obvious resource for the public projection of leaders and a stronger object of media interest.

On the other hand, although these incentives shape leaders' strategies, encouraging a degree of continuity, they do not determine them. Indeed, there have been important differences of style, as well as intensity, in how different leaders use the personal depending on their political circumstances, personality and biography as well as their approaches to political communication. In the case of the two Conservative leaders, whereas the emphasis on Thatcher's personality was focused on her exceptional leadership qualities, which portrayed her as uniquely qualified to lead, Major was presented as an amiable and 'ordinary' guy, with few private qualities that would make him stand out from the crowd. Moreover, although Thatcher's biography was used to authenticate her qualities and values, these were portrayed as incidental to her political convictions and policies (Foley, 2000); in contrast, Major's past was a crucial part of his core message and political identity.

Thatcher has been considered one of the strongest prime ministers of the twentieth century, raising renewed claims of the presidentialisation of British politics. Moreover, as is well known, her era marked a 'quantum leap' in the use of political marketing in British politics (Scammell, 1996: 115). She was also, of course, the first female British prime minister which brings a whole additional set of dimensions, and especially challenges, to role of the personal in the construction of the leader's persona (see Hall Jamieson, 1988; van Zoonen, 2000). Furthermore, following on from Wilson, Thatcher was keen on exploiting a useful contrast with Heath, succeeding where he had failed in using her personal life, and gender, 'to infuse political rhetoric with the common touch' (Nunn, 2002: 47).

It is thus hardly surprising that Thatcher continued to use some of the devices present in the previous era and developed new groundbreaking forms of using the personal sphere for strategic publicity. She appeared regularly on entertainment (including occasionally children's) programmes as well as in mass-circulation weeklies – especially those targeting women – and was the first serving prime minister to appear on a talk show and on the cover of a women's magazine. As Wilson had done before her, Thatcher also allowed cameras to film her in No. 10, including preparing breakfast and praising Marks & Spencer's frozen food (Cockerell, 1988: 300). Moreover, as is well known, she frequently referred to her 'humble' origins as the grocer's daughter from Grantham to emphasise the importance of 'opportunity for all' and to show that she knew 'what it was like to look up the class mountain' (Bruce, 1992: 79). In addition, as part of her highly professionalised approach to political communication, she paid a good deal of attention to her personal appearance and style, including changes to her voice, clothing and haircut. In this regard, she had to trade a fine line between strength, usually associated with masculinity, and the preservation of femininity. So, to avoid being 'stigmatised as unwomanly and unnatural' (Webster, 1990: 88), she combined a portrayal of a respectable and conventional personal life with a glamorous, feminine and highly groomed personal appearance.

But one should not overestimate the use of the personal in the Thatcher era. She indeed used light outlets to shield herself from aggressive interviewing, and selectively employed the personal to attempt to 'humanise' and 'soften' her persona, and to try to appear more in touch with the life and concerns of the 'ordinary' voter; but she was not a strong example of the politicisation of private persona, at least not in its contemporary form. Firstly, the glimpses of her personal life were offered in measured and strategic doses. In particular, she emphasised them prior to her leadership campaign in 1975, where 'Thatcher the housewife' appeared to be 'a woman single-mindedly dedicated to the pursuit of ordinariness' (Webster, 1990: 55); and during the troubled years of her premiership (especially at the height of the miners' strike), when she was increasingly seen as unsympathetic, uncaring and unwilling to listen (Cockerell, 1988: xiii). But apart from when she felt she had little choice but to show the 'other side of the Iron Lady', she was reluctant to give publicity to her personal life, and especially her family. For instance, unlike Heath and later Kinnock and Major, she did not allow her biopic for the General Election in 1983 to be broadcast. Moreover, Gordon Reece's suggestion of producing two Roosevelt-style fireside chats a year using Party Political Broadcast (PPB) time was rejected by Thatcher. Instead, most of the party spots where she appeared were formal and conventional, with obviously scripted and rehearsed speeches with complex rhetorical patterns, almost always in official settings, and with very little in the way of mediated intimacy or 'revelations' (Pearce, 2005). More generally, the exposure and performance of her 'private' persona in public was formal, almost never confessional nor revealing of her 'inner self'.

Secondly, in the construction of her persona, the emphasis was on her remarkable leadership qualities, not on the ordinary or the 'human being'. It is true that earlier on there was a purposeful effort to emphasise personal, and specifically stereotypical female, qualities as proof of her 'supreme ability to juggle home and work' (Nunn, 2002: 86) and 'everyday female common sense' (Nunn, 2002: 16). But by the 1980s she was happy to be depicted as the 'Iron Lady', both because of the political leverage of this portrayal and because it was closer to her sense of self. Thus, the strategy shifted to an emphasis on her 'extraordinary qualities and abilities' (Webster, 1990: 50), and especially her strength, assertiveness and even aggressiveness, focusing on her status – and clear comparative advantage – as incumbent and world (and war) leader. In this sense, it is clear that Thatcher saw, and represented, herself as 'uniquely fitted to lead Britain, endowed with qualities of strength and vision which no-one else can equal' (Webster, 1990: 92). Thus the undertone of her personal story was not of ordinariness, but that of a unique and extraordinary character, which emphasised difference and distance rather than closeness and resemblance, portraying her as 'exceptional rather than an everyday or normal woman ... even inhuman in her capacity and ambition' (Nunn, 2002: 41). This exclusion, paradoxically, was especially marked for women as Thatcher often recommended the opposite path to the one she chose, that of the good housewife and mother, leaving, within Thatcherism, 'no room for a woman like her' (Webster, 1990: 44). In short, the emphasis was ultimately on respect rather than likeability, which was fitting given that the public hardly changed their mind about the latter (Scammell, 1995).

Thirdly, the use of the personal was anything but apolitical or un-ideological. The references to her private life, and especially her past, were at times employed to try to 'soften' her persona. But foremost, they were used to authenticate strong ideological beliefs and values at the core of Thatcherism, especially enterprise, self-discipline, personal responsibility, and competitive individualism. Thus, her preferred emphasis was on her roots, her father, Methodism and the early provincial 'spartan' life as the grocer's daughter, rather than on the details of the (distracting) routines and pleasures of everyday life or the rare glimpses of 'intimacy'.

In short, on the one hand, Thatcher appropriated and further developed some of the devices used previously for the strategic use of the personal, and made some additional concessions to deal with gender expectations. On the other hand, this was not central to her communication strategy. Moreover, the selective use of the personal emphasised exceptional qualities and was at the service of core ideological values. Furthermore, the exposure and performance of her 'private' persona in public was formal, unrevealing, emotionally detached and hardly ever acknowledging error or vulnerability. In fact, one could argue that in many ways her persona 'refers back to an earlier tradition of political discourse; one represented, perhaps, by Winston Churchill, whom she directly invokes' (Pearce, 2005: 81).

Thatcher's successor, John Major, was rather different. Although an important figure in her government, he came to the party's leadership representing a strong break from the past. Moreover, atypically for a prime minister, he was also little known to the general public, which gave him more leeway in the presentation of the self, especially in terms of portraying himself as an 'outsider'. In fact, Major was presented as a 'fresh start' (Busby, 2009: 77), an 'antidote' to the previous leader as 'an integral part of his original appeal had been that he was *not* Margaret Thatcher' (Foley, 2002: 27). Whereas Thatcher was a strong, divisive, one-woman show driven by the power of her convictions, Major was collegial, conciliatory and focused on pragmatic politics. Moreover, if she was respected but rarely liked and her persona anything but ordinary, he emphasised his amiable, courteous and 'ordinary' persona, representing conservatism with a 'human face'.

But although Major played on the image that he was, in contrast to Thatcher (and Kinnock), unconcerned about his image in the media, his professed disdain for paying attention to communication and image 'deserves to be thoroughly debunked' (Scammell, 1995: 242). His 'anti-packaging' approach was a deliberate communication strategy that suited not only his reserved personality but also, crucially, the 'plain-as-pump-water' persona he was trying to portray. Similarly, despite his much emphasised respect for cabinet government, under Major the Conservatives made a strategic decision to run long 'presidential-style' campaigns, especially in 1992 (Foley, 2002). In short, whereas in the case of Thatcher her presidential style of communication and the role of image-making have been probably overstated, for Major it has often been the opposite. Not only did he try to follow in Thatcher's steps, albeit often less successfully in the execution, but also in some regards took it to a new level.

This also applies to the use of the personal in the construction of their public personae. It is true that Major did not use light entertainment outlets, and especially women's magazines, as much or as skilfully as Thatcher did, although as Heath often did he appeared on sports programmes. Yet 'Brixton-to-Westminster' Major emphasised his 'soft' personal traits and made use of his personal life, and specifically of his past, more premeditatedly and in a more central fashion than Thatcher ever did. This was epitomised by a poster for the 1992 campaign, which with the background of a smiling Major, asked: 'What does the Conservative Party offer a working class kid from Brixton? They make him Prime Minister. No wonder that John Major thinks that everyone should have an equal opportunity' (quoted in Allan et al., 1995: 388). Moreover, Major's past was also the star of *The Journey* PEB, which followed on from Heath's (*A Man to Trust*) and Kinnock's (*Kinnock the Movie*) biopics. In this broadcast, Major takes us on a chauffeured drive through his 'success story' (Allan et al., 1995: 376) from Brixton to No. 10, showing 'John Major the man',[6] and how his personal experiences informed and authenticated his political proposals. It is through him that past, present and future, and the personal and the political, are linked. In fact, apart from the final shot, there are neither references to the party nor does any other member appear. Perhaps surprisingly for contemporary eyes, however, neither are there any images of his wife or children, which he requested be deleted (Rosenbaum, 1997: 74), nor open expression of emotions, or intimate or remotely revealing details of his everyday life.

Some parallels could be drawn between the 'grocer's daughter' and the 'Brixton-to-Westminster' journey. However, although both Thatcher and Major came from relatively modest backgrounds, and both emphasised it in the construction of their public personae and their advocacy of conservative values, the use was very different. Thatcher's past helped to explain her qualities and values, but these were portrayed as incidental to her political convictions and policies, which demanded unique strength of leadership and drastic political change (Foley, 2000). In contrast, Major's past was not merely a backdrop but a crucial part of his core message and political identity, which also set him above and slightly apart from his party (Scammell, 1995: 258). Specifically, as in *The Journey*, his political ideas were subsumed under the narrative and meaning of Major's life experiences and his personal journey acted as the living embodiment of 'an opportunity, classless Britain', a living proof of what ordinary people could achieve, and personal guarantee of insightful understanding and protection of those who were less well off (Foley, 2002: 42). But, as a result, he appeared more as a successful example of social mobility and meritocracy than as its driver. In contrast, Thatcher's past informed her values but she did not merely embody them, she pursued them with the aim of radical change.

Moreover, whereas the emphasis on Thatcher's personality was focused on her exceptional leadership qualities, which portrayed her as uniquely qualified to lead, Major was presented, à la Baldwin, as an amiable and 'ordinary' guy, with few private qualities that would make him stand out: plain-speaking, plain-eating and plain-dressing sort; deficient student and even temporarily unemployed; and with a nostalgic love for icons of a traditional notion of Englishness, including cricket, warm beer and the green of county grounds.[7] In fact, Major and his 'cultivated mediocrity and self-styled ordinariness' (Foley, 2002: 156) were, for a while, considered the party's chief assets (Scammell, 1995: 258).

But, although in some ways successful, there were several problems with this strategy, some of which came to be reflected in the media coverage. Firstly, although Major continued to be regarded as likeable and honest, as his premiership progressed, the benefits of the 'antidote' strategy wore out and he was increasingly, and negatively, compared with the 'strong leadership, radical vision and personal power' of Thatcher and 'repeatedly admonished for not developing the same aura of leadership authority' (Foley, 2002: 59). Moreover, the criticisms often took a gendered turn, as his increasingly weak and ineffectual leadership was portrayed, in opposition to Thatcher, as a form of 'lesser masculinity' (Nunn, 2002: 178). Secondly, as reflected in the rise of the references to personal 'soft' qualities (see Chapter 3), the media criticism became not only leader-centred but more personal. As he had personally embodied his politics and government, now his persona came to embody its weaknesses: ordinary, grey, old-fashioned, and (too) amiable and unadventurous. This is not to say that Thatcher was spared criticism, but rather that in her case, having long discounted likeability, these were focused not on the personal but on her relationship with the party, her policies and her leadership qualities.

Conclusion

This chapter has presented a historical journey of the use of the personal in the construction of public personae by British prime ministers, from 'farmer Stan' Baldwin to 'Brixton-to-Westminster' Major. It is tempting to see this journey as a linear path; from a detached authoritative persona based on political performance to the human-leader as 'one of us'. But it is not so simple. In fact, because of the importance of the variations in the style of different leaders and the political circumstances affecting their premierships, the discussion resists easy generalisation about patterns of change. Indeed, in the manner that they have (not) used the personal, Baldwin seems to have in some ways more in common with Major than with his contemporaries, as Churchill does with Thatcher, Attlee does with Brown, and Wilson does with Blair.

But there are, nonetheless, some important conclusions that can be drawn. Firstly, the use of the personal for strategic publicity is not a Blair creation nor, significant as it is, a product of television. This might seem obvious but it is often forgotten. Secondly, the 1960s, especially in the figure of Harold

Wilson, were a crucial watershed in the development of the politicisation of private persona in Britain. This unprecedented emphasis on 'going personal' resulted from a combination of factors specific to Wilson as well as structural socio-political, cultural and technological transformations. It also triggered changes in how the media treated the personal. Thirdly, and an extension of the above, the chapter has underscored that we can only make sense of the evolution of the politicisation of private persona if we understand that it is a result of the complex interaction between structural conditions (and how these have changed), the particularities of leaders and the political context, and the reactive nature of leader competition (which is not the same as a straight 'contagion' effect because it encourages imitation but also 'antidote' strategies). This intricate interplay between the enduring and the idiosyncratic has led, on the one hand, to persistent differences between leaders and, on the other, to a degree of systematic change.

In this sense, for all that the developments resist neat generalisation, there have been some clear changes over time. The use of the personal for strategic publicity has intensified; whereas previously, revealing some selected aspects of the personal was remarkable, over time it became a common practice. Moreover, from the 1960s, the execution has become more professionalised and the aims more encompassing; it shifted from a marginal tactic of image-making to give leaders a 'human' touch, to a core dimension of the communication strategy which is usefully exploited but also needs to be carefully managed. This applies to leaders such as Wilson, who seemed naturally capable of appearing 'human', but also to those to whom it did not come easily, as we saw in the case of Heath – particularly when under pressure from the competition. In fact, as much as Wilson's strategic use of the personal, what marks the period is how it also shaped the construction of Heath's leader persona. Moreover, along with the expansion of politics into 'soft' entertainment outlets, the use of the personal has also become a tool of media management: to gain media exposure, avoid aggressive interviewing and to engage with a different audience.

The style of persona has also changed, along with cultural and techno-logical transformations. Some leaders, such as Attlee and Churchill, hardly tried to develop mediated intimacy or appear as 'one of us'. And even those who did engage with personalisation as a strategy earlier on, such as Baldwin and Macmillan, did so only to a limited degree. The difference and distance between them (the leader) and us (the people) in position, qualities and style remained at the forefront. Moreover, earlier leaders' representation and self-representation were characterised by a great deal of formality, authoritativeness and emotional detachment, which was consistent with dominant normative modes of masculinity, and hence of leadership. Paradoxically, of the more recent leaders, it is the only female British prime minister, Margaret Thatcher, who presents more continuity with this style; albeit with occasional concessions in times of need to try to avoid appearing too 'inhuman' or 'unwomanly', the focus was above all on her remarkable leadership, and hence exceptional, qualities.

The greater use of the personal in the marketing of leaders gradually started to colour media reporting. In the 1940s and 1950s the routine coverage of prime ministers was focused almost exclusively on their political activities. Moreover, bar major political scandals, when touching on the personal the press used a detached and deferential tone, reporting only on the limited aspects of the leader's personal life that he *chose* to reveal. Over time, more 'intimate' details slowly began to appear. Moreover, the more leaders used the personal for strategic publicity, the more incentive the media found to unveil the 'behind the scenes' and to search for traces of 'packaging' and their 'real' selves. The degree of strategic coverage, adversarialism and the search for (in)authenticity was by today's standards trifling; but it is nonetheless possible to recognise in the 1960s the seeds of these characteristics of contemporary political coverage. In addition, the greater visibility of the personal also started to have an impact on the evaluation of suitability for leadership. Within both media and political parties, the idea that a strong 'human' persona – or conversely the lack of one – might be critical to electoral successes began to take root. Quantitatively, however, as we have seen in the previous chapter, it was still very much a minor element of public discourse as politicians were mostly confined to 'hard' news, and 'going personal' was a marginal element of their communication strategies.

In short, the politicisation of private persona is not a recent 'invention' but has evolved over time, becoming more common, professionalised and encompassing in its aims. The media's approach to the personal has also changed; although the quantitative increase has been only minimal, the tone became more inquisitive and less deferential. Moreover, the capacity to appear 'human' started to be used as a criterion of leadership assessment. These changes are related to the socio-political, media and cultural transformations of these decades, which encouraged leaders suited for mediated intimacy to try to take advantage of the potential benefits of 'going personal'. Moreover, the more it was performed, the more other leaders thought it a strategy worth imitating, and the more the media felt compelled and entitled to report on the personal. In consequence, over time the personal lives of leaders became a more attractive element for the construction of public persona and of greater interest to the media.

At the same time, we should not overestimate its importance. The chapter uncovered an increase in its relative prevalence over time but does not claim that it has become the most important dimension of party communication, branding or media reporting. Moreover, the evolution has not been linear, because to what extent and how leaders 'go personal' was (and still is) ultimately dependant on the style and the circumstances of the individuals. Furthermore, although it became more common from the 1960s, until the 1990s using the personal was still by and large an optional strategy, with some leaders using it as part of their core communication approach, others using it only sporadically – especially during campaigns – to 'sort out' image problems, and some ignoring it almost entirely. In this sense, as we shall see in the next chapter, during Blair's era the politicisation of private persona reached new levels of intensity and sophistication, making the personal not just a common, but a routine, element of public discourse, and one more closely entangled with the political. Moreover, being able to reveal 'authentically' the private self has come to be considered a crucial leadership quality. As a result, although how they deal with this issue is still to an extent idiosyncratic, it has become increasingly problematic for leaders to refuse to reveal their private selves.

Notes

1 As Frederick Newman of the *Daily Sketch* put it, Attlee 'was a man who tucked his personality behind a pipe and left colleagues and public to make what they could of all the smoke signals' (quoted in Heasman, 1967: 83).

2 Television ownership grew from a few hundred thousand households in 1945, when Attlee was elected for the first time, to over twelve million ten years later (*Observer*, 15 May 1955).

3 The 'friend' was former *Herald* journalist and Labour sympathiser, Mr Percy Cudlipp.

4 Mrs Attlee's main intervention was to mention, again, that she would be driving her husband during the campaign!

5 It was only from the 1959 election onwards that the BBC, to a large extent as a result of the emergence of the commercial channel ITV, started to include information about the election in its news bulletins. Until then, the BBC avoided talking about the election and suspended most of its political programmes between the dissolution of parliament and polling day.

6 These were the very words used by Chris Patten, Party Chair, to describe the broadcast: 'It was never meant to be glossy; what it was meant to be was an experience of John Major the man … it is about the journey … the road he travelled from Coldharbour Lane to Downing Street' (quoted in Allan et al., 1995: 374).

7 This was expressed, most patently and memorably, in a speech in 1993: '50 years from now Britain will still be the country of long shadows on country grounds, warm beer, invincible green suburbs, dog lovers and pool fillers and – as George Orwell said – "old maids cycling to Holy Communion through the morning mist"'.

5

Tony Blair: the special one

Tony Blair was elected leader of the Labour party in July 1994 replacing the late John Smith. Prior to Smith's sudden death, it was generally assumed that, when the time came, Gordon Brown would become the next leader. Although both Blair and Brown were leading members of the shadow cabinet and hard-core modernisers, Brown was considered more senior. Nonetheless, after Smith's death, Blair came to be regarded as a stronger contender because of his media skills, his young and family-friendly image, and especially his stronger appeal to non-Labour voters. So, realising that Blair had greater support across the party, and after much negotiation, Brown decided not to run. Blair won the leadership election in a landslide and led the party to victory in three consecutive General Elections (1997, 2001 and 2005).

Blair's leadership was clearly remarkable. He was central, both symbolically and practically, to the creation and success of the New Labour brand. He was the longest ever serving Labour prime minister. In addition, as discussed in Chapter 1, it was during his premiership that the presidentialisation trends of the British premiership became consolidated. In these regards, there are some evident parallels with Harold Wilson. Like him, Blair was a moderniser and inherited a party ready for, and in fact already in the process of, change after an 18-year stint in opposition. Both have also been recognised as exceptional media performers and eager students of the lessons from an innovative US Democratic president (JFK and Clinton). Moreover, during both leaderships, Labour caught up with the Conservatives in the use of political marketing. In fact, New Labour is widely considered as one of the most successful and sophisticated examples of the use of public opinion research (especially qualitative), as well as communication techniques and media management, for the strategic re-positioning of a political brand. So it is not surprising to find that Blair made skilful use of his personal life for strategic publicity. In fact, not coincidentally Blair's reign became known as the 'era of spin' and 'celebrity politics', and his persona widely perceived as that of a family man with the 'common touch' – although this was later tainted. Also, as revealed in Chapter 3, it was during his premiership that the references to the personal peaked in the press coverage.

But given the various historical precedents discussed in the previous chapter, key questions remain: what was new, what was different about the use of Blair's personal life in the construction of his public persona? Moreover, to what extent do these differences explain the changes in the patterns of the coverage uncovered in Chapter 3? In many regards, Blair represents continuity. As leaders before him, he strategically used selected aspects of his personal life (e.g. sports, music, parenthood) to 'humanise' his leader persona, present himself as an 'outsider' to the world of professional politics and appear more in touch with the lives and interests of 'ordinary' citizens. Unlike others such as Heath and Thatcher, however, his 'human' side was constitutive to his political identity from the very start, rather than being emphasised in times of wavering popularity in an attempt to improve his image. As others before him, he aligned himself with the symbols and figures of popular culture, as well as often using their expertise. Moreover, even more than Wilson and Thatcher, Blair put great effort into developing relationships with journalists (especially in the tabloids) and keenly embraced the opportunities offered by the use of a wide range of non-traditionally political media outlets such as women's weeklies, chat shows and breakfast TV. These kinds of genres enabled him not only to show his 'human' side but also to avoid tougher questioning, reach a different public and promote coverage focused on his chosen issues and themes. Moreover, New Labour made strategic use of the bargaining power of these attractive 'exclusives' to reward and punish journalists and outlets.

However, there are also some very distinctive dimensions to Blair's use of the personal. Firstly, atypically, especially for a Labour leader, his strategies for developing identification with 'ordinary' citizens were not based on associations with the working class but of 'post-ideological' (read middle-class) aspiration and appeals to 'one nation'. Secondly, his family, only in part because of what were then unusual circumstances (four children living at home including one born while in office), were more central to his public persona, and more present in the public domain, than for any previous leader. Thirdly, Blair was uniquely comfortable at displaying emotional openness in public, which helped to build a sense of intimacy, authenticity and revelation; a feeling that we were getting 'behind the image'. Finally, as New Labour itself, Blair was exceptionally successful at navigating across dualisms. He moved smoothly between news and entertainment formats; between informal and formal discourse; between privateness and publicness; between the authority of leadership and the 'normality' of the human being (Fairclough, 2000). This fluidity not only helped him to align the personal and the political but also conferred naturalness to this connection. This meant that he could not only bring platform and person into line with each other (Finlayson, 2003: 55) and 'anchor the public politician in the "normal" person' (Fairclough, 2000: 7) but also that he was able, with the aid of outstanding media management, to systematically incorporate details of the personal into routine coverage.

This chapter will first analyse Blair's use of the personal, exploring these distinctive dimensions. The following sections will focus on press coverage and aim to uncover to what extent and in which ways this distinctiveness of Blair's communication strategies were reflected in the media's portrayal of the leader. To do so, we will present quantitative content analyses as well as a qualitative exploration of the press coverage of the personal during Blair's premiership.

A very New Labour leader: post-ideological, aspirational and middle class

As we have seen, a leader's personal journey from 'modest' roots to the top job in the country has been a much-exploited dimension of the personal lives of politicians. However, for Tony Blair, unlike for Major and even Thatcher, it was difficult to present himself as an individual with humble origins. He came from a fairly privileged background and was the first prime minister since Douglas-Home to have gone to private school. To leave it at that, however, would be factually accurate but overlook two crucial issues. Firstly, the public 'private' persona of a leader is not simply a marketing invention but nor is it a mirror reflection of their 'real' life: it is a constructed narrative based on selected aspects of their personal life and, crucially, on how it is performed in, and re-interpreted by, the media. Thus, as epitomised by George W. Bush, a personal journey of conquering adversity does not require a poor background (see Busby, 2009; Scammell, 2007). Nor does one have to be a 'regular' guy with an 'ordinary' upbringing to appear in touch with the average citizen. For instance, Blair's personal narrative had elements of the hardship story, as he used his parents' health, and especially his father's stroke (e.g. the 'kitchen' PEB in 1997), to show how he had to overcome personal adversity, and appeared to have much in common, in tastes, habits and aspirations, with 'ordinary' people.

Secondly, to overemphasise the communication limitations resulting from Blair's comfortable background, or even to focus only on how these were cunningly overcome, would be to miss crucial dimensions of what Blair and New Labour represented. New Labour was indeed a sleek communication operation and Blair was a remarkable media performer. Moreover, the information environment had become increasingly chaotic and journalistic culture more adversarial, enhancing the need for management and control. But the distinctiveness of the post-Thatcherite era was not confined to communication. The characteristics and roles of parties, leaders and governments have changed in tune with decreasing partisan affiliation, low turn-outs and declining levels of trusts in political actors and institutions. Moreover, the Left had to re-position itself in relation to the New Right, and in particular in response to the new neo-liberal consensus and the consolidation of an individualistic culture of materialistic aspiration. In this context, New Labour and Blair succeeded because it represented a political, and not just a communicational, shift; a shift that claimed to transcend old dualisms and oppositions: pragmatic, post-ideological, beyond Left and Right, emphasising rights and responsibilities, the role of the state and the individual situated within the community, and with focus on the middle class and 'Middle England' (Finlayson, 2003; Foley, 2000; Leggett, 2005). Moreover, correspondingly, aspiration was essential to New Labour, concentrating on where people wanted to be rather than where they were. In this sense, like Clinton, New Labour and Blair 'sought to distance themselves from their party's core constituencies of the poor and marginalised and to appeal to voters with social and economic aspirations' (Needham, 2005: 352). In Blair's own and much personalised words in a PEB for the 1997 General Election:

> I've always understood, because of dad, why some people who've done very well, come up in life, made it on their own, felt the Tory party was the party that was for them, because it was the party of ambition and aspiration, and that the Labour party somehow wasn't, and I think to an extent, I mean, that's what the Labour party became. It became too stuck in the past, too rooted in the [inaudible] that's where you are, that's where you stay, whereas today I think the position has changed round. What I've always wanted for today's Labour party is to be the party of aspiration [inaudible] say you know you can have a society where there's ambition without a lack of compassion. (From Kimber, 2010)

But although a remarkable political and ideological shift, it was not just a question of policy or 'substance', but also of style. Or rather, of aligning the two, of tallying presentation with New Labour's ideological and policy commitments and of enhancing its 'newness': 'Its form, therefore, is also the content; and it is part of its "pitch" to the electorate' (Finlayson, 2003: 41). And Blair, pivotal in the ideological and political re-invention of Labour, was also central to the re-branding of its stylistic identity, and his persona was crucial to changing 'what it means to be Labour' (Philip Gould).[1] In short, the medium was also the message. However, unlike in Major's case, the aim was not to differentiate Blair from the party, setting him above or apart from it, but to create reciprocal positive associations between the 'new' party, its brand and the leader who personified it. Moreover, Blair's embodiment of the New Labour brand was crucial not only in terms of policies and values, but also through aesthetics and affective elements, which are crucial for the development of boundary differentiators in party and leader branding (Scammell, 2007).

In his early years as leader, Blair was perceived as fresh, different and youthful, the embodiment of both New Labour and a 'new style of politics'. According to polls, a remarkably low 6 per cent (1994) and 8 per cent (1997) of respondents considered Blair out of touch with ordinary people (Ipsos-Mori, 2006b). He was indeed from a new generation of politicians, and hence in some relevant ways different (more informal and emotionally open), but it was also a perception he worked hard at developing. 'This might sound like an odd thing to say, but I don't actually *feel* much like a politician … I feel like *a perfectly normal person*' (quoted in Rentoul, 2001: 284, italics added). Furthermore, Blair appeared to be the personal embodiment of the overcoming of the old dualisms that New Labour claimed to represent. He appealed to 'one nation', which is not only an inclusive appeal but also one associated with the Conservatives (Foley, 2002). In fact, Blair was often regarded as 'half-Tory', a perception he hardly tried to rectify. Moreover, his persona appeared to combine the 'best' features of the Conservative and Labour traditions together with something new: the attributes of a successful businessman (vigorous, active, driven) and those of a social democratic leader (compassionate and caring) (Pearce, 2001: 223), with some 'new man' (in touch with his emotions and a doting, nurturing and more egalitarian family man).

Blair was also – and more importantly was unashamed to appear to be – successful, aspirational and thoroughly middle class, albeit a 1990s metropolitan version of it. And thus, his persona, and his open pride in his middle-class roots and values, personally demonstrated that the party had made 'the mental leap that says that aspiring to middle class is positive' (Mo Mowlam, quoted in Finlayson, 2003: 41). This persona was partly based on Blair's background, professional choices, marriage and so on, and how these were built into his personal narrative and political identity. But it was also a question of communicative style, which reinforced his 'normality' and conveyed values and outlooks generally associated with the 'middle class' and 'middle-England' (Fairclough, 2000: 8).

Blair's accent was clearly middle class but was also adapted to fit the context. He most often used a near-RP (received pronunciation) accent, although less contrived than those of the Queen or Thatcher, and with some personal Northerner touches (Fairclough, 2000: 100). But, when in more off-role modes, his speech had also clearly recognisable elements of Estuary English and on some occasions, arguably, even beyond, in the direction of Cockney (Rosewarne, 1998: 53). Moreover, his overall communication style was adaptable. Blair shifted comfortably back and forth between the public language of politics, or official discourses, and the vernacular language of the 'normal person', most famously in the speech after Diana's death (Fairclough, 2000).[2] The formal and authoritative elements of political language were fused with evocations to common sense and solidarity with the audience, self-deprecating humour and frequent use of conversational elements, such as 'I mean' and 'you know', hesitations and repetitions, colloquialisms, elisions and the use of 'you' instead of 'one' (Fairclough, 2000; see also Finlayson, 2002; Pearce, 2001).

Blair was also unafraid of displaying a degree of emotion in public and to reflect upon his feelings, occasionally even accepting vulnerability and error. In this sense, Blair was quite uniquely suited to respond to the therapeutic culture of contemporary (affluent) societies, where emotional intelligence is increasingly valued (Richards, 2004). Moreover, by revealing (through words but crucially also body language) his inner world of thoughts and emotions and disclosing his subjectivity, he strengthened his claims to openness, sincerity and authenticity (Montgomery, 1999: 13). It is worth noting that this form of honesty is not about morality or one's convictions, but about comfortably expressing, and appearing true to, one's feelings and 'real' self. In other words, it is about managing to enact the conditions of intimate, personal conversations and relationships in the mediated public domain (Montgomery, 1999: 26–7).

This Blair mix, with different measures of public and personal language depending on the context, combined with the mutable accent, the emotional 'sincerity' and the relaxed performances, enabled him – at least in the early years – to appear both authoritative and normal, leader and human, and to integrate the person with the politician. But it was not just his communicative style. His 'normality' was given credibility and depth, as well as coverage, by the selected snippets he revealed about his personal life – sports, pop music, youth rebellion and so on. In this sense, he might not seem unlike other leaders; yet he was different because the main focus was not on his roots or the abstract values he inherited from his father (à la Thatcher or Brown), or on his meritocratic journey (à la Major); instead, he incorporated the personal into the discussion of a range of subjects, emphasising 'normal' talk about everyday life, the mundane and the experiential. Moreover, this portrayal was down to earth and even fallible, empathising with the daily juggling and struggling of 'hard-working families': 'Being a prime minister can be a tough job but I think that being a parent is probably tougher. Sometimes you do not always succeed. But the family to me is more important than anything else.'[3] In fact, in this construction the use of his family, which was based on an archetypical marriage of middle-class professionals with two working parents and a modern hands-on father of four, was crucial. Blair mentioned, and in fact showed, his family more often than any previous prime minister, especially in the early years. There were family Christmas cards, parenting anecdotes of non-sleeping babies and homework tussles, and appealing photo-opportunities. Furthermore, and most distinctively, rather than confining his family to 'lighter' formats and themes, he mentioned them in a wide range of contexts and from different, and often combined, subject positions. As a result, the politician and the person never appeared too far apart. So, for instance, in line with the expectations of the genre, in interviews with David Frost or Des O'Connor the focus was on the person, and thus he made several references to his wife and children and even made jokey (clichéd) comments about his mother-in-law, asserting family closeness (Street, 2000: 85). At the same time, the politician (although not necessarily the *party* leader) also surfaced, as Blair managed to mention the Northern Ireland peace process, his relationship with other heads of government and the seriousness and responsibility of his job, which he compared to the position of the England football manager (see Street, 2000).

In combination, the strategic publicity given to Blair's personal life, and how he combined the subject positions, themes and discourses of the public and the private, enabled him fruitfully to pursue the crucial objectives of the politicisation of private persona. It 'humanised' him, feeding into his image as a family man and 'normal' (middle-class) person and someone with emotional empathy with his audience. It enabled him to demonstrate personal qualities such as reliability, integrity and kindness as well as the virility and the authority of a father figure. It assisted him in embodying and giving coherence to the party message and in authenticating key political values of New Labour. It gave him a fitting platform to reveal his feelings and inner thoughts, hence strengthening his claims to sincerity and authenticity. Finally, but crucially, it also helped him to manage media coverage. As we shall discuss in the next section, the strategic publicity given to his personal life not only made him appealing to a range of 'soft' formats but also generated both event-driven and day-to-day personal coverage in mainstream political media, making exceptional events routine and routine life events exceptional.

Of course, it was not always unproblematic. Blair did not suffer major personal scandals, but nonetheless the high degree of exposure of his personal life encouraged and legitimised the media's exposure and scrutiny of his family, and especially his wife. On occasion he came out relatively unscratched. When his son was found drunk in Leicester Square in July of 2000, just days after Blair had suggested on-the-spot fines for drunken and disorderly behaviour, he responded to the massive media coverage with a mix of personal humility and supportive parenting, combined with a classic touch of self-deprecating humour. In fact, according to his biographer, the episode brought him 'closer to people, making him seem human and fallible again' (Rentoul, 2001: 576). But it became increasingly difficult over time. In addition to political-financial scandals (Ecclestone, Mittal, Geoffrey Robinson) and dubious 'free' holidays, there were recurrent Cherie 'gaffes' and even a 'Cherigate'. Moreover, as epitomised by the relentless press demands to 'come clean' about whether his son had had the MMR vaccine, Blair found it increasingly difficult to uphold the privacy of his family, which he had been determined to protect from 'unwarranted press intrusion'.

More generally, as even the most 'human' of leaders experience after a few years in power, Blair's perception as 'normal' started to decline. Whereas in 1997, only 8 per cent of respondents considered him 'out of touch' with ordinary people, this increased to 32 per cent in 2001 and to 36 per cent in 2005 (Ipsos-Mori, 2006b). Similarly, whereas he was considered 'down to earth' by 30 per cent of the respondents in 1997, this was down to 22 per cent in 2001 and to 15 per cent in 2005 (Ipsos-Mori, 2006b). More broadly, his net 'like' figures went from +48 per cent in 1997 to +32 per cent in 2001 and to only +5 per cent in 2005 (Ipsos-Mori, 2007). Of course, this change did not prevent Labour from winning the 2001 and 2005 elections. Moreover, Thatcher was the longest ever serving prime minister despite her net 'like' figures always being negative (Ipsos-Mori, 2006a). However, the difference is in the trajectory and in the role that their 'likeness' played in their leader personae: 'being seen as in touch was the essence of the New Labour brand and, until the Iraq war, had been personified by Blair' (Scammell, 2007: 187). People idealised Blair in 1997 and hence later felt not only disappointed but hostile towards him; it was as if a relationship had broken up, 'like a damaged love affair' (Langmaid et al., 2006: 6). In other words, unlike Thatcher, who was never really liked, Blair seemed to have radically, and negatively, changed.

This hostility was of course very much influenced by his policies, and especially Iraq and the perceptions that he had lied about the existence of weapons of mass destruction. But it was not just policy; the disappointment was grounded on the mismatch between early (the listening, caring, in-touch Blair) and later perceptions of the leader-person, with the strength of the hostility 'proportionally related to the warmth of their welcome to the younger Blair' (Scammell, 2007: 184). What was perceived by many as a personal and emotional relationship with Blair had been broken. Moreover because, as we have seen, Blair embodied the New Labour brand, when people stopped trusting him and liking him, the brand did not merely lose an important asset but its most defining dimension: 'New Labour had a problem with their leader, but so influential was he as an icon of the brand, the party also had a problem that reached the very core of the brand' (Langmaid et al., 2006: 17). Whether or not the re-connection strategy devised by Langmaid et al. (referred to in the media as the 'masochist strategy') worked is hard to say; but Labour went on to win a third consecutive election, albeit with a campaign more focused on the 'team' and, according to some studies, with Blair losing rather than winning them votes (Evans and Andersen, 2005). But beyond that, and even though it got tainted over the years, there is no doubt that Blair's persona – and how the politician was anchored in the human being – was an important element in New Labour's success. Moreover, as we shall see in the next section, Blair's era changed the role of the personal in public discourse and heavily conditioned the construction of the personae of the leaders that followed.

The role of press coverage

The transformative effects of Blair's era were not only a result of Blair's personality and media skills. Nor, even if it might appear plausible, were they a result of the 'inherent' appeal of his personal, and especially family, life. There is necessarily a transformative mediation between a leader's 'real' personal life and how this is constructed and depicted in the public realm. In other words, a private persona does not simply mirror a leader's personal life, nor does it just reflect how it is constructed and performed by leaders themselves. Media coverage, and how this interrelates with a leader's communication strategy, is crucial and ultimately determines which role the personal plays in public discourse. Moreover, what the media choose to publicise, and how they frame it and interpret it, heavily shapes the perception of a leader's public persona in the public mind (Cornog, 2004: 64). In other words, and as stated earlier, the 'public' private personae of politicians are the result of a battle between who they are, the version(s) of their 'true selves' put forward for public consumption, and the mediated version constructed by, and presented in, the media.

In the case of Blair, it was the combination of the three that made his personal, and especially family, life such a distinctive element of his public persona. Blair's family might have been central to his public persona because it was central to his life. Moreover, with four young children living in Downing Street, including one born while in office, and a high-profile professional wife, his family might have had some 'inherent' newsworthy value. He also clearly emphasised it more and with greater skill than any previous leader, especially because it was not an add-on but a constitutive dimension of his public persona. The leader and the human being were rarely too far apart. For their part, the media took the ball and ran with it, amplifying the publicity given to selected themes of his personal life and routinising its use.

In this sense, the details of Blair's personal life worked as a particular form of 'infotainment' package, offering a steady flow of entertainment-worthy material and appealing touches of 'colour' to the media. Moreover, this particular form of information subsidy not only had the legitimacy normally invested in the figure of prime minister and in this case strengthened by Blair's media skills; it tapped into the media's increasing needs to broaden the content and appeal of political stories, to fill a wider range of sections, and to keep up with the competition. Furthermore, by revealing the 'behind the scenes', it fitted with the media's strategic frames in political coverage and with the increasingly prevailing conventions of revelation, intimacy and authenticity associated with celebrity culture. This is neither to say that the media always reproduced what Blair offered nor that they consistently did so in his preferred terms. As with other PR subsidies, the source is not in total control and it often provoked an adversarial reaction in journalists. But regardless of how this information was re-framed and interpreted, it is clear that the combination of Blair's strategic publicity of the personal and how it tapped into the changing media's values, needs and conventions led to a more prominent and, crucially, routine role of the personal in the coverage of the prime minister and, more broadly, in public discourse.

This stronger role was clearly apparent in the longitudinal trends presented in Chapter 3. The analysis, based on the *Guardian* and *The Times*, showed that there were more references by far to Blair's personal life and qualities than for any previous prime minister. The analysis that follows will expand on these findings, now focusing on the context and content of these references. This investigation is based on three new sets of data, each exploring a different dimension of the phenomenon. The first is a detailed content analysis of an expanded sample of articles of routine coverage of the prime minister, which also includes tabloids. This will enable us to explore further the role of the personal, and especially Blair's family, in everyday coverage. The second is a detailed analysis of all references to Leo, Blair's youngest son, between the announcement of Cherie's Blair pregnancy (19 November 1999) and 30 June 2002 (N=2,356). Because the birth of his son while in office was an out-of-the-ordinary event, it can be considered 'inherently' newsworthy. However, as we shall see, the references to Leo became routinised, continuing to appear in a wide range of contexts well after the birth. Finally, the third part of the analysis focuses on Blair's fiftieth birthday and compares it to that of Major. This event provoked great media interest, and, unlike Major's birthday, came to be constructed as a 'major milestone' in the coverage. The hype was a result of the combination of Downing Street's management of the event and how this tapped into the media's needs and conventions in an increasingly competitive market. As we shall see, however, as well as a remarkable amount of positive coverage, it generated a cynical reaction from journalists to what they perceived as No. 10's manipulation.

The Blairs: the parents of Britain

The first sample includes eight national newspaper titles (both broadsheets and tabloids) and covers the first five years of Blair's premiership (N=450).[4] In this more wide-ranging data set, which includes tabloids, the proportion of articles referring to his personal life and qualities was similar to that of *The Times* and the *Guardian* sample: out of the 450 articles that mentioned Tony Blair, 9 per cent refer to at least one aspect[5] of his personal life (i.e. family life, personal appearance, lifestyle (with holidays a separate category), upbringing and religion).[6] As was the case for the sample in the longitudinal analysis, this figure does not indicate that the phenomenon is present on a massive scale. Nonetheless, the fact that almost one in ten articles about the prime minister gives citizens some kind of information about his personal life confirms that Blair *qua human being* played an important role not only in how he presented himself but also in the media's portrayal.

In terms of content, the evidence indicates that the most common theme was, by far, his family life: 51 per cent of the articles with personal references fall into this category. This theme was followed by personal appearance (24 per cent), holidays (18 per cent) and lifestyle (15 per cent).[7] Often the references to his family life were rather brief. But the more in-depth reporting presented Blair as a perfect stereotype of the 'new man', which is generally characterised as an emotionally expressive, self-aware, and caring person, who is no longer the distant wage-earner but a highly involved father, in touch with, and expressive of, his feelings, and more egalitarian in his dealings with women (Hondagneu-Sotelo and Messner, 1994: 202; Westwood, 1996: 27; see also Smith, 2008). The details about the difficulties and pleasures of bringing up children and the delights of conjugal life were often backed by 'revelatory' quotes from the prime minister himself:

> 'I'm lucky, touch wood; I can't see that ever happening to us [Robin Cook had just divorced]. I'm in love with Cherie. I still feel like that about her' ... Last month, they celebrated their wedding anniversary with a romantic dinner at Chequers and played their song, My Cherie Amour. They reminisced and couldn't believe that 18 years had flown by. (Lee-Potter, *Daily Mail*, 17 April 1998)

> He [Blair] maintains he is always first to get up in the night when Leo cries, which I find hard to believe. 'Oh, I usually do. But he's been doing well

Figure 5.1 Percentage of articles mentioning Blair that refer to his relatives and senior political actors in the *Daily Mail*, the *Guardian*, the *Mirror* and *The Times* (and their Sunday editions), 1997–2002, by newspaper type

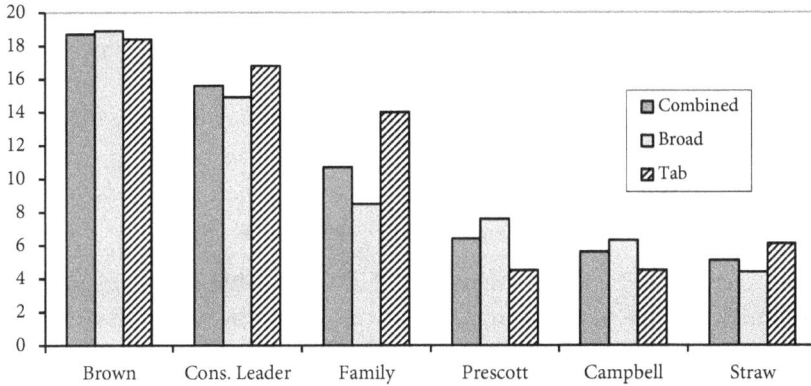

Legend:
- Combined
- Broad
- Tab

X-axis: Brown, Cons. Leader, Family, Prescott, Campbell, Straw

Source: Content analysis by the author

recently, sleeping most nights.' Well done. That must save you and Cherie. I'm sure you must be looking forward very much to having her on the campaign trail this week. 'She is absolutely vital to me. She's a rock of stability.' (Davies, *Mail on Sunday*, 27 May 2001)

The presence of his family in public discourse was also amplified by other references to his wife and children, such as those that mentioned their presence in protocol activities. Out of the total number of articles in the sample (N=450), 11 per cent mentioned one or more relatives. Although some of these articles did not provide details of Blair's personal life, and hence were not included in the index, these kinds of family appearances normalise the presence of the personal in public discourse. Moreover, they can play an important role in the construction of the public persona, particularly in terms of the leader as a 'family man'. In fact, almost half of them (46 per cent) referred to them explicitly as the 'Blair family', giving a distinctive sense of family unity. In contrast, in the case of previous leaders, there were rarely any references to their children, with generally only their spouses mentioned. Moreover, pre-Blair articles practically never refer to the prime ministers' families with equivalent terms to those that were most often used for him, i.e. 'the Blair family' or 'the Blairs'.

The remarkable presence of the Blair family in the coverage is further underlined by the comparison with the presence of senior contemporary political actors. As can be seen in Figure 5.1, although Gordon Brown and the leader of the opposition were mentioned in these articles more often than Blair's relatives, the difference is not as great as one would expect. Furthermore, key political figures such as John Prescott, Alastair Campbell and Jack Straw appeared in the articles mentioning the prime minister less frequently than Blair's family members.[8] This comparison underscores the importance that his family and his personal sphere more generally had in the construction of his public persona. This is not to say that it was pervasive or *the* key defining aspect of his leader persona, but that it was highly prominent.

The routinisation process

The evidence clearly demonstrates that Blair's personal life, and in particular his family, played a noteworthy role in the press coverage. Moreover, the longitudinal evidence established that although not entirely new, the role of the personal was much greater for Blair than for any previous prime minister. However, more detailed analysis reveals that the personal neither replaced everything else nor was present on such a great scale. Firstly, 46 per cent of the articles referring to Blair's personal life did not have domestic or international politics as their main topic (i.e. focus on sports, society, arts, fashion, etc.). This indicates that the personal expanded the mediated presence of the prime minister, stretching the coverage of the political rather than replacing it. Secondly, of the articles coded positively for the index, only 16 per cent had Blair's personal life as the main theme of the piece. Of the rest, 58 per cent were focused on other subjects and mentioned Blair's personal life as a secondary theme and 26 per cent mentioned it only tangentially (i.e. not more than two sentences).

In combination, the location and low salience of the personal references indicates that the personal is less prevalent in political coverage than implied by the overall figures. At the same time, it would be a mistake to ignore these tangential references because they suggest a crucial new dimension in the coverage of the personal, that of routinisation. Even if not so numerous or salient, references to Blair's personal life were ubiquitous and a 'normal' part and parcel of everyday routine media coverage. In other words, during Blair's era, the politicisation of private persona escalated, to a large extent, by the inconspicuous routine incorporation of the personal in public discourse. This suggests that the role of the personal in contemporary political discourse is both more nuanced and more complex than often assumed; most of the time, it is characterised by a drip-drip of constructed familiarity with the leader's personal life rather than a 'shock and awe' of major newsworthy stories or celebrity-like revelations.

The coverage of Leo, Blair's youngest son, perfectly illustrates this process. Because this was in some ways an exceptional event (no other

Figure 5.2 Number of articles per week in all main national daily and Sunday newspapers published in London that mentioned Leo Blair, 19 November 1999 to 30 June 2002

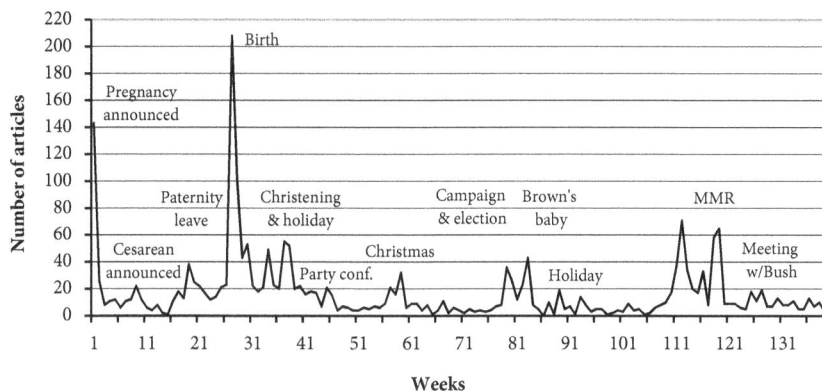

Source: Content analysis by the author

twentieth-century prime minister had a child while in office), it was to an extent expected that Leo would attract some attention from the press. Of course, to say that some press coverage was expected is not to say that it was 'normal'. To accept this interest as normal is to equate unusualness with newsworthiness and to presuppose that an 'interesting' event in a leader's personal life is an all-but inescapable news object, one with inherent appeal and significance. Instead, the fact that it was expected must be understood both as symptomatic of a broader interest in Blair's personal (and especially family) life and as a booster to this interest.

And indeed, as expected, Blair's youngest did attract press attention. Between the announcement of the pregnancy on 19 November 1999 and 30 June 2002 (141 weeks), there were 2,356 articles referring to Leo (55.3 per cent in tabloids and 44.7 per cent in broadsheets) at an average of 2.6 articles per day.[9] But as the analysis of the evolution of the interest shows (Figure 5.2), although the coverage concentrated more heavily on a few 'inherently' newsworthy events (announcement of the pregnancy, birth, christening, etc.), Leo continued to appear in the press long after the novelty period. In other words, he became a 'normal' presence in everyday news. Moreover, fewer than half of these articles (44 per cent) focused on Leo. In the other cases, his presence was not a result of an 'inherent' newsworthiness of events in his life. Instead, the analysis reveals that journalists got used to mentioning Leo in a myriad of contexts, both within and outside political stories, and in relation to the prime minister's multiple and intersecting roles: the person, the politician and the celebrity father.

This multi-purpose use of Leo routinised and normalised the presence of the personal in public discourse, and reinforced Blair's image as family man. In some cases these references were directly related to Blair's role as prime minister, with journalists conjecturing about the impact of his child on his popularity and performance (22 per cent), or using Leo as a 'touch of colour' in the narrative of political stories (25 per cent).[10] But 41 per cent of the references were uncalled for in relation to his prime ministerial role.[11] Leo and the Blairs were referred to as an example of societal trends (e.g. faster intellectual development of contemporary children) and as a proxy for 'ordinary' families (e.g. child-friendly holiday venues). They were also used as an example of celebrity children and parents, e.g. Blair joining David Beckham in the 'joy of fatherhood', and Cherie and Madonna as mature mothers. Moreover, Leo also sparked story ideas, prompting articles in which neither the Blairs nor politics were the focus.

These kinds of references to the Blair family are symptomatic of a routini-sation of the presence of the personal in public discourse. This is a process characterised by low-key recurrence rather than extensive focused attention on the prime minister's personal issues, where the personal 'pops-out' in a wide range of contexts and stories, fulfilling different narrative roles. This routinisation is new and distinctive to Blair's era, and in part explains the rise in the overall presence of the personal. In fact, this routinisation can only be understood as both cause and consequence of the Blair family's high public profile, in what constitutes a self-reinforcing process. Blair's family was 'interesting' both because of its characteristics (novelty but also 'normal') and because of how Blair used it (i.e. routinely and in a range of contexts). But also, the more the personal came to be casually mentioned in the press, the more likely were journalists to start incorporating these elements into the construction of news writing, enhancing its relevance and 'newsworthiness'. Because of this, both politicians and journalists found it more difficult to draw a clear line between private and public. Crucially, the importance of the routinisation process is that its impact goes beyond Blair. The more the personal is incorporated into public discourse, the more likely it is to become part of the common sense assumptions on what constitutes news and political information, or even what is to be considered as of public interest.

The coverage of Leo also underscores the changing definition of the political and the porous boundaries with the personal, which define the politicisation of private persona. Firstly, Leo was mentioned tangentially in stories focused within formal politics (59 per cent) but also in a range of other subjects, including society, fashion and celebrity. In contrast, previous prime ministers and their families were very rarely mentioned outside the politics sections, with the rare exception of sports. This novelty is symptomatic of Blair's celebrity status, his personal life becoming a subject of interest beyond the political sphere. However, this is not so much a result of his attractive and media-friendly 'private' persona as a reflection of a changed media environment, with much-expanded coverage of lifestyle and celebrity subjects and a marked blurring of the boundaries between information and entertainment.

Secondly, Leo's presence (see Figure 5.2) clustered around both personal (e.g. holidays) and political events (e.g. party conference) highlighting both the routine newsworthiness ascribed to Blair's personal life and the extent to which the personal became a 'normal', and hence largely unquestioned, element of the routine reporting of politics. Moreover, the two were at times combined (e.g. paternity leave and children's vaccinations) as Blair's fatherhood, although an obviously personal event, triggered discussion on political issues such as domestic division of labour and masculinity (see also Street, 2000). At the same time, the combination of Blair's use of his family, a high mediated visibility of his personal life, and how this information was played in association with political matters affected the definition of what is regarded as the public interest. One of the best examples of this process was the MMR vaccination crisis. The issue of whether or not the vaccine was safe and the repercussions of parents' refusal received lengthy and persistent coverage from the press. The Blairs refused to publicise any information on this matter on the grounds of Leo's right to privacy. But when the personal is politicised, and the distinction between role and person is blurred, the 'public interest' expands and the right to privacy necessarily becomes challenged. In this context, whether or not the prime minister's son had received the vaccine became such a prominent issue in the debate that almost one in three of all articles that referred to the MMR crisis mentioned Leo Blair (Hargreaves et al., 2003: 22).

In short, the analysis of Leo's presence in the coverage shows that the interest was not just a result of novelty. Once the exceptional had passed, Blair's son remained as a minor but routine element of the press coverage of the prime minister in his multiple and intersecting roles: the person, the politician and the celebrity father. Moreover, Leo was mentioned in the context of both political and personal events, as well as in the intersection of the two, with personal events triggering discussion of political issues, and pushing the boundaries of the public interest. This wide range of references both reinforced the 'naturalness' of the presence of the personal and Blair's image as family man. Moreover, it indicates routinisation; namely a low-key but omnipresent process through which the personal has become part of everyday media discourse.

The prime minister's fiftieth birthday

If the coverage of Leo is the perfect example of the routinisation of the personal, where what was then an atypical event (for a prime minister) muted into an enduring dimension of everyday coverage, Blair's birthday represents the other side of the coin. To contemporary eyes, a prime minister's fiftieth birthday might seem like the kind of event that is 'normal' for the media to cover. But, in fact, this is an occasion that can hardly be regarded as news. And indeed, that it was how it had been considered in the past. So, the contemporary perception of its 'inherent' newsworthiness must be understood as a consequence of the interest in the personal and hence of the phenomenon itself. Thus, the changes both in the coverage and in the perception of its newsworthiness make the birthday an illuminating case study to explore how and why a personal non-event can nowadays trigger remarkable media interest.

Like Blair, John Major also turned fifty while in office and was considered exceptionally young. Moreover, as has been discussed, both purposefully emphasised certain aspects of their personal lives in the construction of their leader personae. However, Blair's birthday drew much greater press coverage and triggered what became almost a media frenzy.

Table 5.1 Coverage of Major's and Blair's fiftieth birthdays in the *Daily Mail*, the *Guardian*, the *Mirror* and *The Times* (and their Sunday editions) over 20 days (birthday plus 17 prior and 2 after)

	N (all articles)	n (mention birthday)	% mention birthday	% birthday focus (n)	Average length*
Major	618	18	3	33 (6)	352
Blair	1149	86	8	66 (57)	861

* Only for articles with the birthday as focus.
Source: Content analysis by the author

As seen in Table 5.1, all quantitative variables show a remarkably stronger interest in Blair's birthday than Major's.[12] Moreover, the analysis of the placement of the stories also indicates the difference in the degree of attributed newsworthiness: five of Blair's articles were cover stories and twenty-one were in the editorial/comment section, as opposed to none and one respectively for Major's sample. Similarly, whereas Major's birthday was found in the headlines of six articles, this was true in sixty of the stories in Blair's sample. Finally, the time-span in which the articles were published (Figure 5.3) also indicates the different degrees of interest. In particular, the spread of Blair's articles is representative of the sense of anticipation

Figure 5.3 Chronological distribution of articles mentioning Major's and Blair's fiftieth birthdays in the *Daily Mail*, the *Guardian*, the *Mirror* and *The Times* (and their Sunday editions)

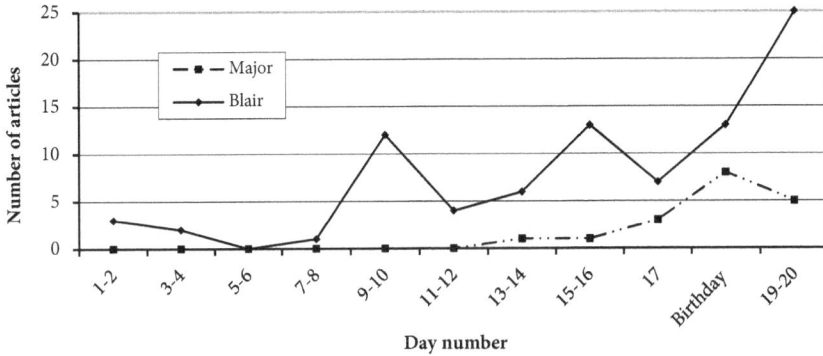

Source: Content analysis by the author

with which the press treated his, but not Major's, birthday. Moreover, this scattered distribution also helped to build and sustain the sense of 'self-evident' importance of the event.

There were also important differences in the content of the pieces. Whereas for Major most articles simply reported that he was turning fifty, nearly half of the articles for Blair included retrospective analyses of his political and especially personal life. Moreover, in Blair's case the predominant narrative was of the *inescapable* importance of turning fifty, which was completely absent on Major's birthday. Expressions such as 'major milestone', 'dreaded landmark', and 'prime of life' were found in a large number of stories relating to Blair. The 'indisputable' importance of the event was also reflected in, and reinforced by, the large number of feature articles commissioned for the occasion by newspapers as well as a range of magazines. Looking at some of the titles, it is plain that Blair's birthday was considered a major event.

Interview. Confident Blair on the world, the nation and his birthday. (Stephens and Newman, *Financial Times*, 28 April 2003)

Loneliness of the long-distance PM. Leadership is a sad affair and Tony Blair, 50 next week, has been changed by the isolation of the office. (Kettle, the *Guardian*, 3 May 2003)

Facing up to the future. Tony Blair is hitting his half-century. (Kay, *Independent*, 3 May 2003)

The Prime Minister at 50; family man on the loneliest road. (Shipman, *Sunday Express*, 4 May 2003)

50 facts about the premier (some of which he'd rather we didn't tell you). (Mulkerrins, *Daily Mail*, 5 May 2003)

Tony Blair at 50: from the novice of '97 to the harder figure of today. Six years in No 10: how the power has changed the man. (White, the *Guardian*, 6 May 2003)

50: A PM in the prime of life: How Anthony Charles Lynton Blair, born in Edinburgh in 1953, grew up to be Prime Minister. (Foster, *Mirror*, 6 May 2003)

Tony Blair: Prime of life. (*The Times*, 6 May 2003)

Most of these pieces followed the style of celebrity profiles, where the private sphere (a star's background, their path to stardom, and their off-screen life) is constructed as the ultimate site of truth for understanding their conduct in the public sphere (Marshall, 1997: 247; Ponce de Leon, 2002: 60). In fact, by scrutinising the past and the present of his personal life, as well as psychological aspects of his character, these birthday special features seem to have attempted to explain Blair's leadership, especially as it coincided with the Iraq war. In other words, it seems that Blair and his politics presented a puzzle that could only be 'solved' by also looking at his personal sphere, that it was only by understanding the man that one could truly decipher the actions of the prime minister. The content of these pieces was not, however, uni-dimensional; it was not the 'triumph' of the father over the prime minister, as the critics of personalisation fear, or vice versa, as some normative theory would hope for. It was a combination of the two in which the person fused with the politician.

In addition to the content, the revelatory tone of these pieces was reinforced by a number of more subtle 'intimacy cues' that enhanced this feeling of mediated intimacy and unparalleled exposure of Blair's 'real self'. Firstly, the pictures included images of Blair as leader alongside others of him with open neck shirt in the garden, playing the guitar, with the family, and showing the domestic environment, with Leo's toys spread across the place. Typically of celebrity profiles, these homely and informal pictures encourage us to believe that 'we are seeing them as they "really" are and that we are getting a privileged look behind the façade of public life' (Becker, 1992: 141). At the same time, the presence of more formal pictures that epitomise the prime ministerial role remind us of how far he was from being just 'one of us'. Secondly, the articles relied heavily on material and information provided by close friends and aides of the prime minister, making it much more 'revealing'. Finally, Blair's rhetorical style, by drawing on the world of ordinary life, emotions, humour and colloqui-alisms, intensified the feeling of rapport with the readers, although without completely excluding the more assertive style conventionally associated with politics.

Moreover, as is common in the treatment of media stars (and especially women), there were plenty of references to how Blair looked and how he had aged, backed by exclusive childhood pictures, before-and-after photo-montages, and even a portrait commissioned from celebrity photographer Ian Rankin (characterised by the press as 'heroin chic') for the *Financial Times*. There were even more obvious links to popular culture with a BBC one-hour tribute programme, called 'Happy Birthday Mr Prime Minister', where Cilla Black followed in the footsteps of Marilyn Monroe, singing Happy Birthday to Blair. The programme was described as 'light-hearted' by the BBC which said it was 'aimed at easing Mr Blair's worries about turning 50'. There was also a full-page ad, published in most national newspapers, by the vitamin supplement brand Sanatogen, where they wished a happy fiftieth birthday to the prime minister. Asked about it, Blair said, 'I wasn't looking forward to reaching 50 and this gloom was before I opened today's newspapers and found I was used – without my permission – to advertise Sanatogen. However, as somebody pointed out this morning, it's better than the impotence advertisements Pele is fronting.' This quote was reproduced by almost every newspaper.

Of course, one could be tempted to think that the remarkable characteristics of the coverage were only a consequence of the special circumstances, i.e. the prime minister's fiftieth birthday. In such an event, it might seem logical and natural to many that the media recapitulated the different aspects of Blair's life and gave him 'star treatment'. In fact, according to the press representation of Blair's birthday, there was a strong sense that '50 is obviously a milestone' (*Sunday Times*, 4 May 2003) and therefore one that journalists had to report. Yet it is worth repeating again: there was nothing remotely comparable – quantitatively or qualitatively – in the coverage of Major's fiftieth birthday just a few years previously. If Blair's fiftieth birthday seemed of self-evident importance and the coverage 'natural', albeit as we shall see simultaneously heavily criticised, it must have been a result of the depth of the changes and how normalised these had become.

The role of No. 10 and the political-media complex

The coverage of Blair's fiftieth birthday compared to Major's cannot be explained by a distinctive appeal of Blair's 'real' personal life, as in the unmediated realm the event is exactly the same. Instead, the interest in Blair's birthday, and more generally in his personal life, must be understood as a result of recent interlinked changes. Changes in the media environment, with an unprecedented degree of competition, including a marked decline in newspaper readership, the steepest ever increase in the number of general interest magazines (PPA Marketing & Research, 2010),[13] and the rising impact of the internet on the nature of coverage in other media; associated changes in journalism, with the broadening of content into soft subjects, the need to make political coverage more appealing, and a greater number of pages to fill with less resources (Davis, 2002; Lewis et al., 2008); the ever-strong links between politics and popular culture and the impact of celebrity culture; and subtle changes in the role of the personal in journalistic conventions, especially through routinisation, by which Blair's personal life came to be regarded as a 'natural' and almost inescapable object of media coverage. Moreover, the remarkable coverage was also idiosyncratic; namely, a result of Blair's distinctive communication strategies and style.

With regard to the latter, it is clear that Downing Street made a concerted effort to transform Blair's birthday into an appealing object of media coverage, feeding into journalists' need for appealing stories and exclusive 'revelations'. The aim was twofold: to encourage coverage of the personal, and hence to emphasise both Blair's 'normality' and his remarkable achievements, and to 'humanise' his leader persona in the midst of heavy personal criticism because of the decision to invade Iraq. To achieve these aims Downing Street agreed 'intimate' interviews with the prime minister with a few selected media, some focused on the birthday (e.g. *Saga* magazine and the *Observer*) and some on the war (e.g. *Vanity Fair* and *The Times*). It also facilitated exclusive access 'behind the scenes' in No. 10, provided family photo albums and authorised contact with those who know the 'real' Blair. The pieces, not by chance, were trailed in advance and published with about a week between each, which built anticipation and ensured sustained personal coverage over a longer period (see Figure 5.3).

The result of No. 10's strategy was not just a few interviews but a remarkable media hype that, as we have seen, greatly amplified the coverage of the birthday and magnified its 'self-evident' importance. It also gave a personal and 'intimate' angle to the coverage of Blair's role in Iraq, with the prime minister 'pouring his heart out' (e.g. the *Sun*) and being pictured making life and death decisions surrounded by his guitar and his children's toys (*The Times*). This hype was encouraged by No. 10, which offered the media 'unmissable' infotainment packages, granted privileged access to key sources, and strategically chose the outlets and timing of publication of exclusive interviews. Moreover, it is apparent that they played on the recycling potential of these pieces, knowing that, in the context of intense competition, quotes and pictures from these articles were likely to be reproduced by a significant number of outlets who could not afford to miss out on a 'good story'. The hype was strengthened by Blair's communicative style, with his remarkable capacity to fluidly combine private and public discourses, to anchor the political in the personal, and to reveal his emotions and 'authentic self' across both mainstream political coverage and softer formats.

But, crucially, we must not overlook the fact that the hype was enacted by the media. No. 10 can do its best to influence but cannot force the coverage. The news management of the birthday only succeeded because it played on what had become journalists' 'natural' impulses in regard to the attributed newsworthiness of the personal. After having routinely incorporated elements from Blair's personal life into reporting about the prime minister during the first six years of his premiership, it was only 'normal' for the birthday to mutate into a major public event. Moreover, the event provoked a news wave because in the context of intense competition different outlets emulated each other's coverage, creating what van Noije defines as a 'self-referential media momentum' (2007: 42). Most newspapers published articles just to report on these interviews and reproduced substantial parts of their content. They also created 'new' stories from a slightly different angle, with fresh quotes and pictures that other outlets felt compelled to reproduce. The interest also triggered other articles about No. 10's strategy and about the coverage itself. The result, characteristic of media hypes about crime, scandal or medical discoveries, was amplification and magnification of the coverage and the event, as hardly any news editor seemed able 'to resist the temptation of such an attractive story; it must be reported, because the competition is doing so' (Vasterman, 2005: 509). This hype resulted in a more pervasive presence of 'birthday talk', which facilitated the transformation of Blair's fiftieth into an 'obviously' important event. It also funnelled the content of the articles that referred to the event, repeating the same appealing personal quotes. Although the original pieces also included plenty of content of a 'straight' political nature, most of the recycling helped, by repeating the same quotes, to underscore the personal material not only in relation to the birthday but also the war in Iraq.

As with other media hypes, the interest in Blair's fiftieth birthday quickly vanished. So in itself, it was a major news event only for a limited period of time. It is in the bigger picture, however, that the birthday coverage is significant. It was symptomatic of the distinctiveness of Blair's era, where the personal became both a routine – which is not to say dominant – dimension of news coverage, and capable of triggering a news wave around an irrelevant personal event. Moreover, the birthday coverage reinforced the belief that personal events can – and probably need to – be managed for political advantage, trailing intimate interviews to generate anticipation and encourage the desired coverage. It also strengthened the perception that they are 'inherently' newsworthy. Furthermore, it continued to normalise the presence of the personal life of leaders in public discourse.

At the same time, in the typical fashion of what has been called an 'incestuous affair' (Swanson, 1997: 1274), journalists, while nurturing this process, simultaneously expressed their resentment at what they perceived as a clear attempt at manipulation. This is typical of contemporary political journalism, especially in the US but also elsewhere, which is characterised by an unending spiral of manipulation and resistance between politicians and journalists that has led to the pervasive presence of the well-documented adversarial culture (Barnett and Gaber, 2001; Blumler, 1997; Cappella and Hall Jamieson, 1997; Hall Jamieson, 1992; Patterson, 1993). On the one hand, journalists seek and need access to and cooperation from politicians. On the other hand, feeling used and in danger of losing their autonomy, they attempt to assert their independence ever more aggressively. However, other elements of journalistic culture prevent them from neglecting what politicians and their spin-doctors have to offer in this relationship of mutual dependence. Politicians are not only a privileged source of exclusive and ready-to-use information, but they have also become savvy about how to offer material that will satisfy journalists' news values and needs in an increasingly competitive market.

In the case of the birthday coverage, it is clear that journalists felt that they could not disregard the opportunity of an exclusive, or even just the chance of reproducing the material offered by Blair in these interviews. However, feeling uncomfortable about the manipulation, and trying to bolster their sense of independence, they took advantage of the occasion to emphasise what they saw as the disgraceful motives of the prime minister. As a result, in addition to the uncritical recycling, they condemned the attention paid by the media to this event and called attention to the prime minister's dubious motives for bolstering the coverage. Although, of course, by so doing they were not only discrediting but also spreading the coverage and potentially the significance attached to the event. This ambivalence resulted in a coverage that evidenced what Kurtz has called journalists' 'split personality' (Kurtz, 1992 in Winch, 1997: 122), which leads them to do what they can to discredit stories they dislike while also responding to some kind of 'uncontrollable force' – represented by the editors, the market or audiences' appetite – that makes them feel compelled to reproduce it (Winch, 1997: 143). This kind of coverage fuelled the presence of two of the most common features of political reporting: adversarialism and cynicism.

Although to an extent we have grown accustomed to the presence of cynicism in political reporting, its presence in the coverage of a personal event such as the prime minister's birthday is not only paradoxical, because there was no need to cover it in the first place, but also, in a sense, particularly unfortunate. On the one hand, it is true that the subject is less important than, for instance, the party's manifesto or education reform.

Thus, being cynical about Blair's intentions in regard to his birthday can be considered less problematic than being so about issues for which the informed engagement of citizens is considered crucial. On the other hand, this cynical reaction to the importance assigned to Blair's birthday – or any other aspect of his personal life – is doubly counterproductive. Firstly, by boosting the coverage devoted to the birthday, journalists are not only failing to defeat, but are actually encouraging, Blair's 'publicity game'. Secondly, by raising the cynical tone and focusing on uncovering the hidden reasons for the birthday 'fuss', they are endangering what is potentially a positive dimension of the politicisation of private persona: to provide a platform for engagement between leaders and citizens, grounded in leaders' openness and authenticity. If the search for uncovering leaders' 'true selves' grows to be fundamentally grounded in the assumption that they are anything but true, this is certainly unlikely to happen, and the responsibility will fall on both journalists and the increasingly 'human' politicians.

Conclusion

Blair's era intensified previous trends but also introduced new transformative features and dynamics to the role of the personal in public discourse. It routinised its use, changed expectations about what a leader 'ought' to reveal about his or her personal life and helped to re-define the boundaries, in journalistic norms, of what is considered of public interest (and not just of interest to the public). This was not just a result of Blair's performative skills, important as they were. In addition to Blair's personal style, the degree and characteristics of the publicity given to Blair's personal life must be understood as the outcome of a complex set of dynamics: transformations in the media environment and associated changes in journalism; the ever-strong links between politics and popular culture and the impact of celebrity culture; and subtle changes in the role of the personal in journalistic conventions. Moreover, and crucially, the remarkable coverage was also idiosyncratic; namely, a result of Blair's distinctive communication strategies and style.

Like other prime ministers before him, Blair used details of his personal life to humanise his leader persona, portray himself as 'normal', and show affinity with the lives of 'ordinary' people, and especially – atypically for a Labour leader – the aspirational middle class. He also, like Wilson and Thatcher, realised the potential of popular culture for generating positive associations and of softer media genres for reaching wider audiences and avoiding aggressive interviewing. But for Blair it was a matter of overall branding rather than just a strategy of 'image making' or media management. Blair selectively exposed details of his personal life from the beginning of his leadership, and did so more systematically and profes-sionally than previous leaders, and as an integral dimension of his, and the 'new' party's, identity. Moreover, he linked it more closely to the political. That is, rather than using it to show 'another side' of the leader, he anchored the political in the personal and the leader in the human being, both person-alising the political and politicising the personal.

Blair was also more willing than most leaders to selectively reveal (innocuous) details of his personal life. In part, these strategically delivered touches of personal 'colour' were attractive to journalists because of the characteristics of Blair's personal life and how he used it. But also, crucially, this stronger interest was a result of the changing conditions of media reporting: the need to broaden the content and appeal of political reporting; the greater interest in strategy and the 'behind the scenes'; the blurring of the boundaries between 'serious' and 'soft' news associated with techno-logical developments, stronger competition and changes in the definitions of the political; and the impact of celebrity culture and its emphasis on the private and the confessional in the quest to reveal the 'real selves' of the famous. Moreover, in the context of unprecedented competition and an expanded media market, there was not only intensified eagerness to secure exclusives but also a great deal of recycling and self-referentiality across media, which amplified the coverage of the personal and augmented its apparent importance.

In fact, during Blair's era there were more references to the personal than for any other previous prime minister: his family was more visible than several senior political figures in his government, and his personal life routinely present in both political and non-political coverage. Moreover, the most ordinary of personal events became exceptional (i.e. fiftieth birthday) and the exceptional became routine (i.e. Leo's birth). However, although greater than in the past, it is crucial to emphasise that the personal was not present on a huge scale, nor did it displace 'serious' reporting in a zero-sum game. Snippets about Blair's personal life were incorporated into political coverage, but they also appeared in a range of previously atypical sections for a prime minister to be mentioned, such as travel and lifestyle, hence expanding his mediated presence beyond the sphere of traditional politics. Moreover, and crucially, most of the articles that referred to Blair's personal life did so only in passing; thus, although frequent, the references to the personal clearly did *not* dominate the coverage. In other words, the role of the personal is significant but is also more nuanced than often assumed: it is not as a result of frequent outbursts of major personal stories and grand revelations, but of generally minor but regular references to the personal; more like a steady drizzle than a tropical storm.

These minor references were, however, important because they helped to create a *sense* of pervasiveness. Moreover, as seen most clearly in the coverage of Blair's youngest son, Leo, they indicate a process of routini-sation. This process was manifested in the unproblematic and unreflexive way in which the media used Blair's personal life as a low-key versatile narrative resource, spread across a variety of sections and topics, both within and outside the sphere of politics and linked to his three overlapping roles: politician, person and celebrity father. This routinisation naturalises the role of personal life in the construction of leader personae. Moreover, it also helps to build up a significant degree of familiarity of citizens with a leader's personal life.

In fact, Blair's personal life came to be regarded as such a 'natural' and almost inescapable object of media interest that such an ordinary event as the prime minister's fiftieth birthday came to be regarded as extraordinary and triggered great media hype. This press interest could seem normal and almost inevitable if it were not for the fact that, as shown by Major's coverage, there is little that is remarkable about turning fifty while in office. In part, the hype was a result of the clever manipulation of the event by No. 10, which generated exclusives greatly reproduced across media. But this strategy only succeeded because it built on journalistic values and commercial needs, and especially because it resonated with the media's conceptions of the newsworthiness of the prime minister's personal life. It was thus neither Blair's spin doctors nor journalists alone, but their interactions, that made it 'normal' for the birthday to become a major story.

This self-reinforcing process makes the politicisation of private persona more likely to endure, taking on a momentum of its own. The more the personal is present in public discourse, the more likely journalists are to regard it as an attractive and uncontroversial resource for news writing. Furthermore, the personal lives of leaders are also more likely to come to be seen as not only of interest to the public but as belonging to the public interest. In other words, the personal grows to be considered to warrant not only publicity but public accountability, and becomes not only part of the conventions of newsworthiness but also of the understanding of journalists' democratic duties. Furthermore, the capacity to reveal and appear 'human' becomes a more important criterion in the media's assessment of leadership. In turn, politicians are also more likely to rely on the personal for the construction of public personae, because of their enhanced belief that it is the road to political success. Citizens, for their part, regardless of how they might decode the information provided and how it might influence their assessment of leaders, are certainly growing used to reading about politicians' personal lives as part of their regular menu of news and entertainment.

Notes

1 From a memorandum Gould wrote in 1994 called 'Consolidating the Blair Identity' reproduced in Fairclough (2000: 96).
2 For in-depth analysis of this speech, and how it exemplifies Blair's communicative style, see Fairclough (2000), Finlayson (2003) and Montgomery (1999).
3 This is a fragment from Blair's speech to the Faith in the Future conference in July 2000, after Euan, his eldest son, was arrested for drunkenness in Leicester Square. Available from: www.guardian.co.uk/uk/2000/jul/07/labour.politics.
4 The sample covered from 30 June 1997 to 30 June 2002 and the titles included were: the *Daily Mail*, the *Mirror*, the *Guardian, The Times* and their Sunday editions. The 450 articles were selected using multi-stage sampling. In the first stage, 15 weeks were randomly selected. Then, for each selected week, a search was carried out in Lexis-Nexis with the key words Blair AND/OR prime minister. After cleaning the hit list (e.g. duplicates), 30 articles were randomly chosen for each week. Letters to the editor and articles shorter than 50 words were excluded.
5 The unit of analysis was the entire article and any reference to one or more of these dimensions meant that the article was coded as positive: each piece is only counted once in the results, regardless of how many dimensions of the index were coded as present.
6 A second person coded a 20 per cent random sub-sample of the articles (i.e. 90 pieces). The overall inter-coder reliability for this chapter, calculated using Holsti's formula, is 0.95, with individual variable scores ranging from 0.87 to 0.99.
7 The total adds to more than 100 because, although counted only once for overall index, each article could have been coded positively for any number of themes.
8 Prescott was the Deputy Prime Minister, Campbell was No. 10 Director of Communications and Strategy, and Jack Straw was Home Secretary (1997–2001) and Foreign Secretary (2001–2006).
9 The analysis is based on *every* article in all main London-based national daily and Sunday newspapers (18 titles) that mentioned Blair's youngest son from the time the pregnancy was announced until 30 June 2002.
10 As it focuses in the exploration of routinisation, the analysis was carried out only on articles that referred to Leo only tangentially (N=1,111).
11 The rest of the references (12 per cent) were coded as 'other'.
12 The difference in the percentages is even more striking given that the conflict in Iraq had greatly increased Blair's overall presence in the newspapers.
13 Since the 1980s, there has been a 135 per cent increase in the number of consumer magazines in the UK market (women, men, public affairs, general interest), with the steepest increase between 1996 and 2000.

6

Gordon Brown and David Cameron

After Blair's era, where the personal became a routine element of public discourse, the question that emerges is: was it a temporary blip, caused by a prime minister exceptionally eager to use, and skilful at using, his personal life for strategic publicity? Or did Blair's era have a long-term impact on the role of the personal? In other words, once Blair stood down, did things go back to 'normal'? The answer is yes and no. On the one hand, there are a set of factors conditioning the use of the personal that are contingent and hence do not apply equally to all leaders. This was the case in the past, as we saw in Chapter 4, and still applies. In this sense, whereas Cameron represents a clear continuity with Blair, Brown – because of personality and political circumstances – was much more reluctant to use the personal in the construction of his public persona. On the other hand what is 'normal' has changed, affecting all politicians regardless of style. During the Blair era, there was a transformation in expectations, within the media and parties, about the role that the personal lives of leaders play, and ought to play, in public discourse. The personal is now often uncritically accepted as a normal element of political coverage and is used in the overall assessment of leadership. Moreover, leaders are expected to be prepared, even to be keen, to reveal, as the ability to expose their 'real' selves has come to be regarded a prerequisite of electoral success.

Following this argument, this chapter will explore how the transformations in the role of the personal experienced during Blair's era have been reflected in the communication strategies and media coverage of his successor (Gordon Brown) and his 'heir' (David Cameron). Specifically, it will look at how they have managed the personal dimension of their public personae, how the media have covered them and how the personal has been employed in the assessment of their leaderships. It will show that, although there are differences, both leaders have had to adapt to the prevalent practices of political communication, where the personal is regarded as a 'normal' feature of public discourse. The first section will look at similarities and differences in the contingent factors affecting the use of the personal for each of the leaders. The second section will focus on Cameron as leader of the opposition, including a comparison of the coverage of his and Blair's rise to their party leaderships. It will show not only that there are important similarities between the two leaders but also that Cameron has in some ways taken 'going personal' even further. The final section is devoted to Brown and will demonstrate that, despite his reluctance, the characteristics of contemporary political communication pushed him to 'comply', even if only partially, with the rules of mediated intimacy. Moreover, the coverage of the personal, although less prominent than for Blair and Cameron, was higher than for any other prime minister except Blair, and the 'human' dimensions of his public persona (or rather lack thereof) were an important element in the media assessment of his leadership.

Blair's legacy: antidote and imitation

In June 2007, after ten years as Chancellor of the Exchequer, Gordon Brown finally replaced Tony Blair as leader of the Labour party and hence as prime minister, a post he held for just under three years. Eighteen month earlier, in December 2005, David Cameron had been elected leader of the Conservative party and would later become, in May 2010, prime minister. These two leaders have remarkably contrasting styles. Brown, although in some ways media and marketing savvy, was reminiscent of earlier modes of leadership: technocratic and heavy on policy detail, strongly reliant on public forms of discourse, emotionally detached, ill at ease in 'off-role' modes, and remarkably reserved – in contemporary terms – about his personal life. He was also undoubtedly a political junkie and policy wonk, obsessively (pre)occupied with work. In contrast, Cameron has an informal rhetorical style, has eagerly and skilfully exploited the opportunities offered by non-traditional and new media formats (including the Internet), and has been more than happy to make the private public and to selectively reveal his emotions. Moreover, he has emphasised the enjoyment he gets from non-political activities such as music, sport, watching James Bond and Star Wars movies, and especially from his family life.

   Their personal biographies are also quite different. Both leaders are married and had a severely disabled child who died while they were in public office; but the similarities do not go much further. Cameron, educated at Eton and Oxford and the son of a stockbroker, had an unmistakably privileged background. In contrast, Brown's upbringing was middle class, albeit not typical: the 'son of the manse', he grew up in the Scottish industrial town of Kirkcaldy and was educated in state schools. He was also heavily involved in politics from a very early age, especially after a rugby accident at the age of 16 forced him to spend months lying in bed in a darkened room and left him blind in one eye. Give the characteristics of their personal lives, and how they might resonate with 'ordinary' people, one would expect Brown's to have been more heavily emphasised. However, as we shall see, it is Cameron who gave more exposure to the personal (although downplaying his past) and it is also his personal life – not Brown's – that received more attention in the media. This shows, as in the case of Blair, that being politically advantageous or newsworthy are not characteristics of the leaders' lives themselves but of the process of mediation.

There were also important differences in the position of their parties and thus in their strategic needs as well as on their takes on Blair's legacy. Cameron became leader of the Conservatives after the party's third consecutive defeat in 2005. He was not the front-runner in the leadership election but was chosen – in many ways similarly to Blair – because of his fresh and young image, media savviness and potential appeal outside the core Conservative vote. As with Labour in 1997, the party was also in need of ideological renewal after a long period out of office, needing to adapt to post-Blairite Britain. As leader of the opposition, Cameron presented himself as a moderniser who was determined to decontaminate the Conservative brand from its association as the 'nasty party': more to the centre ground, more caring, and embracing post-materialistic issues such as ethical consumption, the environment and life–work balance (see Finlayson, 2007; Kerr, 2007; O'Hara, 2007; Quinn, 2008). Moreover, although in policy terms Cameron has been less reformist than might at first have appeared (Bale, 2008), early on in his leadership he promoted the idea that he was the natural and 'true' heir to Blair, and presented himself as the personal embodiment of the Conservative party 'new' values.

In contrast, after 10 years as Chancellor, when Brown became prime minister he was well known and his public persona – including negative traits such as detached, dour and grumpy – was harder to alter. Moreover, Brown's main strategic need was to differentiate his leadership from Tony Blair's while preserving the ideological core of the New Labour project. One of the key tactics for doing so was to present himself as the antidote to Blair, not so much in policy but in style: less 'presidential', anti-spin, anti-celebrity and glamour-less (and thus more collegiate, focused on 'substance' and statesman-like).

These differences are important for explaining how the two leaders have tried to use the personal in the construction of their leader personae. As has been discussed in previous chapters, how the personal is incorporated into the construction of a leader's persona have to do with his or her biography, personality and communicative styles. Moreover, it relates to the strategic needs of the party, as ideally the leader's style should suit the political climate and form a coherent package with the policies and values he or she advocates. The leadership styles of predecessors and of the opposition are also important because leadership dynamics are strongly reactive both in terms of differentiation and imitation (Foley, 2002: 8). In short, there are a set of factors conditioning the use of the personal that are contingent, because they are idiosyncratic to the leader and related to the prevailing political climate.

However, these are not the only factors. If it was all down to personality, then Brown could have moulded himself on Attlee, whom he repeatedly said he identified with. More realistically, and closer in time, one can see strong parallels between Brown and Ted Heath: although reserved characters, they both reacted to accusations of aloofness and dourness – accentuated by the contrast with the opposition leaders – by trying to show a 'softer' side of their personae. There are indeed some similarities between the two leaders in this regard but there are important differences. Both the media criticism of Brown's lack of a 'human' persona, and his attempts to overcome it, were more central than in the case of Heath: they were more prevalent, they extended to day-to-day governing, and they were more entangled with evaluations of leadership and overall government performance. Moreover, whereas previously a 'humanised' leader such as Wilson was considered unusual and innovative, now it is someone reserved like Brown who appears at odds with the times.

So, on the one hand, because of the differences in personality and political circumstances, it was more attractive for Cameron to use the personal. On the other hand, both leaders were conditioned in how they could construct their public personae by the broad socio-political, cultural and media changes that have increased the incentives, as well as the pressures, to show the 'human' side of leaders. Moreover, they have also been affected by the enduring impact of the Blair era, both in terms of the routinisation of the use of the personal in public discourse and beliefs about what makes a leader successful and popular (Langer, 2010).

David Cameron: Blair's 'true' heir

In the case of Cameron, the continuity with Blair is clear. In fact, it would appear that during his period as leader of the opposition the role of the personal was actually more central than during Blair's years, both to Cameron's communication strategy and to media coverage. To test this proposition, and given that Cameron – at the time of writing – has only recently become prime minister, we carried out a comparative content analysis of the coverage of Blair's and Cameron's rise to the leadership of their parties in *The Times* and *Sunday Times*. Although this is obviously a limited sample, it should give us a good indication of change, as well as continuity, in the personal coverage of the two leaders.

The analysis focused on exploring, comparatively, the degree and nature of the politicisation of their private personae. Hence, following the operationalised definition used in previous chapters, the articles were coded for all references to the five dimensions of their personal lives (family life, lifestyle, personal appearance, upbringing and religion) and to their personal 'soft' qualities (e.g. being nice, likeable). Given the leaders' remarkable youth, age was also added but, to preserve comparability, as a separate variable. For similar reasons, references to the schools they attended were also coded separately. As before, for the overall calculations each article was counted only once even if it referred to more than one of the themes in the index. The samples were constructed to include the same four key moments in the leadership election and its aftermath: the start of the race, the official presentations of their candidacies, their acceptance speeches and their first party conference as leaders. Articles were retrieved from NewsBank, and every story that mentioned the leaders in relation to each of these events was analysed: 119 for Tony Blair and 106 for David Cameron.

Reading both sets of articles, the similarities in the overall content are striking. Despite the differences in the candidates' standing in the race and the paper's editorial line (more supportive of Blair than of Cameron), the coverage of the leadership campaigns followed a very similar narrative, almost a template. The paper provided some factual information about key campaign events; discussed policy positions, leadership qualities (experience, record and ability) and the horse race; identified similar challenges (mostly to 'convert rhetoric into reality') and party enemies; and analysed the impact of a 'fresh' leader on the government's electoral strategy. But, above all, the similarities are in the personal characterisations of Blair and Cameron: among frequent accusations of 'style over substance', both were portrayed as media friendly, likeable, good looking, young, modern family men from privileged backgrounds, and regularly identified as part of the Islington/ Notting Hill sets.

Beyond these thematic similarities, the content analysis presented in Table 6.1 shows that the coverage of Cameron's rise to the party leadership paid more attention to his personal life and qualities than in Blair's case. This indicates that, for all Blair's 'specialness', the politicisation of private persona continued to evolve after him; in fact, it actually intensified for Cameron's sample. Partly this could be attributed to Cameron's even younger age and privileged background, both of which drew more attention to his personal life and qualities. But both attributes applied also to Blair. Moreover, excluding those articles that referred only to the leader's youth or school diminishes the proportion but hardly changes the trend: compared to

Blair's sample, there is still an increase of 50 per cent in the proportion of articles referring to the personal in Cameron's set of articles. Furthermore, these results are consistent with the findings of a different study, in that case focused on everyday coverage of the leader of the opposition, which found that, as compared to Blair, 'the Conservative leader has continued, and expanded, the trend' with 40 per cent more articles referring to the personal than in the case of the former prime minister (Langer, 2010: 65). In short, although remarkable, it is clear that the emphasis on the personal in media coverage was not a one-off occurrence unique to Blair.

Table 6.1 Percentage of articles in *The Times* and *Sunday Times* focused on the party leadership election that refer to personal lives and qualities

	Blair (N=119)	Cameron (N=106)
Personal life and personal qualities	31%	50%
Excluding articles referring only to age and/or school	24%	36%

Source: Content analysis by the author

There are also interesting qualitative similarities and differences. Their personal backgrounds are interpreted in eminently political terms, especially in association with their class appeal. Undoubtedly, the British obsession with class is not something new: however, whereas in the past the main emphasis was on the class implications of the party's policies and values, class readings are now more personalised, with greater attention paid to the leader's upbringing, family and personal style. On the other hand, interestingly, there is also a different dimension of politicisation of private persona at play here that reveals links between the personal and the political which, although not most prevalent, are distinctively contemporary. In some articles – especially for Cameron whose privileged background, as a Conservative, is perhaps more problematic – it is suggested that material class attributes can be overwritten by the leader's behaviour in the private sphere. In other words, it is not where you come from, or the values and policies you espouse, but the 'inner self' that might matter the most. This interpretation of the personal, albeit peripheral, substantiates one of the key criticisms of the emphasis on politicians as persons, which it is feared 'obscures the continuing importance of class in advanced industrial societies' (Sennett, 1977: 4):

> Cameron has a classic Tory background: Eton, Oxford and special adviser at the Treasury. His father-in-law is a landed baronet, Sir Reginald Sheffield. But

he has a *genuine concern with issues of poverty*. Many previously *suspicious observers warmed* to the young MP as he *talked movingly* on BBC Question Time about *his oldest child, Ivan, who is severely disabled'*. (Cracknell and Woods, *Sunday Times*, 8 May 2005, italics added)

The press attaches the Eton label to Cameron at every opportunity, but whether a purely negative association still holds true for the population at large is more uncertain. To the extent that Cameron has yet impinged on middle-class consciousness, *he is seen as a polite young chap with a pregnant wife who has an appealing ankle tattoo*. Where he went to school seems a matter of relative indifference: Oppidan, Schmoppidan. (Macintyre, *The Times*, 9 December 2005, italics added)

For both leaders there was also emphasis on their personal appearance and those of their wives. A lot of this is trivial fashion assessment and highlights the difference with the coverage of earlier leaders' wives: their presence in the media is not new, but they now appear more frequently and the tone is more critical and judgemental as well as focused on the motives behind their sartorial choices. Moreover, the look and style of the leaders and their spouses are linked not only to their personal and even sex appeal; more significantly, they are also used by journalists, often in combination with other 'lifestyle' choices, as a way of assessing whether the leaders (and thus their parties and policies) are as new and modern as they claim to be. In other words, it is not style replacing substance, but substance read-off from style:

Fashion-lovers in the Labour party have grown alarmed by the number of Marks & Spencer carrier bags containing standard-issue grey and black suits heading towards Tony Blair's office. They fear that the Labour leader is about to repeat Neil Kinnock's mistake and turn himself into a stuffed shirt. Be true to yourself, Tony, they say; and bring back those casual green jackets you used to wear. (Atticus, *Sunday Times*, 24 July 1994)

Cameron was wearing 'a black Tshirt and drinking a smoothie'. For a fleeting moment, it seemed that a single piece of clothing and a fruit drink were enough to clinch the deal for the new Tories. Had they finally stepped into the 21st century after so many years in the wilderness? [...] Times change. Modern man now is part Jamie Oliver, part Andrew Flintoff. He is Cameron absolutely – the sort of man who slips into his wife's vintage motor on a Saturday morning to buy some Daylesford organic beef at the farmers' market, while James Blunt wails out of his in-car iPod. There are beacons of new Tory-ness all over the pop-cultural landscape. (Flynn, *Sunday Times*, 4 December 2005)

Similarly, their young age is linked to their political experience (or rather lack thereof, especially for Cameron) but also to generational change, and hence to a different type of person and therefore leader: more open, informal and relaxed, and hence 'sincere'. These kinds of links are especially marked in relation to their family lives. It is not only that, according to many of the articles, having young children makes them more 'normal' and more capable of relating to the concerns of 'hard-working families'. It is also about how their personal qualities, as modern (new) men and leaders, are inferred from their more hands-on and emotionally engaged approach to parenthood.

In short, some of the personal elements in the coverage of Blair's and Cameron's rise to party leadership were plainly trivial and hardly linked to the political. In other cases, particularly in relation to their backgrounds, they were more overtly political, especially in terms of class and privilege. But the most interesting cases were those in between, because these kinds of links between the personal and the political are distinctively contemporary. Namely, those articles that drew inferences about the type of leader Blair or Cameron would be, and the policies they might enact, from the kind of private men they appear to be. As in the past, it was in part about whether they are 'in touch' or sufficiently 'ordinary'. But it goes beyond that because the personal was used to uncover not only who they are but what they 'are about', employing it to judge their leadership qualities, policies and their credentials as modernisers. Moreover, it was not just their childhood experiences or their personal journey but also their personal style, consumption patterns and family life that journalists used to assess the credibility of the political project they (re)presented.

How Blair and Cameron used the personal in the construction of their personae was also different from those of earlier leaders such as Baldwin, Wilson, Thatcher and Major (Chapter 4). As they did, but more intensely, Blair and Cameron eagerly and skilfully used non-public affairs outlets to communicate with a broader audience in a more casual style, and regularly referred to their taste in music, love for sports, hobbies and so on. But, distinctively, they used the personal from the start of their careers and as a constitutive element of their political identity and overall branding of themselves and, crucially, of their 'new' parties. Significantly, too, both displayed a degree of emotion in public and mixed formal and informal discourses. Both talked about, and to an extent showed, their families and everyday life, and publicly engaged with new forms of masculinity (see Smith, 2008). Both linked the personal with the political in a range of topics and when speaking not only 'off-role', as persons, but also when positioned as leaders on even the most official of occasions.

It is also important to note that in some ways Cameron has taken 'going personal' further than Blair, setting new milestones in the use of the personal for the construction of a public persona (Langer, 2010). He has talked about the personal as a virtually unavoidable feature of 'modern' politics, going so far as to pronounce that the public is *entitled* to know about a leader's personal life. He not only did the usual light interviews on breakfast TV, women's magazines and so on, but also, via webcameron, self-generated 'intimate chats' while his everyday life – literally – took place publicly in the background. In fact, the channel was launched with what was described as 'a strikingly intimate portrait, complete with Cameron wearing rubber gloves as he talked politics doing the dishes' (Crabtree, *The Wire*, 24 March 2010). Moreover, Cameron's wife has been more willingly in the public eye in wife-role than Cherie Blair ever was. They have also invited cameras to his family home, most famously ITN who filmed Cameron having breakfast with his children. Furthermore, he has placed more emphasis on the experiential side of fatherhood, not only talking – like Blair – about how demanding this 'job' is and the efforts he has had to undertake to make sure his children live a 'normal' life, but also about the satisfaction and self-fulfilment that being a father brings.

In addition, whereas Blair's linking of the personal with the political was strong but often elliptical, Cameron's has been more wide ranging and explicit. Moreover, it was generally expressed not in terms of broad political values but from the insights provided by his experiences as an individual, including as a citizen-consumer. For instance, the ITN interview took place the day before he unveiled a new parental leave plan, both generating publicity for the proposal and authenticating it, by showing live his hands-on fatherhood and personal struggle with work–life balance. He has also repeatedly referred – both in major speeches and media interviews – to his experiences as the father of a severely disabled child (Ivan) as a personal endorsement and emotional authentication of the strength of his support for the NHS and respite care policies. Cameron has also made more explicit emphasis on lifestyle choices, such as cycling, to link personal behaviour to his environmental agenda. Of course, after the official-car-following-bike fiasco this strategy came partially undone, but nonetheless the fact is that Cameron became one of the routine names used by journalists (covering politics but also a range of other subjects from celebrities to ethical living) as the embodiment of green trends (Langer, 2010: 67).

In short, the analysis of the coverage of the election of Blair and Cameron as party leaders shows a noteworthy – albeit not pervasive – degree of attention to the personal. This was also qualitatively distinctive, as it was used to assess not only their 'normality' and character but also their leadership potential and the strength of their policy commitments and the Party's 'new' values. Moreover, the comparative analysis of Blair's and Cameron's coverage shows not only a continuation but in fact an acceleration of the previous trend. This has to do both with the changed characteristics of political communication, where the personal has become a routine element of political discourse, and with what suited Cameron, which in some ways encouraged him to take 'going personal' even further.

Project Gordon 3D

> Tony was a charismatic leader (mostly for the good, I think). It is always difficult to follow leaders like that, and *foolish to try to emulate* them, and of course you would not try. At the moment the voters do not feel they really know you. *The solution is not to try to become more accessible or more likeable or whatever, it is to reveal your true potential as a person and a leader at the right time* … Your *own distinctive charisma* will then emerge.
> (Philip Gould's memo to Gordon Brown, 2007, italics added)

Whereas 'going personal' was a strategy that suited Cameron, this was not the case for Gordon Brown. Although his personal life had interesting dimensions that could have been exploited for publicity purposes, Brown was a reserved character with a communicative style not suited for the politics of 'intimacy'. Moreover, unlike Cameron, for whom Blair's style was a suitable and attractive role model, Brown needed to differentiate himself from his predecessor, presenting himself as an 'antidote' to celebrity and personality politics. For these reasons, Brown was generally reluctant to use the personal for strategic publicity. In fact, his first communication campaign once in No. 10 was the poster, 'Not flash, just Gordon', hoping that, as recommended by Philip Gould in the memo above, his own distinctive charisma would emerge.

Brown's reluctance has been reflected in the media coverage. Figure 3.8 (in Chapter 3), shows the proportion of articles in *The Times* and the *Guardian* with references to the prime ministers' personal lives between 1945 and 2009. As the trend line for both papers shows, starved of a steady flow of stories by the leader's reluctance to reveal, the presence of the personal in the coverage dropped. This decrease indicates that even in the post-Blair era there is still a degree of individual choice on the degree of exposure of the personal, even for a prime minister.

But this picture ignores the structural factors that underpin the development of the politicisation of private persona; these factors can be contained and managed but cannot be eliminated. There is now a normalised assumption that, if they are to succeed, politicians must be prepared to show, and be good at showing, their 'human' side. A reserved leader like Brown can choose not to reveal but this choice is at odds with blurred distinctions between private and public and with contemporary modes of mediated leadership. In fact, as we shall see, the characteristics of contemporary political communication drove him to partly conform, even if grudgingly, with the rules of mediated intimacy; secondly, it meant that, despite his reserve, his personal life was mentioned in the media more than for any other prime minister except Blair; finally, but crucially, it meant that the 'human' dimensions of his public persona (or rather lack thereof) were an important element in the media assessment of his leadership. Let us unpack each of these elements in turn.

Despite his reluctance and Gould's advice to avoid trying to 'become more accessible or more likeable or whatever', Brown gave in to what has come to be considered by many, including it seems himself, an essential requirement of modern leadership: to show a more 'human' side of his persona. In fact, he publicly declared that he felt that he had little choice but to talk about his personal life if people were to understand him and what he does (Langer, 2010). He did not do it routinely, as Cameron and Blair have done, but it was nonetheless considered a necessary dimension of his communication strategy. In fact, as early as 2004, when Brown's team was already preparing for his much-awaited transition to No. 10, his personal pollster, Deborah Mattinson, concluded that:

> GB should show voters the man behind the authoritative Chancellor's persona. Project 3D was so called because its purpose was to develop a more three-dimensional image for GB. Having seen the positive voter reaction [to his appearance on GMTV, where he talked about his son] I believed that GB's personal positioning could and should embrace a wider scope, introducing the private man to a wider audience. Project 3D became my primary focus. It was clearly intended to play a part in developing GB's future prime ministerial position, a crucial piece in the overall jigsaw. (Mattinson, 2010: 140)

The strategy resurfaced in 2006, as part of 'Project Volvo', which was named after the car that focus group members associated with Brown: 'solid, reliable and does what it says on the tin' (Mattinson, 2010: 154). The overall aim was to highlight Brown's 'vision' and policies, but these were intimately tied up with his persona. His advisers identified the need to emphasise his strengths and what made him different from both Blair and Cameron (a serious, substantive 'father-of-the-nation' figure) but also to change, by addressing the '3D problem', his image as 'one-dimensional numbers man' who had few interests outside work and was perceived as both 'old and old fashioned' (Mattinson, 2010: 156–7). The devised strategy was to demonstrate his 'hinterland', emphasise his 'back story', and prioritise daytime TV and 'personal "tie-off" visits', where he should use 'everyday language and examples of real people', as well as to encourage him to work on his fitness, haircut and wardrobe (Mattinson, 2010: 158).

In step with this strategy (dubbed by the press as Project Gordon), Brown started to speak more frequently about his formative experiences (especially his rugby accident), his parents and how his Presbyterian upbringing gave him a 'moral compass'. He also gave a number of 'confessional' interviews, where he talked about his youth, family life and enjoyment of popular culture. Moreover, at the Labour Party Conference in 2008, while asserting his sons' right to privacy ('My children aren't props, they are people'), Brown not only made references to his upbringing but was also introduced to the stage by his wife. She repeated the act in 2009, when she heralded him as 'my husband, my hero'. More generally, Sarah Brown (a former PR executive) developed a very high public profile not only for her charity work but, as one journalist evocatively put it, as 'Brown's special envoy to planet normal' (Wintour, the *Guardian*, 8 July 2009: 1), trying to show the public her husband's 'real self'. The strategy was repeated during the long campaign for the 2010 General Election, where Sarah played a very visible role, including an interview with her husband on GMTV.

It is true that Brown's use of the personal for strategic publicity was intermittent and low-key, especially in comparison to Blair and Cameron. Nonetheless, these attempts at 'going personal' show how the routine politicisation of private persona, and the factors that encourage it, conditions the construction of a leader's public persona, regardless of their personality. In other words, leaders still have a choice, and there will always be differences in how and to what extent they use the personal; but this choice is heavily constrained by the imperatives imposed by the routine presence of the personal in public discourse and by the fact that a 'human' dimension of persona has come to be considered, by advisers and journalists alike, a pre-requisite of contemporary leadership.

Moreover, Brown's reluctance did not stop the media from trying to uncover his 'true self'. As we have seen, the personal is now embedded as a routine component of public discourse across genres. As a result, even in the absence of fresh personal 'news', the personal will still be mentioned. This is clear in the case of Brown. Even though he only rarely fed the press with 'intimate' information, as seen in Figure 3.8 (Chapter 3), the proportion of articles referring to his personal life did not return to the lower levels of Major, who for all his greyness was more willing to emphasise the personal than Brown ever was. In other words, for all Brown's reserve, and because it has become a routine feature of news writing across sections and subjects, the presence of the personal has not gone back to pre-Blair levels.

Furthermore, beyond these figures, which reveal the routine picture, it is important to note that there was also a series of short-lived media hypes about Brown's personal sphere, which increased the feeling of pervasiveness of the personal. These waves were triggered by rare minor personal revelations, whose content was greatly amplified by cross-media recycling. For instance, Brown's interview with Piers Morgan in February 2010, where he became emotional ('wept' according to the press) about the death of his daughter on national TV, was mentioned in over 90 articles (and this is only in the national papers) in the two weeks before and after it was shown, and was still being mentioned three months after the event. Similarly, Brown's supposed 'dithering' about his favourite biscuit in a webchat on Mumsnet (a parenting website) became a story in almost every news outlet and travelled as far as China and the Middle East. Moreover, 'biscuitgate', a furore about Brown's supposed failure to answer a question which was never actually put to him, was still sporadically mentioned more than six months after the event.[1]

The fact is that, in the current media environment, a single personal quote can be reproduced in dozens of pieces and has a long shelf-life, as journalists re-use it later in different contexts. Of course, cross-media recycling of 'newsworthy' media events is not new. However, the news value of these kinds of events has increased because of the routine media interest in the personal. Moreover, the media – as a result of technological changes and market conditions – are now more deeply entwined and imitative and, as a result, self-referentiality across outlets is now more intense (Hart, 1998: 185). Self-referentiality is also strengthened by the leaders' competing (and highly reactive) communication strategies and the comparisons – about their personalities, their performances and the public's reactions – that events of similar kinds generate in the media (e.g. all three main leaders appeared on Mumsnet).

In combination, the intense but sporadic media hypes, often originated outside news and public affairs but greatly reproduced across media, and the low-key but routine references to a leader's family, hobbies and so on have helped to create a sense of pervasiveness of the personal. Under current conditions, this applies even for a leader like Brown, who was mostly reluctant to engage with the politicisation of private persona. The levels are lower than for the keener Blair and Cameron. But they are substantially higher than for a comparable leader such as Heath, both because of techno-logical, market and journalistic changes in the media and because dealing with the '3D problem' was, arguably unavoidably, more central to Brown's than to Heath's communication strategy.

Even more significant than the degree of coverage of the personal is how the politicisation of private persona has affected the media's assessment of leadership and government performance. The public 'private' persona of leaders is *not* the only, or even the most prevalent, explanation of success and failure. Moreover, it can be considered what Schudson (1995: 133) calls a 'fundamental attribution error' whereby journalists explain causality focusing on human actors a reader can love or hate, while minimising the more fundamental impact of more abstract factors. But even if an attribution error, the fact is that the personal is now deeply entangled with the overall assessment of leadership, as well as with the interpretation of political accomplishments and fiascos. This was particularly marked in the case of Brown, precisely because of his reluctance to reveal and his inability to appear at ease when performing mediated intimacy. His lack of a 'human' side and his poor performance of intimacy were considered not just a personality flaw or a communication problem, but a shortcoming of leadership leaving many to quickly dismiss Brown 'as a liability on the grounds that he was distant, out of touch and devoid of effective outreach' (Foley, 2009: 508).

These changes, and Brown's difficulties, are reflected in Figures 3.7 and 3.8 (Chapter 3). Whereas the proportion of articles referring to his personal life is lower than for Blair, the relationship is inverted for personal 'soft' qualities. What this indicates is that the lack of personal information does not mean that his public 'private' persona becomes 'invisible' but that its absence, and what it appears to say about the leader, is highlighted as a shortcoming. Similarly, an analysis of the press coverage marking the first year of Brown's leadership shows how, without being the only, or even the most prevalent, criteria of evaluation, 'the personal has become an important element in the media's assessment of the performance and popularity of parties and leaders' (Langer, 2010: 69). This analysis showed that although most pieces explained Labour's and Brown's escalating unpopularity on traditional political grounds (90 per cent) and as a result of his political performance and his flaws as leader such as indecisiveness and secrecy (85 per cent), 45 per cent of the articles also mentioned the 'human' dimensions of Brown's leader persona as one of the potential explanations for his increasing unpopularity. These character traits (e.g. aloofness, dourness), which were in the early days regarded by many commentators as a positive contrast to Blair's slickness and showmanship, came often to be considered as flaws. Moreover, and most interestingly, questions about Brown's personal qualities and life, and about how these were enacted in his communication strategy and media performances, became an integral element of the overall narrative of the leader's unpopularity and failure. For example, Brown's 'biscuitgate' on Mumsnet became, especially in the right-wing press, another obvious 'proof' of his dithering, insincerity and non-normality:

> He attracted avoidable mockery by taking days to reply after being asked (12 times) last Friday, during a webchat with a parents' networking site, to name his favourite biscuit. After a weekend wrestling with his soul he revealed that it was any chocolate biscuit. On the very same day, when the UN Human Rights Council debated the biased Goldstone report on the Gaza conflict, Britain was initially minded to abstain. But in the end it couldn't decide even

to do that, and Britain didn't manage to vote at all – along with such countries as Angola and Kyrgyzstan. (Leader column, *The Times*, October 21 2009)

It took more than 24 hours for the Prime Minister to come clean, with an unnervingly vague comment on the messaging service Twitter that he liked 'absolutely anything with a bit of chocolate on it', which, if anything, made the whole half-coated digestive debacle worse. Let's be blunt. Not having a favourite biscuit is unnatural – freakishly so. While it's entirely possible to negotiate adult life without a favourite football team or holiday destination, only robots (and Gordon Brown) can't name their favourite biscuit. Which possibly tells us all we need to know about our beleaguered premier. The joy of biscuits is that they strip people down to their very essence. (Woods, *Daily Telegraph*, October 20 2009)

Even David Cameron brought it up at Prime Minister's Questions (21 October 2009):

The way to stop these strikes and this militancy is to show some leadership, some backbone and some courage. Are we really going to spend another six months with a Prime Minister who cannot give a straight answer, who cannot pass his own legislation, and who sits in his bunker not even able to decide what sort of biscuits he wants to eat?

This is a rather extreme example and, ironically, one based on a 'gaffe' that never actually happened. But it pointedly illustrates a more general point. The personal is rarely a predominant element in the coverage of politics and has not replaced the discussion of leadership qualities, party politics or policy. Moreover, its prevalence depends to an extent on the willingness of the leader to reveal. But, at the same time, the personal is now a routine element of public discourse and it is expected of leaders to be able to show their 'real selves' in public. Furthermore, whether successful or unsuccessful at this task, the personal is now entangled with the media's assessment of leadership. This evaluation will be based on a range of issues, most of which are political in a traditional sense. It will also depend on the strength of the government of the day because, if everything else is on track, this weakness might be overlooked or even appraised as a refreshing difference from 'sleeker' leaders. But the force of the expectations of contemporary leadership is never too far from the surface. Eventually, as popularity falters and the novelty wears off, the use of personal criteria tends to re-emerge, comparing unfavourably those who embraced the 'antidote' strategy with other more 'human' leaders. As a consequence, parties and leaders are likely to become increasingly convinced that a 'humanised' persona is a precondition of popularity reinforcing the cycle. For the media, the assessments of the leader *qua* human being are now often part of the explanation of success and failure both because they are meant to reveal the leader's real self, and hence his 'true' motivations and intentions, and because of the media's belief in their impact on citizens' evaluation – paradoxically given the lack of evidence of strong direct effects of personal qualities on voting behaviour. It is also a more appealing journalistic narrative to explain a government's (un)popularity than the abstract complexities of intra-party bargaining, policy negotiations and institutional power structures.

In the case of Brown, the media's emphasis on his personal qualities had partly to do with the overall weakness of his premiership. His inability to appear 'human' was also starker because of the style of his predecessor and the opposition leader. Moreover, it was an obvious, and narratively interesting, focus of criticism, which served to encapsulate much broader and more complex leadership and political weaknesses. It was not the only criterion and, had his government being more popular, it might well have been considered a minor flaw or even – as it was during his brief 'honeymoon' period – as a positive contrast to Blair and Cameron. But, instead, it became an attractive and easy means to criticise him. Moreover, it made everything else more difficult because, as the medium is also the message, it also hindered Brown's capacity to communicate about issues and policies. Moreover, this often-mentioned liability weakened his position in the eyes of the media and the party.

Of course, the problem was not that Brown was necessarily any less 'human' than Blair and Cameron. He appeared so because of his reluctance to reveal as well as his inability to perform sincerity:

> Sincerity is a form of self-display without concealment, involving the disclosure of subjectivity. If, however, a discourse of sincerity is adopted in the mediated public sphere, the speaker needs to inhabit his or her words in such a way that the emotion disclosed can be recovered almost independently of the words through which it is staked. There needs to be some other, preferably spontaneous or reflex, signal of the emotion if the performative paradox is to be avoided. (Montgomery, 1999: 26)

In part, this inability was a result of his awkward body language, related to his physical disabilities (in his eyes but also in his mouth movements) as a consequence of his rugby accident. But it goes well beyond that. Brown, even when factually 'intimate', appeared to conceal his feelings and hence part of his private self. As a result, his 'personal revelations' often appeared as hypocritical performances of 'someone who is always holding something back' (Runciman, 2006a), making it hard for people to believe that he was being sincere, 'real'. Moreover, Brown tended to use public forms of discourse (formal, abstract and impersonal) even when talking about his personal life, hence objectifying the personal and appearing contrived and ill at ease.[2] In addition, there was also an issue of content. The infrequent references to his family were rarely about his role as parent or husband, and did not engage, unlike Blair and Cameron, with the mundane aspects of everyday life. Instead, his personal disclosure was more 'son of the manse' than 'new man' (Smith, 2008), mostly revolving around the influence of his father on his work ethic and commitment to public service, or what he called his 'moral compass'. For instance, note the differences in the quotes below, selected by the journalist to characterise the leaders *qua* human beings. Whereas Brown's is defined by the abstract mention of his childhood and detached hints of emotionality, Cameron's offers a detailed and intimate narration of a snapshot of his everyday family life:

Brown on Brown:
I attended the local state primary school in Kirkcaldy a few streets away from where I lived – and then I took the school bus to the local secondary school up the hill. And I have school friends I have kept in touch with all my life who have shared the good times and comforted me in the bad times.

Cameron on Cameron:
I'm happy in the job. And I do feel I still spend enough time with the family. Last night I got home at seven and read *Noddy* for the millionth time to Elwyn and put the children to bed and then Sam and I had supper together and just watched television. That doesn't happen every night, admittedly. (*The Observer*, 11 April 2010: 22)

The point is that even when forced into the terrain of intimacy, Brown did not dovetail the personal with the political. He tended to redirect the focus away from the private sphere, and toward the impersonal, abstract, and emotionally detached discourse of policy and the strictly political. In short, even when 'intimate', he quickly re-positioned himself as citizen and leader, and away from the private 'feeling' person. There was hardly any open acknowledgment of vulnerability, grief or pleasure; of what makes personal experiences unique, defiant of abstraction and generalisation. Moreover, instead of anchoring the political in the personal, the latter appeared – in Brown's public discourse and in his view of politics – as all but irrelevant. At the same time, irrelevant as it might have felt, it is clear he could not entirely escape the need to reveal, and politicise, his private persona.

Conclusion

Tony Blair was clearly exceptional and so was the politicisation of private persona during his era as prime minister. But this is not to say that once he stood down the presence of the personal in public discourse went back to 'normal'. It could not, because 'normal' has changed. Firstly, the personal is now embedded as a routine component of public discourse, including in 'intimate' personal profiles, lifestyle and fashion stories, celebrity-like coverage and so on but also casually fused with more traditional political reporting. Moreover, as a result of technological changes and market conditions, the media are now more deeply entwined and imitative, and hence even insignificant personal 'revelations' made to minor outlets are greatly amplified by self-referentiality, augmenting the *sense* of pervasiveness of the personal. *Sense* is fundamental here because the personal is, in fact, rarely a predominant element in the coverage of politics and has not replaced the discussion of leadership qualities, party politics or policy. Nonetheless, it appears pervasive because it is routinely present, spread across media genres and outlets, and it has permeated into most facets of public discourse. Secondly, although the assessment of leadership performance depends on multiple other factors, most of which continue to be categorically political, the performance of the leader *qua* human being is now part of the explanation of a leader's success or failure. Finally, unsurprisingly, it has now come to be expected that most politicians will be willing, even if reluctantly, to respond to media demands to expose their private selves in public. Moreover, many also will proactively use their personal lives for strategic publicity. This is in part a result of the demands of the conditions of mediation; but also of the fact that there is an increasing need for leaders to embody the party and its values, personally authenticate its policies, and generate a degree of identification and emotional connection with citizens, which requires them to walk a tightrope between being normal and 'real' enough for citizens to identify with them, and extraordinary enough to lead them. These needs influence how leaders construct their personae as well as, arguably, who parties select as their leaders.

These factors heavily condition, but do not determine, the role of the personal in relation to individual leaders. There is still a degree of choice in how much and in which ways leaders use the personal, affecting also how it is reported by the media. As a result, although the personal is now more present in public discourse than in the past, the degree and nature of the politicisation of private persona still depends on a politician's biography, personality, communicative styles and strategic needs.

As we have seen, in the case of Cameron, because of his personal style and tactical needs, he heavily used the personal in the construction of his public persona. In many regards he did so in similar ways to Blair, and differently from those leaders who preceded them. Both used the personal as a constitutive element of their political identity and their brand and, vitally, of the 'reinvention' of their parties. Both, distinctively, were able and willing to display emotion publically, mix formal and informal discourses, casually discuss their domestic lives and families, and identified themselves with novel forms of masculinity and fatherhood. Moreover, both linked the personal with the political in a range of occasions, when speaking about a variety of subjects and when positioned both 'off-role' (e.g. in soft genres) and 'on-role' (e.g. party conferences). Furthermore, in some regards, Cameron pushed 'going personal' beyond the point that Blair had. He used the internet to produce 'intimate' broadcasts, acknowledged interest in his private life and beliefs as a citizen entitlement, publicised his family life even more openly, and made more explicit links between his private life and his political beliefs. This was reflected in the coverage, where there was not only a continuation of the trends identified in Blair's premiership but in fact an acceleration, with a 50 per cent increase in the proportion of references to the personal. In addition to reporting the plainly trivial and the more overtly political, the media used Blair's and Cameron's presentation of their private selves to judge them not only as 'human beings' but also to assess their leadership qualities, policy proposals and their credentials as modernisers.

In contrast to Cameron, Brown was much less inclined to use the personal. But he could not entirely escape media interest and, more importantly, the assumption that, if they are to succeed, politicians must be willing to show, and be good at showing, their 'human' side. In fact, the nature of contemporary political communication, especially post-Blair, compelled him to 'comply', if only partially, with the expectations of mediated intimacy. Moreover, despite his reserve, his personal life still received more coverage than for any other prime minister except Blair.

In addition, and crucially, the (lack of a) 'human' dimension to Brown's public persona was central to the media assessment of his leadership, with more references to his personal qualities than for any other prime minister. His incapacity to appear at ease performing mediated intimacy was more notable because of the negative contrast with the styles of the most obvious points of comparison, Blair and Cameron. Moreover, for journalists the personal was both a simpler and more appealing way to articulate their criticisms about Brown and his government than concentrating exclusively on more complex and abstract political and leadership weaknesses. But the prominence of these criticisms was also a result of the fact that the willingness to reveal, and the ability to do it 'authentically', have come to be considered not just an asset but a basic requirement of contemporary leadership. Brown fell short because of his reluctance to expose the private, his failure to combine the personal with the political and his inability to perform sincerity. In other words, his private 'feeling' person was, for Brown, something that in an ideal world had neither place nor relevance in the public sphere.

Brown's distaste for the emotional and the personal raises interesting questions in relation to normative debates. In some ways, he appears like an ideal figure for those who yearn for public discourse to preserve the key characteristics that make it, in theory, radically distinct from the sphere of the private. A sphere of impersonality, where people talk and act as impartial reasoners or detached generalisers, abstracting from particular experiences, histories, feelings, desires and interests (Young, 1990: 100). No self-disclosure, intimacy or sharing of feelings; no confusion between public and private life (Sennett, 1977). Could then Brown's reluctance and incapacity to reveal be considered democratic assets? This is a difficult question. It was clearly costly at the personal level, because it was at odds with contemporary expectations of leadership. As a result, it made it harder for him to perform as a leader and pushed him, even if unenthusiastically, to conform to the demands of mediated intimacy. This encouraged scripted revelations, and hence affected, and ineffective, (pseudo) 'authenticity'. It also raises issues about the impact on the recruitment and selection of leaders. Even if, as research generally indicates, most voters are only marginally influenced by their perceptions of the 'soft' personal qualities of leaders, the greater the role of the personal in public discourse and in the assessment of leadership, the more difficult the conditions become for those politicians who are unhappy or unable to play the personal game.

But to claim that the ideal is for a leader, and more broadly political discourse, to be 'purely public' (impersonal, emotionless, exclusively focused on facts and policy) is to ignore other important dimensions of democratic life, specifically engagement and mobilisation. The impersonal abstraction of 'proper' political discourse makes it distinct from the personal sphere but also from the way that most people talk and this is precisely what many disengaged citizens 'find disingenuous and alienating' (Coleman, 2006: 469). Conversely, the aesthetic, affective, mundane and entertaining dimensions of the portrayal of leaders as 'human beings' might make politics more appealing, help citizens to develop a degree of identification with leaders, and foster novel forms of emotional resonance between citizens and those elected to represent them; possibly more than if these elements are absent. Moreover, the discussion of the personal can help – as was the case on occasions with Blair and Cameron – to generate coverage and engaging narratives for the debate of political issues such as the gender division of domestic labour, and link 'high' politics with the politics of everyday life. On the other hand, and this will be explored in the conclusion, *if* the personal becomes a *predominant* subject of the discussion of politics and key criterion of leadership assessment, it does raise some troubling questions about the impact on the recruitment of political elites, the accountability of those in power and a potential de-politicisation of the solution to structural societal problems.

Notes

1 Mumsnet explained that due to technical reasons, Brown actually never received the question and hence could not have (failed to) answered it. Nonetheless, by then the story had taken a life of its own and was widely reproduced. Downing Street even felt obliged to do a press release and Brown later posted an answer on Twitter: 'I missed Mumsnet question about biscuits: the answer is absolutely anything with a bit of chocolate on it, but trying v hard to cut down'.

2 See van Zoonen and Holtz-Bacha (2000) for a more general discussion about 'personalised objectified discourse'.

Conclusion

Redefining personalisation

The main aims of this book have been twofold: first, to unpack and re-define the concept of the personalisation of politics; second, to provide empirical evidence offering a historical perspective on the question of the person-alisation of politics in the UK, and to explore in depth how the process of the politicisation of private persona has evolved over time, particularly in relation to Tony Blair, as it is during his era that the phenomenon experienced the most marked shift.

The book argued that in order to understand, investigate and grasp the consequences of the personalisation of politics it is necessary to redefine it *as a multi-dimensional concept.* The commonplace idea that person-alisation refers to the (increasing) importance of leaders is a misleading generalisation of a complex process. This book demonstrated that *presiden-tialisation of power* and *personality politics* are two distinctive dimensions of personalisation, which are indeed related and frequently overlap in their empirical manifestation but which are not identical in their characteristics or causes. As a result of these differences, and as shown in the UK case, it is neither necessary nor inevitable for both dimensions to be manifested to the same extent. In fact, whereas presidentialisation trends have been present – albeit fluctuating – since the 1960s, the intensification of personality politics is a more recent phenomenon. Importantly, the implications of each of these dimensions of personalisation for democratic politics are different, with concerns about presidentialisation focusing more on the imbalances in the distribution of power and the displacement of political parties, and personality politics on the impact on the quality of political discourse, the rationality of electoral behaviour and the recruitment and assessment of leaders.

Moreover, personality politics itself is not a single unitary concept: it contains elements which, both conceptually and empirically, are best understood when distinguished. Personality politics is used as a broad, and often ill-defined, term. It is applied to virtually all and every reference, explicit or implied, to the leader's personality, from his or her intelligence and integrity, to his or her ability to communicate in 'human' English to his or her passion for the *X Factor*. In contrast, this book has demonstrated that it is important to distinguish between the emphasis, on the one hand, on leadership qualities (competence, strength, etc.) and on the other on personal qualities and personal life. We can think of this distinction as the difference between the leader as statesman and the leader as 'human being'. The emphasis on the latter was defined here as the *politicisation of private persona*, and has been the main focus of this work. This concept refers specifically to the emphasis not *just* on leaders or their leadership qualities but on their personal lives and on qualities that are not directly related to their capacity for governing, and that are generally rooted in the private sphere of politicians and are meant to reveal their 'authentic' selves.

This distinction is anything but straightforward: these categories are better thought of not only as situated on a scale but also, as a result of how personalisation is developing, as increasingly overlapping. We cannot easily distinguish between 'relevant' leadership or political qualities and seemingly 'irrelevant' personal information because the two are brought together in the construction of the persona, the presentation of policy and in the evaluations of leadership. And yet, their analytical separation is important. It enabled us to conduct a systematic empirical investigation to uncover how the boundaries between the personal and the political, and public and private, have changed over time. Moreover, the distinction helps to address the strong and distinctive normative concerns associated with the politicisation of private persona. Whereas an emphasis on leadership qualities is generally recognised as an acceptable feature of modern, de-aligned mediated politics, this is not the case with the emphasis on the 'private' personal.

This book has argued that this aspect of personalisation, namely the emphasis on the personal lives and qualities of politicians, is highly significant, even if we can only detect thus far limited direct effects on electoral choices. It matters greatly because of its impact on the characteristics of public discourse and its wider implications for the political process. One does not need to consider the personal as mutually exclusive from, or in rigid opposition to, the political to realise the significance of the phenomenon; as a matter of fact, quite the opposite. The importance of the process of politicisation of private persona lies precisely in the fact that it links the personal and the political, and the private and the public, in leaders' personae, and in the impact this has on the (re)drawing of the mutable and permeable boundaries between these spheres in journalistic conventions, public discourse and the political process more generally. Moreover, by personalising the political, the politicisation of private persona also provides potential benefits, as it offers alternative forms of connection between leaders and citizens, which can, potentially, help citizens to re-engage with their representatives and the democratic process, including its more 'rational' dimensions.

The empirical evidence

As a whole, the book has explored three central questions: to what extent is politics nowadays more personalised than in the past, what is distinctive about contemporary forms of personalisation, and how enduring are these changes? The combined evidence reveals a complex picture, which challenges both those who see personalisation as a pervasive and escalating phenomenon, a forgone conclusion, and those who can see almost no change at all, because of the existence of historical precedents and the lack of clear linear trends.

With regard to presidentialisation, the review of the evidence (Chapter 1) revealed a strengthening of the autonomy and power resources of the prime minister within the party and the executive. However, it is also clear that even though the process of presidentialisation can bolster their authority, no prime minister is unconditionally powerful. They are still constrained by other actors within and outside the executive, as well as at the sub-national and – increasingly – supranational level. Moreover, the capacity to exercise their authority is still dependent on their skills and abilities, which vary from leader to leader, and on their, inevitably fluctuating, degree of popularity (Heffernan, 2003). If, or rather when, it decreases, the leader becomes weaker within the party, affecting also his or her standing within the executive and his or her command of the legislature. This has, to an extent, always been the case but it is now more acute because of the shift to professional-electoral parties, the permanent campaign and, crucially, the inflated personalised accountability vested in leaders.

The conclusions are less clear-cut for the electoral face of presidentialisation. On the one hand, it is now accepted that leaders have an important influence on electoral choices, both directly and indirectly, even though independent effects rarely determine the overall winners of elections. On the other hand, as for other dimensions of personalisation, the evidence concerning increase over time is more ambiguous, with several studies showing mixed or negative results. At the same time, however, there are indications of change in indirect effects because the assessment of leaders has become increasingly entangled with the evaluation of issue competence, policy proposals and party image. Moreover, regardless of what research shows, the belief that leaders have an increasing potential to sway votes and are crucial for the party's electoral success, has affected who they select as leaders, how they campaign and how much freedom of manoeuvre they afford them, both during elections and, crucially, in government.

The evidence, perhaps most unexpectedly, was also inconclusive for the media dimension of the electoral face. Although leaders are clearly predominant in both press and broadcasting coverage of campaigns, for the more stringent – but essential – test of presidentialisation (i.e. systematic increase over time) the data is not clear-cut. Overall, there are some indications of an increase in the relative visibility of the leaders vis-à-vis the parties and their spokespersons but, especially relative to party colleagues, it less clear and systematic than conventional wisdom suggests. Earlier surges as well as variations associated with the particularities of the campaign are at least as remarkable as the overall upward trend.

These conclusions are reinforced by the analysis of the role of the prime ministers in everyday coverage, from Attlee to Brown, presented in Chapter 3. The analysis indicates an overall upward trend in the prime ministers' salience, particularly in their absolute visibility. Although this growth is to a large extent a consequence of an increase in pagination, rather than of presidentialisation, it must still be taken into account because it has expanded the presence of the prime ministers in public discourse. Moreover, leaders are nowadays also appearing outside the political sections of the newspapers, hence contributing to the sense of their ubiquity. In addition, and perhaps most telling, there has been a very clear growth in the power the media ascribe to the prime ministers: increasingly premiers not only lead but also, in the eyes of the press, personify and 'own' government.

However, as for campaign coverage, most indicators do not show the consistent and sizeable growth that the insistent talk about the presidentialisation of British politics has led us to expect. Firstly, leaders have been predominant in the day-to-day coverage for the entire period under study and, if one had to identify a single defining period, it would not be the 1980s or 1990s but the 1960s. Secondly, although noteworthy in absolute terms, the growth in leaders' visibility over time has not been as substantial as expected. Thirdly, the trends show a good degree of fluctuation, indicating that regardless of the impact of structural changes, the degree of personalisation still varies according to the style of each prime minister and the political context. Finally, although the prominence of leaders vis-à-vis their parties has also increased, there is no doubt that the latter still play a crucial role in British politics and, thus, in media coverage.

In contrast, there is a clear shift over time, and especially since the 1990s, in relation to personality politics, and specifically in regard to the politicisation of private persona. This is revealed by evidence of the combination of two changes. Firstly, the media's appraisal of character has taken a personal turn. Until fairly recently, it was essentially restricted to qualities and skills directly associated with the fitness to govern. Nowadays, however, it also includes emotional, temperamental and psychological dimensions, which, as noted in Chapter 3, denotes a shift towards the private sphere, the inner self and the leader as 'human being'. Secondly, there has been an increase in the references to the personal lives of the prime ministers, a trend which started during Wilson's era (although it remained generally low until Major), peaked with Blair and, although it decreased during Brown's years, did not go back to previous levels.

The changes between Blair and his predecessors go beyond the quantitative increase, as demonstrated by the analysis of the coverage of his youngest son, Leo, and of his fiftieth birthday (Chapter 5). On the one hand, a seemingly remarkable event (i.e. having a child while in office) became, due to its enduring persistence in public discourse, part of the routine coverage of the prime minister. Leo's journalistic appeal continued after the novelty periods of the pregnancy and birth; it mutated into a versatile narrative resource, used by journalists when writing about a surprisingly wide range of topics, both within and outside political coverage and linked to Blair in his role both as prime minister, and 'ordinary' and celebrity father. What is of most significance about this routinisation process is that it subtly blurs the boundaries between what is perceived to be of a personal or political nature, and what is considered to belong to the public and private spheres, naturalising the role of personal life in public discourse.

On the other hand, and not by chance, such an ordinary event as the prime minister's fiftieth birthday came to be regarded as extraordinary. Blair's birthday was considered worthy not only of a remarkable amount of coverage but also of coverage that denoted a great sense of excitement and anticipation and of personal and political significance. This might appear to be a typical press reaction for an event of this kind. However, as shown by the coverage of Major's birthday a few years earlier, turning fifty in No. 10 is not inherently newsworthy. What this difference reveals is that the degree of interest in, and the nature of the representation of, personal events in the mediated realm are not a given but the outcome of a complex and self-reinforcing set of dynamics. In other words, Blair's birthday was not 'born' but constructed, by his communication team and the media's routinised interest in the personal, into a 'natural' and all-but-inescapable object of media attention.

The changes in the role of the personal in public discourse during the Blair era are important. However, the emphasis on the politicisation of private persona should not be interpreted as arguing that the phenomenon has provoked a radical transformation in the characteristics of political discourse. The phenomenon is not entirely new, nor does it have a linear trajectory or systematically replace other elements of political coverage such as the discussion of issues and policies or strategy and process. Moreover, it is not present on a vast scale. In fact, the expansion of the role of the personal is taking place neither through an avalanche of celebrity-like stories about prime ministers nor by a straight displacement of the 'truly' political, but due to its inconspicuous and routine incorporation in public discourse.

This is clear from the evidence. In spite of the high overall visibility of leaders in the coverage, references to their personal lives and associated personal qualities are not as prominent as often imagined. Even in the case of Tony Blair, who is regarded as a paradigmatic case of the politicisation of private persona and who was indeed found to be the peak of this trend so far, only nine per cent of the articles (in tabloids and broadsheets) made references to these issues. This figure, although certainly noteworthy, is not large enough to claim that the personal has taken over the political. Moreover, two other crucial findings reinforce this interpretation. Firstly, Blair's personal life played a minor role in the content and narrative of 84 per cent of the pieces where it was mentioned. Secondly, a significant number (more than 40 per cent) of the personal references were found in articles that had their focus on non-political – at least narrowly defined – subjects, which indicates that references to Blair's personal life have extended and diversified his presence in the public realm. Moreover, given that Blair has been so far the peak of the trend, this data might not be taken as evidence of a structural escalation of the phenomenon, and hence one with long-term implications, but as an indication of Blair's exceptionalism.

Shall we then simply conclude that the politicisation of private persona is a minor and rather insignificant phenomenon, perhaps remarkable only in relation to the 'king of spin'? Surely not. The fact that it is not quantitatively massive does not mean it is insignificant. The fact that there are historical precedents does not mean that the phenomenon cannot be in many ways new. The fact that personalities of leaders and the political circumstances do clearly make a difference does not mean that changes are merely contingent. In fact, the combined evidence reveals the importance and enduring character of the politicisation of private persona. Moreover, it underscores the importance of analysing the phenomenon in historical context and in association with the other dimensions of personalisation, as well as the need to regard it as a complex, and for most part subtle, process.

Firstly, as we have seen, this dimension of personalisation is distinctively contemporary. In the past not only was the personal rarely mentioned but, when referring to it, the press used a detached and deferential tone, reporting only on the limited aspects of the prime minister's personal life that he or she *chose* to reveal (Chapter 4). No search for revelations, inner lives and feelings, or the 'authentic' selves of politicians. Over time, the press started to incorporate some colourful, and occasionally 'revealing', details about the leaders' personal lives in political reporting. But these were still rare, as until the 1990s journalistic culture (especially in broadcasting) was largely deferential, and the interest in celebrities and the urge to expose the 'real' self of the famous nowhere near today's. Moreover, nowadays the media market is more competitive than ever, and the boundaries between news and entertainment increasingly blurred. Contemporary media are also more deeply entwined and imitative. As a result, even the most minor 'revelations' published in small outlets often end up appearing, because of media's self-referentiality, 'everywhere'. This is not to say that the personal has become the most predominant element in the coverage of politics. But it is to say that it appears pervasive because it has permeated into most facets of public discourse.

Secondly, although Blair was in some ways exceptional, when he left office the role of the personal did not go back to the previous levels because 'normal' had changed (Chapter 6). In fact, the presence of the personal actually increased for Cameron compared to Blair. Moreover, although there was a decrease in the case of Brown, the levels of personal coverage were substantially higher for him than for the equally reluctant Heath and, more telling, than for Major, who was more prepared to 'go personal' than Brown ever was.

Thirdly, the politician as human being, and how this is performed, has become increasingly incorporated into the media's assessment of leadership and even government performance. By and large, this evaluation is still dominated by downright political factors; but, distinctively to our era, assessments of the leader *qua* human being now often play an important role in the interpretative narratives of leaders' rise and fall in popularity. Moreover, this is linked with the analysis of their political positions and values. Indeed, in the cases of Blair's and Cameron's election to the party leadership, the media used the personal not only to offer a portrayal of them as 'human beings' but also to infer their leadership qualities, scrutinise the validity of their reputation as modernisers, and to test the degree of personal conviction behind, and hence strength of, their policy proposals. In part, there was little novel about this: journalists have long used the personal to judge whether leaders are 'ordinary' or 'in touch' enough. But it went further because the personal was used to infer and test not only who they were but what they 'were about'. Similarly, but in a negative way, the critical assessments of Brown's 'human' side, his psychological and emotional traits and communicative style, became entwined with other, more political, factors in journalistic explanations of the leader's unpopularity and failure. In short, the public and the private, and personal and political qualities have become increasingly hard to distinguish.

The changes are not limited to media coverage but very much reflect on, and are influenced by, the transformations over time in how leaders use the personal for the construction of their public personae (Chapters 4 to

6). The use of the personal for strategic publicity is not a Blair invention nor, important as it is, a product of television. In some ways, it is as old as politics itself. But there have been critical changes in how this is carried out. Moreover, and as importantly, there is now a strong belief that, if they are to succeed, leaders need to let the public see their 'real selves'. This belief arises to some extent as a consequence of the conditions of mediation, which make it costly to 'conceal' and have convinced politicians and their advisers that a degree of personal revelation is almost unavoidable. But it is not only a protective strategy to try to manage media demands. Leaders are also responding, proactively, to the need to act as brand differentiators; to embody, in public and in private, in substance and in style, the party and its values; to authenticate its policies; and to create an opportunity for personal identification and emotional connection with voters, which requires of them to tread a difficult path, under the glaring lights of relentless mediated visibility, between appearing normal enough to be identified with, and extraordinary enough to lead.

As a result, whereas a few decades ago using selected snippets of their personal lives for strategic publicity was considered remarkable, this practice has become more common and encompassing over time. The differences are particularly evident when comparing Wilson, who undoubtedly marked a watershed in the use of the personal in British politics, and Blair (and by extension Cameron). Like other prime ministers before them, both Wilson and Blair strategically used selected details of their personal lives – and especially their families – to soften their personae, portray 'normality', and demonstrate affinity with the lives of 'ordinary' people. Both understood the positive potential of the figures and symbols of popular culture and used softer media genres for appearing 'off-role', reaching wider audiences and evading probing questions. Moreover, both were helped in this task by their exceptional skills as media performers.

However, for Blair, it was not just a question of 'image making' or media management but of overall branding. In fact, the personal was a constitutive dimension not only of his political identity but also of that of the 'new' party, as his persona was considered crucial to changing what it meant to be Labour. In other words, the medium was also the message and a way of authenticating and linking, through even the smallest of details, functional attributes (i.e. political values and policies) and the, often intangible but crucial, aesthetics and emotional elements of the New Labour brand.

Again, as in the case of the media coverage, there was something exceptional about Blair. His communicative style, media skills and personal life encouraged and enabled him to make intense use of the personal for the construction of his public persona. But even if exceptional, the causes and effects are in many ways enduring. For all the problems that the over-emphasis on 'spin' caused him and the party, Blair became a role model of the successful leader persona. Moreover, the use the personal came to be expected and its presence in public discourse routinised. In addition, and crucially, the role of the personal during Blair's era was related to socio-political, cultural, technological and media transformations, which created greater incentives, as well as pressures, to show the 'human' side of leaders. Because the political climate is in permanent flux, not all these conditions are wholly immutable; but nor are most of these transformations, which are predominantly structural, about to be undone. In particular, it is clear that the increasing impact of the internet in all facets of political communication presents even greater opportunities to exploit the personal, as well risks. It puts pressure on leaders to utilise the medium to develop millions of 'intimate' connections, selectively disclose the personal and to show, authentically, their 'real selves'. This is in part because of the characteristics of the medium which, as much as or more than television, is best suited for an emotionally open, conversational and confessional style; but also because, in combination with a range of new technologies, it has provoked an even more radical blurring of the boundaries between the front and the back stage. There are now not only millions of potential amateur 'journalists' able to expose, but also intense cross-media integration, as even radio and press interviews are now shown online with footage revealing the interviewee's interaction with those in the studio, his or her body language, style of dress and so on. Furthermore, the availability of massive quantities of material, which is perennially accessible at the click of a mouse, increases self-referentially across media.

This is not to say that every leader will now use the personal to the same extent or in the same way. The degree and style of politicians' use of the personal, and how the media cover it, is a result of the interaction between structural conditions (and how these have gradually changed over time) and short-term factors. This was evident in the comparison between how Brown and Cameron dealt with the personal (Chapter 6). Cameron, as opposition leader, followed in Blair's footsteps, and in some ways has taken 'going personal' even further, including extensively using the internet to self-generate mediated intimacy. In fact, webcameron is a telling example of the blurring of the boundaries between private and public, the personal and political, and style and substance. Most of the clips were heavy on political material, albeit not on policy detail. But many of the clips also offered a combination of the personal and the political, in content as well as in style, because of the DIY fliming, the informal language and the locations where they were shot, including the leader's house. Moreover, the very existence of webcameron was devised to demonstrate that the new young leader was in touch with new technologies, and thus with all its associated meanings.

In other words, what is communicated and how it is communicated cannot be neatly separated; nor can the public and private, or the personal and the political. All elements have to reinforce each other in a consistent and credible way, and have the right resonance, both rationally and emotionally.

Brown was a different kettle of fish. Because of personality, (in)abilities and political circumstances he was clearly less inclined to draw on the personal for the construction of his public persona. His use of the personal for strategic publicity was hence more uncommon than in the cases of Blair and Cameron. It was also more problematic because of his reluctance to reveal, the failure to dovetail the personal with the political, the concealment of his feelings and his reliance on public discourse on even the more personal occasions. Nonetheless, the fact that, despite his lack of enthusiasm and obvious inability, Brown still felt the need to 'go personal' demonstrates how the routine politicisation of private persona, and the factors that encourage it, condition the construction of a leader's public persona, regardless of his or her personality. The degree will vary across leaders because of the impact of idiosyncratic elements, including the individual characteristics of the main leaders, their degree of popularity and the political context, which unsurprisingly often vary from election to election. Moreover, the leadership style 'in fashion' is subject to a degree of short-term volatility. But leaders' choices are greatly shaped by the conditions of mediation, the need to personally embody the party, its values and policies, and especially by the fact that to be perceived as emotionally open, 'normal' and likeable have come to be considered key attributes, and often pre-conditions, of successful leaders' personae. In the words of Brown's personal pollster:

> Is it possible to be a successful politician nowadays without attracting some level of public warmth? My judgement would be that is not [...] voters want more from their politicians. No longer content for them to be the remote and one-dimensional figure that Mrs Thatcher typified back in the 1980s, voters now demand to see politicians in the round: to know about their backgrounds, their families, their hobbies, their homes – to get to know them as people. (Mattinson, 2010: 263 and 287)

This does not mean that these are the predominant criteria used by citizens when making decisions at the ballot box. Pollsters are fully aware that strength and experience, as well as policies and party images, remain crucial. Moreover, academic research has shown that the evaluation of leaders is only one among multiple influences on electoral behaviour (Denver, 2003; King, 2002c; McAllister, 2007; Mughan, 2000; Ohr and Oscarsson, 2010). Furthermore, within this, the perception of their personal lives and qualities appear to have only a marginal influence, compared to political leadership qualities (Bean, 1993; Bean and Mughan, 1989; Jones and Hudson, 1996;

Just et al., 1996; Miller et al., 1986; Ohr and Oscarsson, 2010). It is true that these kinds of studies are likely to underestimate the impact of the personal. Citizens' evaluations of leaders are a complex process, in which different kind of attributes, and the rational and the emotional, are not neatly separated; instead, the perceptions of the personal qualities of the leaders are interlinked with the assessment of their leadership qualities, policies and the images of the parties (Just et al., 1996). Moreover, some research has shown that the effects are stronger if personal information is more prevalent, and especially if it is negative (Bucy, 2000; Miller et al., 1986; Ohr and Oscarsson, 2010; but see Bean, 1993). But even with these caveats, the fact is that academic research has found no conclusive evidence that a reserved, aloof or unlikeable leader cannot be elected.

Yet, this is in many ways irrelevant because the strongest impact of the politicisation of private persona is not on citizens but on journalists and on politicians and their advisers, affecting whom parties choose as leaders and how their personae are constructed. It is of course not the only consideration; but being unable to appear 'human' and successfully politicise the personal have come to be regarded as a clear liability for a British leader in the twenty-first century. And in many ways, regardless of what we know about electoral behaviour, it is the case. Even if at times they might be able to get away with it, it is harder to develop any positive leadership attributes or successfully promote policies when the medium, i.e. the leader, is on the one hand both predominant and increasingly presented as embodying the party and 'owning' government and policies, and on the other is such an easy target for criticism.

The implications for democratic politics

The implications of the politicisation of private persona for democratic politics are important and deserve thorough consideration. As a matter of fact, my interest in this subject sprung precisely from the normative debates associated with the phenomenon: firstly, from the dissatisfaction with the discussions of normative issues that often lack definitional clarity and a solid empirical basis; and, secondly, with a reluctance to accept rigid distinctions between 'proper' and 'improper' political discourse, and hence to agree, unquestioningly, that the inclusion of the personal must be damaging for democracy. This is both a restricted and restricting view of politics. Although these assumptions are now more often challenged, there is still not enough recognition in political communication that the personal, as well as the aesthetic and the emotional, are legitimate dimensions of politics, which can play a positive role.

At the same time, over the course of this research it became increasingly clear that this can only be a starting point. Firstly, the problems of representative democracy are obviously too profound and multifaceted to imagine that trust and engagement would be automatically restored, if only politicians could be more expressive, authentic and 'human'. Secondly, challenging narrow definitions of 'proper' political discourse, and hence citizenship, is important but is only the first step. The fact that it is not intrinsically negative does not mean that, in practice, the politicisation of private persona cannot have detrimental implications. Rigid notions of what political discourse should be are problematic, but so is a position that in challenging this assumption gives way to an unquestioned embracing of the inclusion of the personal. Instead, it is necessary to recognise that although in some ways the politicisation of private persona is harmless and even potentially positive, in other ways it is normatively worrying. This is not because of its trivial nature, but precisely because of the very political implications of the phenomenon.

Firstly, the empirical findings demonstrate that some of the concerns are overstated. The personal has not become such a predominant feature of the coverage of politics, even if it is on the increase and more entangled with the selection and assessment of leaders. This, as demonstrated in the case of Blair (Chapter 5), is the case not only for broadsheets but also for tabloids. Moreover, the inclusion of the personal does not lead to a systematic replacement of the politician with the human being. Instead, the personal has diversified the presence of leaders in the public realm, pushing them outside the narrow confines of the political pages. In some ways this makes them more like celebrities, potentially trivialising the content of political discourse. But with the ongoing transformations in the understanding of what constitutes the political and the increasing importance of more individualised and less institutional forms of citizens' engagement with politics (including as consumers), it is ever more difficult to insist on rigid boundaries between the personal and the political, or to assert that a leader's experiences, conduct and choices in the private sphere can be summarily rejected as apolitical or trivial. In this regard, although in some cases the discussion of the personal is plainly superfluous, it can and does also help to generate engaging narratives for the debate of issues such as paternity leave or green lifestyle choices, and link 'high' politics with the politics of everyday life. Although this is less common than those who advocate the potential of the phenomenon might hope, it is still a positive development.

Secondly, the emphasis on the personal can contribute to providing an alternative platform of connection between citizens and the 'humanised' politicians; one that deals better with our ambivalence towards leaders, that is more firmly grounded in the emotional dimensions of politics, that invites the shortening of distance and unnecessary deference, and that might attract and engage people who are not that interested in formal politics. In short, it may help citizens to feel that, even if not like them, leaders are at least living on the same planet and sharing the same discursive universe (see Coleman, 2003: 754–7). It is for these reasons that advocating the superiority of 'purely public' discourse (impersonal, emotionless, exclusively focused on facts and policy) is misguided. In fact, the spheres of the public and the private need to be 'confused' because rigid barriers make politics an exclusive sport, an insider's activity practised by alien creatures from a world that seems to have nothing in common with people's everyday lives and experiences. Furthermore, a more personalised connection does not need to undermine 'good' judgement because the affective dimension of politics not only encourages mobilisation but can facilitate, as opposed to inhibiting, rationality and deliberation (Brennan and Hamlin, 2000; Marcus, 2002; Marcus et al., 2000).

But there are also reasons for concern. Although in principle the politicisation of private persona can make a positive contribution to engagement and mobilisation, the practice is more complex. In fact, there are reasons to argue that the greater the politicisation of leaders' private personae, the greater the chances for citizens to feel that leaders are falling short. At the end of the continuum, the chances of scandal are heightened, as a result in part of the technological capability of the media to expose, but also because of the sense of the 'self-evident' importance of leaders' personal behaviour. But even if leaders manage to remain scandal-free, there is a significant risk of disillusionment.

On the one hand, the more refusing to reveal becomes regarded as a leadership liability, the more leaders such as Brown will feel the need to, reluctantly, reveal the 'inner self'. This encourages scripted and forced 'authenticity', which citizens unsurprisingly find off-putting. On the other hand, it is a difficult undertaking even for those who are comfortable with mediated intimacy. The positive potential of the emphasis on the 'human' dimensions of the political persona relates to the personal nature of what is emphasised, but also to emotional reflexivity and authenticity. This requires leaders to be prepared to acknowledge vulnerability, to own up to (inevitable) errors, to appear unscripted, and to maintain a high level of consistency between staged and unstaged and on and off role performances. This is possible to achieve for some leaders, some of the time, but the strength quickly becomes a weakness. Politics requires compromise, which can be easily perceived as personal dishonesty. Moreover, the longer leaders are in power, the less 'normal' and 'sincere' they (appear to) become. This is in part a result of the exceptional nature of the role they perform and of relentless mediated visibility; but also, crucially, because of the 'split personality' of journalists. The media encourages this process through the routine emphasis on the personal while, at the same time, in a culture of (celebrity) revelation and remarkable adversarialism, constantly highlighting politicians' spurious motives for their 'humanness' and searching for inconsistency and damaging revelations. Moreover, citizens themselves are increasingly cynical: 'As a rule, politicians' motives are presumed insincere ... his car is chosen for "its image", he does charity work or even attends a football match purely to make a vote-winning point' (Mattinson, 2010: 250). The combination of unremitting mediated visibility and a high degree of negativity is not exactly promising. In fact, it is reasonable to fear that the pursuit of appearing more 'human', 'real' or 'authentic' might result in a poorer perception of leaders' personae, in both the extraordinary and ordinary components needed to nourish leadership, and lead to further disenchantment and mistrust between citizens and politicians.

There are other reasons for concern, which have to do not with engagement and mobilisation but with the accountability of those in power. One can identify or not with someone's lifestyle and personal experiences, empathise or not with their feelings, and agree or disagree with their motivations, but leaders cannot be held accountable for these in the same terms as for their political choices and actions. It is all a matter of degree, but *if* the personal became a *predominant* subject in the discussion of politics and a central dimension of leadership assessment it could make it easier to bypass the examination of hard facts, as the emphasis shifts from the validity of arguments and the judgement of outcomes to questions of personal sincerity (Hart, 1998; Runciman, 2008; Sennett, 1977). As we saw in the case of Cameron's rise to leadership, there are signs that the credibility of political values and policy proposals are being read off from the personal motivations and feelings of the leaders. There might be a relationship between the two, but Cameron's deep-felt emotions about his late disabled son cannot substitute for the analysis of his proposals for reform of the NHS, and their very material implications. Similarly, in the debate about the invasion of Iraq, Blair's personal sincerity (or lack thereof) about his motivations and the emotional difficulties of the decision acquired at times an independent value in the analysis of the political act (see Runciman, 2006b).

The emphasis on the personal and the experiential can also encourage the framing of societal problems as matters of primarily individual, and in many ways consumer-like, choices. Moreover, it suggests that a leader's role and responsibilities are equivalent to those of ordinary citizens (e.g. 'hard-felt' quasi-paternal pain about a soldier's death or the 'moral' duty of home recycling) even though the power to provoke change is patently unequal. As a result, there is a risk of a de-politicisation of the solutions to what are structural problems of collective importance that require government action.

To be clear: the inclusion of the personal does not necessarily entail de-politicisation; it contains the potential for both politicisation and de-politicisation. It politicises, in a narrow sense, because the personal is used in the construction of personae, the presentation of policy and in the assessment of leadership. It also politicises because, as discussed above, it can contribute to bringing some issues into the sphere of public debate. But as Hay points out, there are different arenas where the political takes place, and hence levels of politicisation. Expanding restrictive definitions of the political is important but 'whether or not a particular issue or set of concerns has been incorporated into the formal political process is phenomenally significant in its own terms' (2008: 65). If an issue is presented essentially as a matter of individual choice and personal duty then this is to an extent de-politicising because it displaces responsibility away from the formal political realm. This is why the politicisation of private persona is to an important extent different from the feminist conception of the 'personal is political'. The feminist version was about including previously excluded issues into the sphere of government action; in contrast, placing the emphasis on leaders' personal behaviour might invert the relationship. Of course, the downgrading of the role of the state and government is a result of much broader ideological shifts, associated with neo-liberalism. Nonetheless, personalised discourse can play a subtle role in masking the ideological roots and political implications of looking at societal problems through the eyes of the individual.

Finally, the politicisation of private persona also raises issues about the recruitment and selection of leaders. Because of understandable concerns about invasion of privacy and the need for a 'suitable' past, the greater focus on the personal might also discourage many capable individuals from running for public office. Moreover, even though research shows that 'soft' personal qualities have a limited impact on voters' choices, the more the media emphasises the personal in their evaluation of leaders, the more difficult it is to succeed for those who, because of their past, personal choice or inability, are uncomfortable with 'going personal'. This need not lead to the selection of incompetent leaders, because the ability to reveal, 'sincerely' and attractively, their private selves is not incompatible with possessing 'hard' leadership qualities. Moreover, we know that generally citizens expect a leader to combine both types of qualities. But the emphasis on the inner lives of politicians makes it, nonetheless, harder (and perhaps too hard) to succeed for those who are reluctant or unable to reveal.

In practice, the degree of difficulty has to do in part with the features of their personal lives, character and communicative style, and even primary physical characteristics (Corner, 2000: 394). But questions also need to be asked about whether the politicisation of private persona could engender a systematic bias against groups that might find it inherently more difficult to adapt to this requirement of contemporary leadership. There is, clearly, a gender dimension. Family life, sports and personal appearance are all minefields for women; and so is, paradoxically, the expression of emotions, which are valued in men as a revelation of their 'softer' side but are often interpreted as weakness or even as lack of control in women (see Hall Jamieson, 1988; van Zoonen, 2000). Arguably, and again paradoxically, there might also be class dimensions. Although humble roots are an obvious useful resource for conveying 'ordinariness', the assessment of a politician's lifestyle, personal appearance and communicative style (such as accent and body language) are likely to be filtered by white urban middle class codes prevalent in journalism. Similarly, emotional expressiveness and open pride in hands-on parenthood, characteristics associated with the figure of the 'new man', are partially a result of generational change; but this is also, essentially, a white middle-class construct (Gill, 2003; Hondagneu-Sotelo and Messner, 1994; Westwood, 1996). Of course, it is not to say that any of these groups had an easy path to leadership in the past; but to emphasise that transformations that might appear as an opportunity to make representation more representative might, in practice, not be so.

In short, nowadays the personal sphere of politicians plays an important role in public discourse, although not one as pervasive as is often imagined. Moreover, in principle, this inclusion should be normatively welcomed. But politics do not take place in a laboratory, where one can add, under controlled conditions, a beneficial element to the 'mix'. Instead, in practice, because of how it is mediated and strategically performed, the politicisation of private persona is likely – at best – to only sporadically and fleetingly contribute to restore the relationship between citizens and representatives. At the same time, it also raises a set of other troubling questions about accountability, de-politicisation and the recruitment of elites. As a result, although not intrinsically detrimental and in some regards potentially beneficial, the politicisation of private persona requires our attention because the way it influences politics is, even if partly ambiguous, normatively unsettling.

Looking ahead: new realities and future research

The 2010 General Election appears to have been another archetypal example of personalisation. Cameron was not only the face and, with his close allies, the brain of the campaign but also framed the election as a choice between 'Cameron and the Conservatives and five more years of Gordon Brown' (www.conservatives.com). Moreover, despite Labour's attempts, the 2010 campaign demonstrated that is now harder than ever to 'hide' an unpopular leader behind 'the team'. Furthermore, of course, the campaign was dominated by the TV leaders' debates, a first in the UK. Early empirical evidence (Scammell and Beckett, 2010) suggests that this might have been the most leader-focused campaign ever, which would chime with findings of the effects of debates on the nature of coverage elsewhere (Reinemann and Wilke, 2007). Whether these effects will last, or will be just another transient peak, remains to be seen. However, although the debates do not appear to have made a strong impact on electoral behaviour, they certainly changed the nature of the campaign and will be a factor in how parties elect future leaders.

The campaign was not only leader-centred but moreover the personal seemed to have played a striking role: the strong presence of the leaders' wives, the 'style-watches', the emphasis on upbringing and class, the references to their parents and children in the debates, and so on. Moreover, signs of routinisation were present as in, for instance, a BBC studio discussion of party proposals for constitutional reform, with background footage that included Brown with his wife and a Cameron family snapshot. Furthermore, as in the case of Blair's birthday (Chapter 5), the campaign offered powerful examples of the impact of recycling across media as well as the imitative effect. For example, there was substantial cross-coverage of Brown's 'teary' interview with Piers Morgan. Media 'recycling' greatly spread the interest in, and the prevalence in the public realm of, what was originally said in the programme, starting even before it was broadcast. Moreover, Cameron responded by doing his own version, or rather two, with an 'intimate' interview for STV broadcast the following day in Scotland and a 'special' with Trevor MacDonald. Nick Clegg also 'obliged', appearing with his (much more reluctant) wife at the family home in a special profile with Mary Nightingale, discussing his earlier comment in GQ magazine that he slept with 'no more than 30' women before his marriage, how they met while they were studying in Belgium, and how it was 'love at first sight'.

But we have learnt that if one is not to overestimate the significance of striking instances of interest in the personal they need to be investigated in the context of the overall coverage, as well as during the routine of day-to-day politics (i.e. outside campaigning periods). High-profile examples do not equal pervasiveness. On the other hand, this research has shown that in order not to underestimate the importance of the phenomenon one must also pay attention to the more subtle details, and explore the minor and seemingly banal mentions of leaders' personal lives as well as the intimacy cues 'hidden' in the rhetoric, narrative and form of the texts. This is crucial because, as we have seen, they greatly contribute to the sense of pervasiveness, newsworthiness and significance of the personal, but they are generally not captured in quantitative studies.

It therefore follows that it is important in future research to expand and complement the approach used in this book. The focus here has been on newspapers, and hence on print media and news and current affairs. This was a deliberate choice to enable the provision of much-needed systematic evidence over time. But it has resulted in the exclusion of other media, especially television and the internet, as well as other genres such as gossip magazines and talk shows, which could be considered in principle as more fertile grounds for the politicisation of private persona. The overall magnitude and characteristics of the phenomenon are unlikely to differ greatly, or at least not within news and current affairs. But the knowledge of how the phenomenon adapts to the technological requirements, professional conventions and routines, and discursive characteristics of different media and genres is fundamental for achieving an in-depth understanding of the process of the politicisation of private persona. Moreover, 'soft' and public affairs genres need to be explored in combination to enable us to understand the process of cross-fertilisation across outlets, which is a key reason why there is such a *sense* of pervasiveness of the personal, which is not confirmed quantitatively.

But if the 2010 election was special, the outcome was even more so. At the time of writing, British politics seems to be going through a seismic shift. New Labour is out of power and has been replaced by the first peace-time coalition government since 1931. This potentially has radical implications for all dimensions of personalisation, and especially for presidentialisation. Although all indicators suggested that Cameron would be a prime minister in the Blair mould, the coalition has made this more problematic. In fact, given that there are two parties in government one might expect a potential reversal in presidentialisation trends. The coalition will create more pressure for collegiality within the executive, because if the government is to survive, Liberal Democrat ministers need to be consulted and incorporated in the decision-making process (Blick and Jones, 2010). Moreover, under the coalition some of the prime ministerial prerogatives have been curtailed: Cameron cannot hire and fire ministers unilaterally nor, if the fixed-term Parliament Bill is passed, call an election. The presence of a coalition is also likely to demand more consultation within the parties, in the hope that decisions that are a result of inter-party bargaining do not cause revolt among MPs, who will feel less attached to the government's fortunes than would normally be the case, especially among Lib-Dems. Moreover, media coverage is likely to be less leader-centred, not only because of the dual (albeit unequal) leadership, but also because of the always newsworthy attraction of potential cabinet and party conflict.

This is not to say, however, that there will simply be a return to 'normal' forms of cabinet government. Although common in other European countries, coalition governments have not been the norm in the UK and so this cannot be interpreted simply as the 'elastic band' snapping back. Moreover, even though the changed conditions invite more inclusiveness and collegiality, not all of the trends associated with presidentialisation will magically disappear. Even if more dormant, the expectations of authoritative, centralised and public leadership will remain (Heffernan, 2010). Moreover, the cabinet as a whole might play a stronger public role but is unlikely to set the agenda or make, rather than rubber-stamp, critical policies. In fact, the tendency to make key decisions in bilaterals and 'kitchen cabinets' will probably continue, although now in a more bipartisan fashion, with 'inner cabinets' of top figures from both parties (including the formalised coalition committee) and frequent bilaterals between Cameron and Clegg. Furthermore, it is to be expected that Cameron will, as his predecessors, take advantage of the strengthened resources of No. 10 and continue to rely on special and other external advisers.

The relationship with parliament and the party will also be affected; but it will not necessarily weaken the prime minister. With regard to the former, even if the rate of rebellion grows (and there is evidence that it already has; see Cowley and Stuart, 2010 in Pack, 2010), dominance might in fact be stronger than usual as the coalition has a majority of 37 seats, which limits the blackmail potential of backbench MPs in both parties (Dunleavy, 2010). The control of the party, and especially of those on the Right, could appear now to be more difficult. However, the presence of the Lib-Dems might in fact make it easier to sideline defiant voices within the party. Moreover, in opposition, Cameron was successful at controlling the party from the top, and this might continue. As Heffernan highlights, Cameron often used 'going public' strategies, looking for the direct support of the grassroots and the electorate at large, while at the same time asserting a strong person-alised control over the party, including the incorporation of A-lists, ruthless reprimanding of off-message MPs, and the personalised management of the expenses scandal (Heffernan, 2010). Moreover, he made a public virtue of his 'toughness', emphasising it as an indicator of a reformed party and his abilities as leader (although was in practice greatly helped by the calming effect on party dissent of a long spell in opposition). The dominance of the leadership continued during the formation of the coalition when, unlike Clegg, Cameron did not consult with the party at large.

The electoral face is harder to call, in part because it is not known whether the coalition will last 5 years. But it is not just that. It is also unclear whether, as has become increasingly common, the prime minister will be made personally accountable for the successes and failures of the government or whether, as a result of the coalition, praise and blame will be more widely distributed. If unity starts to falter, will the prime minister manage to present himself as above partisan adversarialism, profitably using 'going public' strategies (e.g. Cameron direct) to build new alliances and personal electoral support, against the disruptive forces of 'old politics'? Or will his authority depend mostly on how successful and united the government as a whole is perceived to be? With regard to media coverage, the coalition has countervailing effects. On the one hand, the prime minister's mediated visibility relative to colleagues and parties is likely to decrease, as a result of the semi-dual leadership, the greater potential for intra- and inter- party conflict, and the incentives to emphasise cabinet collective responsibility. On the other hand, the media's tendency to focus on leaders, reinforced by the prime minister's need to have a personalised communication strategy and his dominant role on national and international stages, will continue to make him – and to a lesser extent Nick Clegg – a predominant figure, magnifying his role in government. In fact, at least in its early days, the success of the coalition was reported as not so much the result of political agreement but of the personal relationship (and even chemistry) between the two leaders.

In short, it is difficult to predict how presidentialisation trends will evolve under a coalition government, both because of novelty and because these trends are always to an extent contingent on the context, and the government's and the leader's performances. However, one thing is clear. If before presidentialisation trends led to 'an emergent hybrid' that fused some dimensions of presidential politics with forms of parliamentary democracy and cabinet government (Foley, 2000: 351), now the distinctiveness of the hybrid is bound to be even starker. Coalition government makes the UK system even less strictly comparable to the US, but without necessarily reducing the centrality of leader(s), the resources of the prime minister, or his attempts to obtain personalised support and to bypass troublesome factions in the party. At the same time, as usual, the prime minister's authority and power will be conditioned by his skills, popularity and standing in the party (Heffernan, 2005a); but now, distinctively, also by another party leader's fortunes and ability to control his MPs.

In addition to the coalition, there are other elements of the current political climate that raise questions about the enduring nature of the trends uncovered in this research. In this case, however, they relate not so much to presidentialisation as to the politicisation of private persona. The UK is moving from an era of affluence and 'sunshine' politics, where parties and leaders fought each other to see who could appear 'softer' and 'nicer', to an 'era of austerity'. In the current climate, Cameron appears at times to be less like the early Blair and more like Thatcher, emphasising toughness over likability and kindness, although with more stress on pragmatism than ideology. This raises the question of to what extent the politicisation of private persona might be associated only with affluent times. The fact is that the emphasis on the personal, and its entanglement with leadership assessment, will not simply stop, because as we have seen it is a result of structural socio-political, cultural and technological developments and has become normalised in public discourse. Moreover, it is still important for leaders to appear in-touch and authentic, and to try to benefit from the advantages of off-role situations and soft genres. Nonetheless, in times of crisis and austerity, there might be weaker incentives for leaders to use the personal for strategic publicity, relying more instead on traditional political qualities and their portrayal as strong leaders. This should not be surprising. Both dimensions of leadership are important but the emphasis varies according to not only the leader and the context but the broader political climate, as well as by structural and cultural variables.

For these reasons, there is an imperative need to develop more longitudinal studies and especially to strengthen the comparative dimension of research on personalisation, systematically investigating patterns over time and across countries. In relation to presidentialisation, this research agenda has been slowly developing in the last few years (e.g. Bennister, 2008; Helms, 2005; King, 2002c; Poguntke and Webb, 2005b). But comparative studies regarding personality politics and the politicisation of private persona have been much rarer (Campus, 2010; Krogstad and Storvik, 2006; Stanyer and Wring, 2004b). On the one hand, it is clear that there are important trends associated with the politicisation of private persona that have been manifested across cultures, making it possibly a 'global' phenomenon (Stanyer and Wring, 2004a: 5). This includes, inter alia, the weakening of ideology and rise in partisan dealignment, disenchantment with representative democracy, the increasing mediatisation of politics, the high competitiveness of media systems, the weakening of deference and the rise of celebrity culture. But how do these factors interact with endogenous conditions, and hence affect the nature of the phenomenon? In order to answer this question it is necessary to develop a comparative agenda with studies exploring similarities and differences in how the phenomenon has developed in different national cultures. Beyond the descriptive aspects, it is crucial to focus on investigating the effects of both cross-national trends and the endogenous cultural and systemic factors that affect the prevalence and nature of the phenomenon, following a similar path to the second generation of studies on 'Americanisation'. In other words, it is necessary to investigate which variables encourage and temper partial convergence in the role of the personal qualities and lives of leaders in public discourse, and how these have changed over time.

In this regard, there are the obvious structural differences that affect all dimensions of personalisation, including the political system, the party and electoral system, the media system and the legal provisions on privacy. Some of these differences have been tempered by broad trends affecting most Western democracies, but have not been overridden, and hence they do not influence all countries equally. For instance, the degree of commercialisation of the media system, and hence its impact on the extent and tone of political coverage compared to 'infotainment' and 'soft' genres, is a result of broad technological and political changes; but it is nonetheless tempered in national contexts by the presence of strong public service broadcasting. Conversely, the presence of a strong tabloid culture in mainstream media makes the emphasis on the personal more likely, and so does a highly developed magazine market. Equally, how much the personal is used for strategic publicity will be affected by the degree of development of political marketing but also by cultural understandings of the personal and the political and the importance of lifestyle politics, as well as the prevalence of therapeutic culture, which are both to a degree associated with affluence.

At the same time, the impact of transnational trends seems to be becoming more acute, leading to greater convergence. For instance, Kuhn concluded in 2004 that a combination of legal, media and socio-cultural factors have meant that in France 'the distinction between private and public has been well – some might argue too well – respected by journalists' and emphasised that there were still strikingly marked cross-cultural divergences in the ways in which the private lives of politicians were mediatised (Kuhn, 2004: 24). By 2007, however, although still highlighting the relevance of differences across countries, he emphasises that even in France 'what once was – or at least appeared to be – a clear frontier between the public and private spheres has become blurred and open to dispute' (Kuhn, 2007: 186). There also seems to be growing convergence in how the personae of leaders are constructed and assessed, with Barisione finding an increasing 'process of standardisation of political leadership in contemporary democracies' (2009b: 54) with the same prerequisites present across countries. Yet it is also clear that culture still matters, leading to national variations. For instance, whereas charisma in France is still associated with heroism and eroticism, in Norway the emphasis is on ordinariness, sobriety and conspicuous modesty (Krogstad and Storvik, 2006). There are also likely to be variations depending on gender and Left–Right orientations of leaders.

In short, the findings for the UK cannot be automatically extrapolated to other countries as they are in part a result of national characteristics. But there are other causes (e.g. impact of television and the internet, partisan dealignment) which are common to most Western democracies, hence suggesting that the phenomenon will increasingly be manifested beyond national borders. The degree and nature of the convergence will depend on a combination of transnational trends (common endogenous factors and a degree of 'global' imitation) and how these are filtered by systemic and cultural differences. Moreover, as we have seen, the role of individual leaders also has to be taken into account. In other countries as in the UK, some politicians will take more advantage of the opportunities of 'going personal' than others, tempering or strengthening structural trends. But, although to an extent idiosyncratic, potential enduring effects also have to be investigated, because exceptional leaders such as Blair can encourage imitation and help to normalise the role of the personal in public discourse.

The research agenda also needs to pay much greater attention to citizens. It is imperative to develop studies focused on pursuing a better understanding of how leaders' personae, and in particular the role of the personal, are assessed by the public. This is not so much about the impact of leaders (and different dimensions of their personae) on electoral behaviour, although more qualitative studies addressing this specific issue, especially outside the US, would be useful. Instead, it is about exploring to what extent, under which conditions and in which ways citizens consider the personal relevant; and how this is linked to our inherent ambivalence towards leaders, and the conflicting expectations of embodying both ordinariness and extraordinariness we place on them. Moreover, it is necessary to explore how evaluations of the personal relate to perceptions of politicians' degree of symbolic, and even descriptive, representation. Although the assumption is that, in tune with the evaluations of celebrities, citizens now value authenticity over resemblance, and sincerity or the 'real' over flawlessness, this has rarely been empirically tested for politicians (but see Coleman, 2003, 2006). This a crucial gap because the positive potential of a greater emphasis on the personal rests, at least partly, on citizens (and journalists and academia) embracing the idea of the 'good enough leader' (Corner, 2000: 399; Samuels, 2001: 77–84) and accepting, or at least tolerating, vulnerability and failure, as well as difference. However, we have scant understanding of to what extent, and under which conditions, this is the case.

Finally, more research is needed on discourses of privacy and the public interest. The boundaries between public and private are ill-defined, and have clearly been greatly affected by technological developments (Thompson, 2000). But they are also cultural constructs and there is currently much uncertainty about 'where the dividing line is or where it should be drawn' (Kuhn, 2007: 186). Therefore, how the boundaries between the public and private spheres of public figures (including but not restricted to politicians) are constructed in media discourses, on which grounds these are legitimised, and how they reflect and shape public understandings of what belongs to the 'public interest', is crucial if one is to understand one of the key processes that have led to the development of the politicisation of private persona. This kind of analysis would help us to reflect on how the distinction between public and private, and the personal and the political are (re)constructed in everyday discourse, subtly transforming key parameters: of what is regarded as routine components of 'proper' reporting, what politicians are (not) expected to reveal, and on which issues leaders are considered accountable. These processes might seem peripheral to the study of personalisation and to the debate about its implications for democratic politics. However, they are crucial because they seem to be changing not only the construction of leaders' personae and how politics is discussed and presented, but also, and not more or less than, the very definitions of public and private.

References

Aarts, K., A. Blais and H. Schmitt, eds. 2010. *Political Leaders and Democratic Elections*. Oxford: Oxford University Press.

Adam, S. and M. Maier. 2010. Personalization of Politics: A Critical Review and Agenda for Research. In *Communication Yearbook 34*, ed. C. Salmon. Oxford: Routledge.

Allan, S., K. Atkinson and M. Montgomery. 1995. Time and the Politics of Nostalgia. An Analysis of the Conservative Party Election Broadcast 'The Journey'. *Time & Society* 4 (3): 365–395.

Allen, G. 2003. *The Last Prime Minister. Being Honest About the UK Presidency*. London: Societas.

Bale, T. 2008. 'A Bit Less Bunny-Hugging and a Bit More Bunny-Boiling'? Qualifying Conservative Party Change under David Cameron. *British Politics* 3 (3): 270–299.

Barisione, M. 2009a. So, What Difference Do Leaders Make? Candidates' Images and the 'Conditionality' of Leader Effects on Voting. *Journal of Elections, Public Opinion & Parties* 19 (4): 473–500.

——. 2009b. Valence Image and the Standardisation of Democratic Political Leadership. *Leadership* 5 (1): 41–60.

Barker, R. 2001. *Legitimating Identities. The Self-Presentation of Rulers and Subjects*. Cambridge: Cambridge University Press.

Barnett, S. and I. Gaber. 2001. *Westminster Tales: The Twenty-first-century Crisis in British Political Journalism*. London: Continuum.

Bartle, J. and I. Crewe. 2002. The Impact of Party Leaders in Britain: Strong Assumptions, Weak Evidence. In *Leaders' Personalities and the Outcomes of Democratic Elections*, ed. A. King. Oxford: Oxford University Press.

Bartle, J. and D. Griffiths, eds. 2001. *Political Communications Transformed. From Morrison to Mandelson*. Basingstoke: Palgrave.

Bean, C. 1993. The Electoral Influence of Party Leader Images in Australia and New Zealand. *Comparative Political Studies* 26 (1): 111–132.

Bean, C. and A. Mughan. 1989. Leadership Effects in Parliamentary

Elections in Australia and Britain. *American Political Science Review* 83 (4): 1165–1179.

Becker, K. E. 1992. Photojournalism and the Tabloid Press. In *Journalism and Popular Culture*, ed. P. Dahlgren and C. Sparks. London: Sage.

Bennett, L. and R. Entman, eds. 2001. *Mediated Politics. Communication in the Future of Democracy.* Cambridge: Cambridge University Press.

Bennett, L. 1998. The UnCivic Culture: Communication, Identity, and the Rise of Lifestyle Politics. *PS: Political Science and Politics* 31 (4): 740–761.

Bennister, M. 2008. Blair and Howard: Predominant Prime Ministers Compared. *Parliamentary Affairs* 61 (2): 334–355.

Bevir, M. and R. A. W. Rhodes. 2006. Prime Ministers, Presidentialism and Westminster Smokescreens. *Political Studies* 54 (4): 671–690.

Blick, A. and G. Jones. 2010. *The Centre of Central Government.* LSE Public Policy Group Working Paper No. 3. London: Public Policy Group. London School of Economics.

Blumler, J. 1997. Origins of the Crisis of Communication for Citizenship. *Political Communication* 14 (4): 395–404.

Blumler, J. and D. Kavanagh. 1999. The Third Age of Political Communication: Influences and Features. *Political Communication* 16 (3): 209–230.

Blumler, J. and M. Gurevitch. 1995. *The Crisis of Public Communication.* London and New York: Routledge.

Braudy, L. 1986. *The Frenzy of Renown. Fame and Its History.* Oxford: Oxford University Press.

Brennan, G. and A. Hamlin. 2000. *Democratic Devices and Desires.* Cambridge: Cambridge University Press.

Bruce, B. 1992. *Images of Power.* London: Kogan Page Limited.

Bucy, E. P. 2000. Emotional and Evaluative Consequences of Inappropriate Leader Displays. *Communication Research* 27 (2): 194–226.

Burch, M. and I. Holliday. 2004. The Blair Government and the Core Executive. *Government and Opposition* 39 (1): 1–21.

Busby, R. 2009. *Marketing the Populist Politician. The Demotic Democrat.* Basingstoke: Palgrave.

Butler, D. 1995. *British General Elections since 1945.* Second edn. London: Wiley-Blackwell.

Butler, D. and R. Rose. 1960. *The British General Election of 1959.* New York: St Martin's Press.

Calhoun, C. ed. 1997. *Habermas and the Public Sphere.* Cambridge, MA: MIT Press.

Campus, D. 2010. Mediatization and Personalization of Politics in Italy and France: The Cases of Berlusconi and Sarkozy. *International Journal of Press/Politics* 15 (2): 219–235.

Cappella, J. N. and K. Hall Jamieson. 1997. *Spiral of Cynicism. The Press and the Public Good*. New York: Oxford University Press.

Castells, M. 2009. *Communication Power*. Oxford: Oxford University Press.

Clarke, H. and M. Stewart. 1995. Economic Evaluations, Prime Ministerial Approval and Governing Party Support: Rival Models Reconsidered. *British Journal of Political Science* 25 (2): 145–170.

Clarke, H. et al. 2004. *Political Choice in Britain*. New York: Oxford University Press.

——. 2009. *Performance Politics and the British Voter*. Cambridge: Cambridge University Press.

Cockerell, M. 1988. *Live from Number 10*. London: Faber and Faber.

——. 1989. Prime Ministers on Television. *Contemporary British History* 2 (5): 2–4.

Coleman, S. 2003. A Tale of Two Houses: The House of Commons, the *Big Brother* House and the People at Home. *Parliamentary Affairs* 56 (4): 733–758.

——. 2006. How the Other Half Votes. *Big Brother* Viewers and the 2005 General Election. *International Journal of Cultural Studies* 9 (4): 457–479.

Cornejo, V. 2008. *The Search for Authenticity: Some Implications for Political Communication*. Working Paper No. 33. Messina: Centro Interuniversitario per le ricerche sulla Sociologia del Diritto e delle Istituzioni Giuridiche (CIRSDIG).

Corner, J. 2000. Mediated Persona and Political Culture. Dimensions of Structure and Process. *European Journal of Cultural Studies* 3 (3): 386–402.

Corner, J. and D. Pels. 2003a. Introduction. In *Media and the Restyling of Politics*, ed. J. Corner and D. Pels. London: Sage.

——, eds. 2003b. *Media and the Restyling of Politics*. London: Sage.

Cornog, E. 2004. *The Power and the Story*. New York: The Penguin Press.

Couldry, N. 2004. Theorising Media as Practice. *Social Semiotics* 14 (2): 115–132.

Cowley, P. and M. Stuart. 2005. Parliament: Hunting for Votes. *Parliamentary Affairs* 58 (2): 258–271.

Crewe, I. and A. King. 1994. Are British Elections Becoming More 'Presidential'? In *Elections at Home and Abroad*, ed. K. Jennings and T. Mann. Michigan: Michigan University Press.

Crossman, R. 1963. Introduction. In *The English Constitution by Walter Bagehot*, ed. R. Crossman. London: Fontana.

Curran, J. and J. Seaton. 1981. *Power without Responsibility: The Press and Broadcasting in Britain*. First edn. London: Routledge.

Curtice, J. and S. Holmberg. 2005. Party Leaders and Party Choice. In

The European Voter. A Comparative Study of Modern Democracies. Oxford: Oxford University Press.

Curtice, J. and S. Hunjan. 2006. *The Impact of Leadership Evaluations on Voting Behaviour: Do the Rules Matter?* Working Paper No. 110. Oxford: Centre for Research into Elections and Social Trends.

Dalton, R. and M. Wattenberg, eds. 2000. *Parties without Partisans. Political Change in Advanced Industrial Democracies.* New York: Oxford University Press.

Dalton, R., I. McAllister and M. Wattenberg. 2000. The Consequences of Partisan Dealignment. In *Parties without Partisans. Political Change in Advanced Industrialised Democracies*, ed. R. Dalton and M. P. Wattenberg. New York: Oxford University Press.

Davis, A. 2002. *Public Relations Democracy: Public Relations, Politics and the Mass Media in Britain.* Manchester: Manchester University Press.

de la Torre, C. 2009. The History of a Controversy: Populism in Latin American Politics. Paper read at 'Populism of the Twenty-First Century'. Woodrow Wilson International Center for Scholars, at Washington DC, US.

Deacon, D. 2007. Yesterday's Papers and Today's Technology: Digital Newspaper Archives and 'Push Button' Content Analysis. *European Journal of Communication* 22 (1): 5–25.

Deacon, D., P. Golding and M. Billig. 2001. Press and Broadcasting: 'Real Issues' and Real Coverage. In *Britain Votes 2001*, ed. P. Norris. New York: Oxford University Press.

Deacon, D. et al. 2005. *Reporting the 2005 UK General Election for the UK Electoral Commission.* Electoral Commission.

Denver, D. 2003. *Elections and Voters in Britain.* Basingstoke: Palgrave.

———. 2010. The Results: How Britain Voted. *Parliamentary Affairs* 63 (4): 588–606.

Dunleavy, P. 2010. *The Parliamentary Arithmetic Shows that the Cameron-Clegg Coalition is Almost Immune to Rebellions.* Blog. Available from http://blogs.lse.ac.uk/politicsandpolicy/?p=2425 (accessed 20 August 2010).

Dunleavy, P. et al. 2006. Britain Beyond Blair – Party Politics and Leadership Succession. In *Developments in British Politics 8*, ed. P. Dunleavy, R. Heffernan, P. Cowley and C. Hay. Basingstoke: Palgrave.

Elcock, H. 2001. *Political Leadership.* Cheltenham: Edward Elgar.

Elshtain, J. B. 1997. The Displacement of Politics. In *Public and Private in Thought and Practice: Perspectives on a Grand Dichotomy*, ed. J. A. Weintraub and K. Kumar. Chicago: University of Chicago Press.

Evans, G. and R. Andersen. 2005. The Impact of Party Leaders: How Blair Lost Labour Votes. *Parliamentary Affairs* 58 (4): 818–836.

Fairclough, N. 2000. *New Labour, New Language?* New York: Routledge.

Finlayson, A. 2002. Elements of the Blairite Image of Leadership. *Parliamentary Affairs* 55 (3): 586–599.

——. 2003. *Making Sense of New Labour.* London: Lawrence & Wishart.

——. 2007. Making Sense of David Cameron. *Public Policy Research* 14 (1): 3–10.

Flinders, M. 2005. Majoritarian Democracy in Britain: New Labour and the Constitution'. *West European Politics* 28(1): 61–93.

Foley, M. 1993. *The Rise of the British Presidency.* Manchester: Manchester University Press.

——. 2000. *The British Presidency.* Manchester: Manchester University Press.

——. 2002. *John Major, Tony Blair and a Conflict of Leadership.* Manchester: Manchester University Press.

——. 2004. Presidential Attribution as an Agency of Prime Ministerial Critique in a Parliamentary Democracy: The Case of Tony Blair. *The British Journal of Politics and International Relations* 6 (3): 292–311.

——. 2008. The Presidential Dynamics of Leadership Decline in Contemporary British Politics: the Illustrative Case of Tony Blair. *Contemporary Politics* 14 (1): 53–69.

——. 2009. Gordon Brown and the Role of Compounded Crisis in the Pathology of Leadership Decline. *British Politics* 4 (4): 498–513.

Francis, M. 2002. Tears, Tantrums, and Bared Teeth: The Emotional Economy of Three Conservative Prime Ministers, 1951–1963. *Journal of British Studies* 41 (3): 354–387.

Franklin, B. 2004. *Packaging Politics. Political Communications in Britain's Media Democracy.* Second edn. London: Edward Arnold.

Gaffney, J. 2001. Imagined Relationships: Political Leadership in Contemporary Democracies. *Parliamentary Affairs* 54: 120–133.

Gamson, J. 1994. *Claims to Fame: Celebrity in Contemporary America.* Berkeley: University of California Press.

Giddens, A. 1991. *Modernity and Self Identity: Self and Society in the Late Modern Age.* Cambridge: Polity Press in association with Blackwell.

Gill, R. 2003. Power and the Production of Subjects: A Genealogy of the New Man and the New Lad. In *Masculinity and Men's Lifestyle Magazines,* ed. B. Benwell. London: Blackwell.

Goffman, E. 1959. *The Presentation of Self in Everyday Life.* 1991 edn. Harmondsworth: Penguin.

Goodard, P., M. Scammell and H. Semetko. 1998. Too Much of a Good Thing? Television in the 1997 Campaign. In *Political Communications. Why Labour Won the General Election of 1997,* ed. I. Crewe, B. Gosschalk and J. Bartle. London: Frank Cass Publishers.

Gould, P. 1999. *The Unfinished Revolution: How the Modernisers Saved the Labour Party.* London: Abacus.

Grbeša, M. 2008. Personality Politics in Croatia. PhD thesis, Department of Communication Sciences University of Ljubljana, Ljubljana.

Green, J. 2007. When Voters and Parties Agree: Valence Issues and Party Competition. *Political Studies* 55 (3): 629–655.

Hacker, K. ed. 2004. *Presidential Candidate Images.* Oxford: Rowman & Littlefield Publishers.

Hague, R. and M. Harrop. 2010. *Comparative Government and Politics.* Eighth edn. Basingstoke: Palgrave.

Hall Jamieson, K. 1988. *Eloquence in an Electronic Age. The Transformation of Political Speechmaking.* New York: Oxford University Press.

———. 1992. *Dirty Politics: Deception, Distraction, and Democracy.* New York: Oxford University Press.

Hall Jamieson, K. and P. Waldman. 2003. *The Press Effect.* New York: Oxford University Press.

Hardin, R. 1999. Do We Want Trust in Government? In *Democracy & Trust*, ed. M. Warren. Cambridge: Cambridge University Press.

Hargreaves, I., J. Lewis and T. Speers. 2003. *Towards a Better Map. Science, the Public and the Media.* Report to the Economic and Social Research Council. Swindon: ESRC.

Harrison, M. 1965. Television and Radio. In *The British General Election of 1964*, ed. D. Butler and A. King. London: Macmillan.

———. 1966. Television and Radio. In *The British General Election of 1966*, ed. D. Butler and A. King. London: Macmillan.

———. 1971. Broadcasting. In *The British General Election of 1970*, ed. D. Butler and M. Pinto-Duschinsky. London: Macmillan.

———. 1974. Television and Radio. In *The British General Election of February 1974*, ed. D. Butler and D. Kavanagh. London: Macmillan.

———. 1975. On the Air. In *The British General Election of October 1974*, ed. D. Butler and D. Kavanagh. London: Macmillan.

———. 1985. Broadcasting. In *The British General Election of 1983*, ed. D. Butler and D. Kavanagh. London: Macmillan.

———. 1988. Broadcasting. In *The British General Election 1987*, ed. D. Butler and D. Kavanagh. London: Macmillan.

———. 1993. Politics on the Air. In *The British General Election of 1992*, ed. D. Butler and D. Kavanagh. London: Macmillan.

———. 1998. Politics on the Air. In *The British General Election of 1998*, ed. D. Butler and D. Kavanagh. London: Macmillan.

———. 2002. Politics on the Air. In *The British General Election of 2001*, ed. D. Butler and D. Kavanagh. London: Palgrave Macmillan.

——. 2005. On the Air. In *The British General Election of 2005*, ed. D. Kavanagh and D. Butler. London: Palgrave Macmillan.

Harrop, M. 2001. The Rise of Campaign Professionalism. In *Political Communications Transformed. From Morrison to Mandelson*, ed. J. Bartle and D. Griffiths. Basingstoke: Palgrave.

Harrop, M. and M. Scammell. 1993. A Tabloid War. In *The British General Election of 1992*, ed. D. Butler and D. Kavanagh. London: Macmillan.

Hart, R. 1987. *The Sound of Leadership: Presidential Communication in the Modern Age*. Chicago: University of Chicago Press.

——. 1998. The Search for Intimacy in American Politics. In *The Public Voice in a Democracy at Risk*, ed. M. Salvador and P. Sias. Westport: Greenwood Press.

Hart, R., D. Smith-Howell and J. Llewellyn. 1996. News, Psychology, and Presidential Politics. In *The Psychology of Political Communication*, ed. A. Crigler. Ann Arbor: University of Michigan Press.

Hay, C. 2008. *Why We Hate Politics*. Cambridge: Polity Press.

Heasman, D. J. 1967. 'My station and its duties' – The Attlee Version. *Parliamentary Affairs* 21: 75–84.

Heffernan, R. 2003. Prime Ministerial Predominance? Core Executive Politics in the UK. *The British Journal of Politics & International Relations* 5 (3): 347–372.

——. 2005a. Exploring (and Explaining) the British Prime Minister. *The British Journal of Politics & International Relations* 7 (4): 605–620.

——. 2005b. Why the Prime Minister Cannot be a President: Comparing Institutional Imperatives in Britain and America. *Parliamentary Affairs* 58 (1): 53–70.

——. 2006. The Prime Minister and the News Media: Political Communication as a Leadership Resource. *Parliamentary Affairs* 59 (4): 582–598.

——. 2010. The Predominant Party Leader as Predominant Prime Minister? David Cameron in Downing Street. Paper read at the Annual Conference of the American Political Studies Association, at Washington DC, 2–5 September.

Heffernan, R. and P. Webb. 2005. The British Prime Minister: Much More Than 'First Among Equals'. In *The Presidentialization of Politics. A Comparative Study of Modern Democracies*, ed. T. Poguntke and P. Webb. Oxford: Oxford University Press.

Helms, L. 2005. The Presidentialisation of Political Leadership: British Notions and German Observations. *The Political Quarterly* 76 (3): 430–438.

——. 2008. Governing in the Media Age: The Impact of the Mass Media on Executive Leadership in Contemporary Democracies. *Government and Opposition* 43 (1): 26–54.

Hill, A. 2002. Big Brother: The Real Audience. *Television & New Media* 3 (3): 323–340.

Hobsbawm, J. and J. Lloyd. 2008. *The Power of the Commentariat*. London: Editorial Intelligence Ltd.

Holmberg, S. and H. Oscarsson. 2010. Party Leader Effects on the Vote. In *Political Leaders and Democratic Elections*, ed. K. Aarts, A. Blais and H. Schmitt. Oxford: Oxford University Press.

Holmes, S. and S. Redmond, eds. 2006. *Framing Celebrity*. London and New York: Routledge.

Holtz-Bacha, C. 2004. Germany: How the Private Life of Politicians got into the Media. *Parliamentary Affairs* 57 (1): 41–52.

Hondagneu-Sotelo, P. and M. A. Messner. 1994. Gender Displays and Men's Power. In *Theorizing Masculinities*, ed. H. Brod and M. Kaufman. Thousand Oaks, CA: Sage.

Howard, A. and R. West. 1965. *The Making of the Prime Minister*. London: Jonathan Cape.

Inglehart, R. 1990. *Culture Shift in Advanced Industrial Society*. Princeton: Princeton University Press.

———. 1997. *Modernization and Postmodernization: Cultural, Economic, and Political Change in 43 Societies*. Princeton: Princeton University Press.

Ipsos-Mori. 2006a. *Conservative Leader Image*. Available from www.ipsos -mori.com/researchpublications/researcharchive/poll.aspx?oItemID= 58&view=wide (accessed February 2010).

———. 2006b. *Labour Leader Image*. Available from www.ipsos -mori.com/researchpublications/researcharchive/poll.aspx?oItemID= 59&view=wide (accessed February 2010).

———. 2007. *Like Him? Like His Policies? Trends 1984–2007*. Available from www.ipsos-mori.com/researchpublications/researcharchive/poll.aspx? oItemId=2398&view=wide (accessed February 2010).

Jones, B. and P. Norton. 2010. *Politics UK*. Seventh edn. Edinburgh: Pearson.

Jones, G. 1964. The Prime Minister's Power. *Parliamentary Affairs* 18 (2): 167–185.

Jones, P. and J. Hudson. 1996. The Quality of Political Leadership: A Case Study of John Major. *The British Journal of Politics and International Relations* 26: 229–244.

Just, M. and A. N. Crigler. 2000. Leadership Image-Building: After Clinton and Watergate. *Political Psychology* 21 (1): 179–198.

Just, M. et al. 1996. *Crosstalk: Citizens, Candidates, and the Media in a Presidential Campaign*. Chicago: University of Chicago Press.

Kaase, M. 1994. Is There Personalization in Politics? Candidates and Voting

Behavior in Germany. *International Political Science Review* 15 (3): 211–230.

Karvonen, L. 2009. *The Personalisation of Politics. A Study of Parliamentary Democracies.* Colchester: ECPR Press.

Kavanagh, D. and A. Seldom. 2008. *The Powers Behind the Prime Minister: The Hidden Influence of Number Ten.* London: Harper Collins.

Kernell, S. 1997. *Going Public: New Strategies of Presidential Leadership.* Washington DC: CQ Press.

Kerr, P. 2007. Cameron Chameleon and the Current State of Britain's 'Consensus'. *Parliamentary Affairs* 60 (1): 46–65.

Kimber, R. 2010. Party Election Broadcasts transcripts. Available from www.politicsresources.net/area/uk/peb.htm (accessed 5 July 2010).

King, A. 2002a. Conclusions and Implications. In *Leaders' Personalities and the Outcomes of Democratic Elections*, ed. A. King. Oxford: Oxford University Press.

——. 2002b. Do Leaders' Personalities Really Matter? In *Leaders' Personalities and the Outcomes of Democratic Elections*, ed. A. King. Oxford: Oxford University Press.

——, ed. 2002c. *Leaders' Personalities and the Outcomes of Democratic Elections.* Oxford: Oxford University Press.

Kirchheimer, O. 1966. The Transformation of Western European Party Systems. In *Political Parties and Political Development*, ed. J. La Palombara and M. Weiner. Princeton: Princeton University Press.

Kleinnijenhuis, J. et al. 2001. Issues and Personalities in German and Dutch Television News: Patterns and Effects. *European Journal of Communication* 16 (3): 337–359.

Krogstad, A. and A. Storvik. 2006. Seductive Heroes and Ordinary Human Beings: Charismatic Political Leadership in France and Norway. In *Comparative Studies of Social and Political Elites*, ed. F. Engelstad and T. Gulbrandsen. Oslo: JAI Press Inc.

Kuhn, R. 2004. 'Vive La Différence'? The Mediation of Politicians' Public Images and Private Lives in France. *Parliamentary Affairs* 57 (1): 24–40.

——. 2007. The Public and the Private in Contemporary French Politics. *French Cultural Studies* 18 (2): 185–200.

Langer, A. I. 2007. A Historical Exploration of the Personalisation of Politics in the Print Media: The British Prime Ministers (1945–1999). *Parliamentary Affairs* 60 (3): 371–387.

——. 2010. The Politicization of Private Persona: Exceptional Leaders or the New Rule? The Case of the United Kingdom and the Blair Effect. *International Journal of Press/Politics* 15 (1): 60–76.

Langmaid, R., C. Trevail and B. Hayman. 2006. Reconnecting the Prime Minister. Paper read at the Annual Conference of the Market Research Society, the Barbican Centre, London, 5–6 November.

Leggett, W. 2005. It's the *Culture*, Stupid! New Labour's Progressive Consensus. *The Political Quarterly* 76 (4): 550–557.

Lewis, J. et al. 2008. *The Quality and Independence of British Journalism. Tracking the Changes Over 20 Years*. Cardiff: Cardiff School of Journalism.

Lichtenberg, J. 1989. The Politics of Character and the Character of Journalism. Discussion Paper D-2. The Joan Shorenstein Barone Center.

Lilleker, D. 2005. The Impact of Political Marketing on Internal Party Democracy. *Parliamentary Affairs* 58 (3): 570–584.

Livingstone, S. and P. Lunt. 1993. *Talk on Television: Audience Participation and Public Debate*. London and New York: Routledge.

Lupia, A. and M. McCubbins. 1998. *The Democratic Dilemma*. Cambridge: Cambridge University Press.

Mackintosh, J. P. 1962. *The British Cabinet*. London: Stevens.

Mair, P. 2000. Partyless Democracy. *New Left Review* 2 (March–April): 21–36.

Manin, B. 1997. *The Principles of Representative Government*. Cambridge: Cambridge University Press.

Marcus, G. 2002. *The Sentimental Citizen: Emotion in Democratic Politics*. University Park, PA: Pennsylvania State University Press.

Marcus, G., R. Neuman and M. MacKuen. 2000. *Affective Intelligence and Political Judgment*. Chicago: University of Chicago Press.

Marquand, D. 2000. Revisiting the Blair Paradox. *New Left Review* 3 (May–June): 73–79.

Marshall, P. D. 1997. *Celebrity and Power. Fame in Contemporary Culture*. Minneapolis: Minnesota University Press.

Mattinson, D. 2010. *Talking to a Brick Wall*. London: Biteback Publishing.

Mazzoleni, G. 2000. A Return to Civic and Political Engagement Promoted by Personalized Political Leadership? *Political Communication* 17: 325–328.

Mazzoleni, G. and W. Schulz. 1999. 'Mediatization' of Politics: A Challenge for Democracy? *Political Communication* 16 (3): 247–261.

McAllister, I. 1996. Leaders. In *Comparing Democracies. Elections and Voting in Global Perspective.*, ed. L. LeDuc, R. Noemi and P. Norris. London: Sage.

———. 2007. The Personalization of Politics. In *The Oxford Handbook of Political Behaviour*, ed. R. Dalton and H. Klingemann. Oxford: Oxford University Press.

McCallum, R. B. and A. Readman. 1947. *The British General Election of 1945.* London: Cumberlege.

Meyer, T. 2002. *Media Democracy. How the Media Colonize Politics.* Cambridge: Polity Press.

Meyrowitz, J. 1985. *No Sense of Place. The Impact of Electronic Media on Social Behaviour.* New York: Oxford University Press.

Miles, P. and M. Smith. 1987. *Cinema, Literature and Society: Elite and Mass Culture in Interwar Britain.* Worcester: Billing & Sons.

Miller, A., M. Wattenberg and O. Malanchuck. 1986. Schematic Assessment of Presidential Candidates. *American Political Science Review* 80 (2): 521–540.

Montgomery, M. 1999. Speaking Sincerely: Public Reactions to the Death of Diana. *Language and Literature* 8 (1): 5–33.

Mouffe, C. 1996. Democracy, Power, and the 'Political'. In *Democracy and Difference: Contesting the Boundaries of the Political*, ed. S. Benhabib. Princeton: Princeton University Press.

Mughan, A. 2000. *Media and the Presidentialization of Parliamentary Elections.* New York: St. Martin's Press.

———. 2005. On the Conditionality of Leader Effects. Paper read at the 2005 annual EPOP meeting, the University of Essex , 9–11 September.

Needham, C. 2005. Brand Leaders: Clinton, Blair and the Limitations of the Permanent Campaign. *Political Studies* 53 (2): 343–361.

Neuman, R. W. et al., eds. 2007. *The Affect Effect.* Chicago: University of Chicago Press.

Norris, P. 1998. The Battle for the Campaign Agenda. In *New Labour Triumphs: Britain at the Polls*, ed. A. King et al. Chatham: Chatham House.

Norton, P. 2005. *Parliament in British Politics.* Basingtoke: Palgrave Macmillan.

Nunn, H. 2002. *Thatcher, Politics and Fantasy.* London: Lawrence and Wishart Limited.

O'Donnell, G. 1994. Delegative Democracy. *Journal of Democracy* 5 (1): 55–69.

Offe, C. 1999. How Can We Trust Our Fellow Citizens? In *Democracy & Trust*, ed. M. Warren. Cambridge: Cambridge University Press.

O'Hara, K. 2007. *After Blair: David Cameron and the Conservative Tradition.* Cambridge: Icon Books.

Ohr, D. 2010. Changing Patterns in Political Communication. In *Political Leaders and Democratic Elections*, ed. K. Aarts, A. Blais and H. Schmitt. Oxford: Oxford University Press.

Ohr, D. and H. Oscarsson 2010. Leader Traits, Leader Images, and Vote Choice. In *Political Leaders and Democratic Elections*, ed. K. Aarts, A. Blais and H. Schmitt. Oxford: Oxford University Press.

Pack, M. 2010. *How Often are Coalition MPs Rebelling?* Blog. Available from www.markpack.org.uk/how-often-are-coalition-mps-rebelling/ (accessed 20 November 2010).

Panebianco, A. 1988. *Political Parties: Organisation and Power.* Cambridge: Cambridge University Press.

Pasquino, G. 2007. The Five Faces of Silvio Berlusconi: The Knight of Anti-politics. *Modern Italy* 12 (1): 39–54.

Patterson, T. E. 1993. *Out of Order.* First edn. New York: A. Knopf.

Pearce, M. 2001. 'Getting Behind the Image': Personality Politics in a Labour Party Election Broadcast. *Language and Literature* 10 (3): 211–228.

———. 2005. Informalization in UK Party Election Broadcasts 1966–97. *Language and Literature* 14 (1): 65–90.

Pels, D. 2003. Aesthetic Representation and Political Style: Re-balancing Identity and Difference in Media Democracy. In *The Media and the Restyling of Politics*, ed. J. Corner and D. Pels. London: Sage.

Pilsworth, M. 1979. Balanced Broadcasting. In *The British General Election of 1979*, ed. D. Butler and D. Kavanagh. London: Macmillan.

Pimlott, B. 1992. *Harold Wilson.* London: HarperCollins.

Poguntke, T. and P. Webb. 2005a. The Presidentialization of Politics in Democratic Societies: A Framework for Analysis. In *The Presidentialization of Politics. A Comparative Study of Modern Democracies*, ed. T. Poguntke and P. Webb. Oxford: Oxford University Press.

———, eds. 2005b. *The Presidentialization of Politics. A Comparative Study of Modern Democracies.* Oxford: Oxford University Press.

Ponce de Leon, C. L. 2002. *Self-Exposure: Human-Interest Journalism and the Emergence of Celebrity in America, 1890–1940.* Chapel Hill: University of North Carolina Press.

Popkin, S. L. 1991. *The Reasoning Voter: Communication and Persuasion in Presidential Campaigns.* Chicago: University of Chicago Press.

PPA Marketing & Research. 2010. *Number of Consumer Magazine Titles in the UK 1980–2009.* Available from www.ppamarketing.net/public/downloads/BRADnumberofconsumertitles1980–2009.ppt#257,1 (accessed 6 July 2010).

Quinn, T. 2008. The Conservative Party and the 'Centre Ground' of British Politics. *Journal of Elections, Public Opinion & Parties* 18 (2).

Rahat, G. and T. Sheafer. 2007. The Personalization(s) of Politics: Israel 1949–2003. *Political Communication* 24 (1): 65–80.

Redmond, S. 2006. Intimate Fame Everywhere. In *Framing Celebrity*, ed. S. Holmes and S. Redmond. London and New York: Routledge.

Reinemann, C. and J. Wilke. 2007. It's the Debates, Stupid! How the Introduction of Televised Debates Changed the Portrayal of Chancellor

Candidates in the German Press, 1949–2005. *Harvard International Journal of Press/Politics* 12 (4): 92–111.

Rentoul, J. 2001. *Tony Blair: Prime Minister.* Second edn. London: Little, Brown and Company.

Rhodes, A. W., J. Wanna and P. Weller. 2009. *Comparing Westminster.* Oxford: Oxford University Press.

Rhodes, R. A. W. 2000. New Labour's Civil Service: Summing up Joining-up. *The Political Quarterly* 71 (2): 151–166.

Richards, B. 2004. The Emotional Deficit in Political Communication. *Political Communication* 21 (3): 339–352.

——. 2007. *Emotional Governance: Politics, Media and Terror.* Basingstoke: Palgrave.

Rico, G. 2007. The Nature of Leadership Effects in the 2004 Spanish General Election. Paper read at ECPR Workshop on Political Leadership, the University of Helsinki, Finland, 7–12 May.

Roncarolo, F. 2004. Mediation of Italian Politics and the Marketing of Leaders' Private Lives. *Parliamentary Affairs* 57 (1): 108–117.

Rose, R. 1980. British Government: The Job at the Top. In *Presidents and Prime Ministers*, ed. R. Rose and E. Suleiman. Washington DC: American Enterprise Institute for Public Policy Research.

——. 2001. *The Prime Minister in a Shrinking World.* Cambridge: Polity Press.

Rosenbaum, M. 1997. *From Soapbox to Soundbite: Party Political Campaigning in Britain Since 1945.* Basingstoke: Macmillan.

Rosewarne, D. 1998. Tony Blair and William Hague: Two Northerners Heading South. *English Today* 14 (04): 53–54.

Ruddock, A. 2006. Invisible Centers: Boris Johnson, Authenticity, Cultural Citizenship and a Centrifugal Model of Media Power. *Social Semiotics* 16 (2): 263–282.

——. 2007. Get a Real Job: Authenticity on the Performance, Reception and Study of Celebrity. *Particip@tions* 4 (1).

Runciman, D. 2006a. Liars, Hypocrites and Crybabies. *London Review of Books* 28 (21): 8–10.

——. 2006b. *The Politics of Good Intentions.* Princeton: Princeton University Press.

——. 2008. *Political Hypocrisy: The Mask of Power, from Hobbes to Orwell and Beyond.* Princeton: Princeton University Press.

Samuels, A. 2001. *Politics on the Couch. Citizenship and the Internal Life.* London: Profile Books.

Scammell, M. 1995. *Designer Politics: How Elections are Won.* Basingstoke: Macmillan.

——. 1996. The Odd Couple: Marketing and Maggie. *European Journal of Marketing* 30 (10/11): 114–126.

———. 2001. Media and Media Management. In *The Blair Effect*, ed. A. Seldon. London: Little Brown.

———. 2007. Political Brands and Consumer Citizens: The Rebranding of Tony Blair. *The ANNALS of the American Academy of Political and Social Science* 611 (1): 176–192.

Scammell, M. and C. Beckett. 2010. Labour No More: The Press. In *The British General Election of 2010*, ed. D. Kavanagh and P. Cowley. Basingstoke: Palgrave Macmillan.

Scammell, M. and M. Harrop. 1998. The Press. In *The British General Election of 1997*, ed. D. Butler and D. Kavanagh. London: Palgrave.

Scammell, M. and A. I. Langer. 2006. Political Advertising: Why is it so Boring? *Media, Culture and Society* 28 (5): 763–784.

———. 2007. Political Advertising in the UK. In *Handbook of Political Advertising*, ed. L. Kaid and C. Holtz-Bacha. New York: Sage.

Scammell, M. and H. Semetko. 2008. Election News Coverage in the UK. In *The Handbook of Elections News Coverage Around the World*, ed. J. Stromback and L. Lee Kaid. New York: Routledge.

Scarrow, S., P. Webb and D. Farrell. 2000. From Social Integration to Electoral Contestation. The Changing Distribution of Power within Political Parties. In *Parties without Partisans. Political Change in Advanced Industrial Democracies*, ed. R. Dalton and M. Wattenberg. New York: Oxford University Press.

Schmitt, H. and D. Ohr. 2000. Are Party Leaders Becoming More Important in German Elections? Leader Effects on the Vote in Germany, 1961–1998. Paper read at the 2000 Annual Meeting of the American Political Science Association, Marriot Wardman Park, Washington DC, August 31–September 3.

Schudson, M. 1995. *The Power of News*. Cambridge, MA: Harvard University Press.

Schulz, W. and R. Zeh. 2004. The Changing Election Coverage of German Television. Paper read at 54th Annual Conference of the International Communication Association, at New Orleans.

Seaton, J. 2003. Public, Private and the Media. *The Political Quarterly* 74 (2): 174–183.

Semetko, H., M. Scammell and T. Nossiter. 1994. The Media's Coverage of the Campaign. In *Labour's Last Chance? The 1992 Election and Beyond*, ed. A. Heath, R. Jowell and J. Curtice. Aldershot: Dartmouth.

Sennett, R. 1977. *The Fall of Public Man*. 1986 edn. New York, London: Faber and Faber.

Seyomour-Ure, C. 1994. The Media in Postwar British Politics. *Parliamentary Affairs* 47 (4): 530–548.

———. 1995. Characters and Assassinations: Portrayals of John Major and

Neil Kinnock in The Daily Mirror and The Sun. In *Political Communications. The General Election Campaign of 1992*, ed. I. Crewe and B. Gosschalk. Cambridge: Cambridge University Press.

——. 1996. *The British Press and Broadcasting since 1945*. Second edn. Oxford: Blackwell.

——. 1998. Leaders and Leading Articles: Characterisation of John Major and Tony Blair in the Editorials of the National Daily Press. In *Political Communications. Why Labour Won the General Election of 1997*, ed. I. Crewe, B. Gosschalk and J. Bartle. London: Frank Cass Publishers.

Sigelman, L. 2001. The Presentation of Self in Presidential Life: Onstage and Backstage with Johnson and Nixon. *Political Communication* 18 (1): 1–22.

Sigelman, L. and D. Bullock. 1991. Candidates, Issues, Horse Races, and Hoopla: Presidential Campaign Coverage, 1888–1988. *American Politics Research* 19 (1): 5–32.

Smith, A. 2008. New Man or Son of the Manse? Gordon Brown as Reluctant Celebrity Father. *British Politics* 3: 556–575.

Smith, M. 1999. *The Core Executive in Britain*. Basingstoke: Palgrave Macmillan.

Stanyer, J. 2007. *Modern Political Communication*. Cambridge: Polity.

Stanyer, J. and D. Wring. 2004a. Public Images, Private Lives: An Introduction. *Parliamentary Affairs* 57 (1): 1–8.

——. 2004b. Public Images, Private Lives: The Mediation of Politicians around the Globe. *Parliamentary Affairs* 57 (1): 1–235.

Stewart, M. and H. Clarke. 1992. The (Un)Importance of Party Leaders: Leader Images and Party Choice in the 1987 British Election. *Journal of Politics* 54 (2): 47–470.

Street, J. 2000. Prime Time Politics: Popular Culture and Politicians in the UK. *Javnost – The Public* 7 (2): 75–90.

——. 2001. *Mass Media, Politics, and Democracy*. Hampshire, New York: Palgrave.

——. 2003. The Celebrity Politician: Political Style and Popular Culture. In *Media and the Restyling of Politics*, ed. J. Corner and D. Pels. London: Sage.

——. 2004. Celebrity Politicians: Popular Culture and Political Representation. *The British Journal of Politics and International Relations* 6 (4): 435–452.

Swanson, D. 1997. The Political-Media Complex at 50: Putting the 1996 Presidential Campaign in Context. *American Behavioral Scientist* 40 (8): 1264–1282.

Swanson, D. and P. Mancini, eds. 1996. *Politics, Media and Modern Democracy*. Westport, CT: Praeger.

Taylor, A. 2005. Stanley Baldwin, Heresthetics and the Realignment of British Politics. *British Journal of Political Science* 35 (3): 429–463.

Thompson, J. B. 2000. *Political Scandal: Power and Visibility in the Media Age*. Cambridge: Polity Press.

van Noije, L. 2007. *The Democratic Deficit Closer to Home*. Amsterdam: Vrije Universiteit.

van Zoonen, L. 1998a. The Ethics of Making Private Life Public. In *The Media in Question. Popular Cultures and Public Interests*, ed. K. Brants, J. Hermes and L. van Zoonen. London: Sage.

——. 1998b. 'Finally, I Have My Mother Back': Politicians and Their Families in Popular Culture. *The Harvard International Journal of Press/Politics* 3 (1): 48–64.

——. 2000. Broken Hearts, Broken Dreams? Politicians and their Families in Popular Culture. In *Gender, Politics and Communication*, ed. A. Sreberny and E. van Zoonen. Cresskill, NJ: Hampton Press.

——. 2004. Imagining the Fan Democracy. *European Journal of Communication* 19 (1): 39–52.

——. 2005. *Entertaining the Citizen: When Politics and Popular Culture Converge*. Maryland: Rowman & Littlefield.

van Zoonen, L. and C. Holtz-Bacha. 2000. Personalisation in Dutch and German Politics: The Case of Talk Show. *Javnost – The Public* 7 (2): 45–56.

Vasterman, P. L. M. 2005. Media-Hype: Self-Reinforcing News Waves, Journalistic Standards and the Construction of Social Problems. *European Journal of Communication* 20 (4): 508–530.

Warner, M. 2002. *Publics and Counterpublics*. New York: Zone Books.

Wattenberg, M. 1991. *The Rise of Candidate-Centered Politics: Presidential Elections of the 1980s*. Cambridge, MA: Harvard University Press.

——. 2004. Elections: Personal Popularity in US Presidential Elections. *Presidential Studies Quarterly* 34 (1): 143–155.

Webb, P. 2000. *The Modern British Party System*. London: Sage.

Webb, P. and T. Poguntke. 2005. The Presidentialization of Contemporary Democratic Politics: Evidence, Causes and Consequences. In *The Presidentialization of Politics. A Comparative Study of Modern Democracies*, ed. T. Poguntke and P. Webb. Oxford: Oxford University Press.

Weber, M. 1968. *Economy and Society, and Outline of Interpretative Sociology*, ed. G. Roth and C. Wittich. Berkeley: University of California Press.

Webster, W. 1990. *Not a Man to Match Her. The Marketing of a Prime Minister.* London: The Women's Press Limited.

West, D. and J. Orman. 2002. *Celebrity Politics*. New Jersey: Prentice Hall.

Westwood, S. 1996. 'Feckless' Fathers: Masculinities and the British State. In *Understanding Masculinities: Social Relations and Cultural Arenas*, ed. M. Mac an Ghaill. Philadelphia: Open University Press.

Wieten, J. 1988. The Press the Papers Wanted? The Case of Post-War Newsprint Rationing in the Netherlands and Britain. *European Journal of Communication* 3 (4): 431–455.

Williamson, P. 1982. 'Safety First': Baldwin, the Conservative Party and the 1929 General Election. *The Historical Journal* 25 (2): 385–409.

——. 1999. *Stanley Baldwin: Conservative Leadership and National Values*. Cambridge: Cambridge University Press.

Winch, S. P. 1997. *Mapping the Cultural Space of Journalism: How Journalists Distinguish News from Entertainment*. Westport, CT: Praeger.

Wring, D. 1996. Political Marketing and Party Development in Britain: A 'Secret' History. *European Journal of Marketing* 30 (10/11): 92–103.

——. 2005. *The Politics of Marketing the Labour Party*. London: Palgrave.

Young, I. M. 1990. *Justice and the Politics of Difference*. Princeton: Princeton University Press.

——. 1996. Communication and the Other: Beyond Deliberative Democracy. In *Democracy and Difference: Contesting the Boundaries of the Political*, ed. S. Benhabib. Princeton, NJ: Princeton University Press.

Zaller, J. 1998. Monica Lewinsky's Contribution to Political Science. *PS: Political Studies* 31 (2): 182–189.

Index

EU authorised representative for GPSR:
Easy Access System Europe, Mustamäe tee 50,
10621 Tallinn, Estonia
gpsr.requests@easproject.com

www.ingramcontent.com/pod-product-compliance
Lightning Source LLC
Chambersburg PA
CBHW052004270326
41929CB00015B/2787